IMAGERY AND
DAYDREAM
METHODS
IN PSYCHOTHERAPY
AND BEHAVIOR
MODIFICATION

DISCARD

PERSONALITY AND PSYCHOPATHOLOGY
A Series of Monographs, Texts, and Treatises

David T. Lykken, Editor

1. The Anatomy of Achievement Motivation, *Heinz Heckhausen.* 1966°

2. Cues, Decisions, and Diagnoses: A Systems-Analytic Approach to the Diagnosis of Psychopathology, *Peter E. Nathan.* 1967°

3. Human Adaptation and Its Failures, *Leslie Phillips.* 1968°

4. Schizophrenia: Research and Theory, *William E. Broen, Jr.* 1968°

5. Fears and Phobias, *I. M. Marks.* 1969

6. Language of Emotion, *Joel R. Davitz.* 1969

7. Feelings and Emotions, *Magda Arnold.* 1970

8. Rhythms of Dialogue, *Joseph Jaffe* and *Stanley Feldstein.* 1970

9. Character Structure and Impulsiveness, *David Kipnis.* 1971

10. The Control of Aggression and Violence: Cognitive and Physiological Factors, *Jerome L. Singer* (Ed.). 1971

11. The Attraction Paradigm, *Donn Byrne.* 1971

12. Objective Personality Assessment: Changing Perspectives, *James N. Butcher* (Ed.). 1972

13. Schizophrenia and Genetics, *Irving I. Gottesman* and *James Shields,* 1972°

14. Imagery and Daydream Methods in Psychotherapy and Behavior Modification, *Jerome L. Singer.* 1974

15. Experimental Approaches to Psychopathology, *Mitchell L. Kietzman, Samuel Sutton,* and *Joseph Zubin* (Eds.). 1975

16. Coping and Defending: Processes of Self-Environment Organization, *Norma Haan.* 1977

°Titles initiated during the series editorship of Brendan Maher.

IMAGERY AND DAYDREAM METHODS IN PSYCHOTHERAPY AND BEHAVIOR MODIFICATION

JEROME L. SINGER 68684

Department of Psychology
Yale University
New Haven, Connecticut

ACADEMIC PRESS   New York San Francisco London

A Subsidiary of Harcourt Brace Jovanovich, Publishers

ACADEMIC PRESS, INC.
111 Fifth Avenue, New York, New York 10003

United Kingdom Edition published by
ACADEMIC PRESS, INC. (LONDON) LTD.
24/28 Oval Road, London NW1

Library of Congress Cataloging in Publication Data

Singer, Jerome L
    Imagery and daydream.

    (Personality and psychopathology, no.)
    Bibliography: p.
    1. Imagery (Psychology)   2. Psychotherapy.
3. Behavior therapy.   I. Title.   [DNLM: 1.   Behavior
therapy.   2.   Fantasy.   3.   Imagination.   4.   Psychotherapy.   W1 PE861 / WM420 S6173i]
RC480.5.S53   616.8'914   74-1625
ISBN 0-12-646665-3

CONTENTS

v

PREFACE

This book has emerged from the confluence of two major streams in my own professional career—my concern with the nature of daydreaming and related imaginal processes as a theoretical and research issue in psychology and my involvement as a clinical practicioner in psychoanalytically oriented psychotherapy. The former of these trends has led me to seek ways in which the laboratory studies of fantasy processes could begin to be expanded to practical areas. My clinical experience has increasingly suggested that unless the practice of psychotherapy or behavior modification could be based reasonably solidly upon a foundation of scientific research and theory, we run the risk of increasing faddism, mysticism, and denominational splitting that would leave clinical psychology or mental health practice more generally open to the charge of being a mixture of quackery and half-baked religion. The major thesis of this book is to show that one important factor in psychotherapeutic practice, the reliance upon the client's imagery and daydreaming capacities, can be examined across various schools and shown to relate ultimately to some basic principles of human information processing and emotion that are susceptible to scientific research and scrutiny.

The book incorporates a survey of the range of uses of imagery and fantasy processes in psychotherapy and behavior modification. As such, it brings together material not previously assembled or examined in juxtaposition except in very brief sections of books by Richardson (1969), Horowitz (1970), and in several articles I had written (Singer,

1971a, b, 1972c). Much of the content presented here will be new to many readers if my experience from lecturing at various hospitals or universities around the country is any indication. The book should be of interest to clinical practitioners and to psychiatric residents, to psychology graduate students, social work students, and mental health specialists from various disciplines as an introduction to the many ingenious ways that human imagery can be used for symptom relief and psychological change. For the more theoretically or research-oriented professional or student it will point the way also to the important new developments in the scientific study of imagery and fantasy processes as a potential underpinning for clinical practice. Examples of specific research relating to the particular imagery approaches of various behavior modification and psychodynamic psychotherapies are included, along with indications of new directions needed for study. Wherever feasible, case material is included from the literature of various treatment approaches as well as that from my own practice. In drawing on my own case material I have modified details or combined information from several different patients to preserve the privacy of clients.

The book includes an extensive review of psychotherapeutic uses of imagery from classical psychoanalysis through the various European mental imagery techniques and the behavior therapies such as systematic desensitization, covert conditioning, symbolic modeling, and positive emotive imagery. Wherever possible, I have tried to present a reasonably objective description of the proponent's position concerning a specific technique. At the same time I have maintained my viewpoint, which may be called a cognitive–affective orientation with close ties to the theoretical work of Silvan Tomkins and, more generally, the cognitive orientations of Jean Piaget, Kurt Lewin, Heinz Werner, and Ernst Schachtel, among others, and to the social learning and interpersonal orientations of Harry Stack Sullivan, Julian Rotter, and Albert Bandura. In my effort to point to some of the commonalities across the range of therapeutic approaches, I have also used the cognitive–affective orientation as a framework for the loosely systematic approach to imagery and fantasy presented in the later chapters. My earlier works, *Daydreaming* and *The Child's World of Make Believe* (Singer, 1966, 1973), present some of my own research and theorizing in more detail for the interested reader.

ACKNOWLEDGMENTS

This book reflects a variety of personal experiences as a clinician, researcher, and teacher; acknowledgments to my patients, numerous research collaborators, and students would take up a chapter in itself. I do feel I must specifically acknowledge my long-time research collaborator, John Antrobus, for years of mutual examination of research issues. I have had useful discussions with Drs. Mardi Horowitz, Arthur Arkin, Joseph Cautela, Hanscarl Leuner, Paul Kosbab, and Arthur Feiner, as representatives of the various psychoanalytic, European mental imagery, and behavior modification orientations. I had the privilege of attending the Third International Congress of Mental Imagery Techniques held in Cortina d'Ampezzo, Italy with Dr. Sheldon Korchin, where we had personal encounters with important representatives of that movement, who included Drs. Frétigny, Virel, Rigo, and Rigo-Uberto. My contacts with the late Dr. Sydney Segal have enriched my knowledge of imagery research. My discussions and research collaborations with my wife, Dr. Dorothy Singer, have been of important value in helping me shape my direction and persistence in continuing this work.

Important help in preparation of this manuscript has come from Bruce Singer and David Diamond for bibliographic and indexing chores. The manuscript was typed in its various phases by Delores Hyslop, Barbara Frederickson, and Audrey Klein, all of whom I thank most sincerely.

CHAPTER I

THE REVIVAL OF PSYCHOLOGICAL AND PSYCHIATRIC INTEREST IN IMAGERY

> *To dismiss the most central fact of man's being because it is inner and subjective is to make the hugest subjective falsification possible — one that leaves out the really critical half of man's nature. For without that underlying subjective flux, as experienced in floating imagery, dreams, bodily impulses, formative ideas, projections, and symbols, the world that is open to human experience can be neither described nor rationally understood. When our age learns that lesson, it will have made the first move toward redeeming for human use the mechanized and electrified wasteland that is now being bulldozed, at man's expense and to his permanent loss, for the benefit of the Megamachine.*
>
> Lewis Mumford (1967, pp. 75–76)

Human consciousness, the subtle interplay of fleeting images, perceptions of the immediate environment, memories of long-gone events, and daydreams of future or impossible prospects, all carried along on the stream of thought, represent a true miracle of our experience of being. How strange that what is at once so obviously a part of what we

1

are and what we experience has been so completely ruled out as a subject of scientific study by psychology, the very field whose existence
originated in the attempt to understand such inner phenomena. For almost 50 years in this century, as Robert Holt (1964) has so ably documented, psychologists under the sway of behaviorism largely ignored
the study of man's imagery and fantasy processes. American spirit
reflected in the technology of mass production and the empiricism of
the business world was manifest also in the American psychologists'
ingenious emphasis on the overt response, the bar press of the pigeon,
the maze running of the white rat, and the twitches of the conditioned
human eyelid. Europe, devastated by war and social disorganization
during the same half century, never repressed inner experiences to the
same extent, but lagged far behind in the development of a scientific
technology for studying behavior.

While attention to images and fantasies was limited largely to psychiatrists studying the mentally ill or to psychoanalysts engaged in intensive scrutiny of a small number of individuals, these disciplines made
relatively little contribution to our formal understanding of the nature
of imagery or fantasy processes. The genius and increasing influence of
Freud and Jung and their relatively small bands of followers kept aloft
the torch of intrapsychic inquiry in Europe, as well as in the United
States. The limitations of the clinical method, nevertheless, prevented
their work from contributing systematically to scientific knowledge of
images and fantasies. Although Jung's influence was restricted largely
to a small enclave around Zurich, it occasionally was felt elsewhere in
Europe — in the development of some of the imagery techniques in psychotherapy — and his work affected prominent literary figures, most no-
tably James Joyce. The far greater influence of Freud upon international scientific and literary developments need not be elaborated here.
The rather formal structure which psychoanalysis took on during the
first half of this century largely deemphasized any extended exploration
of the imagery modalities or elaborated fantasy either as a psychotherapeutic tool or as an independent subject for research.

Despite Freud's great contributions to the theory of the psychology
of the dream process, the nature of primary and secondary thought,
and his discovery of the transference phenomena, relatively little importance was placed on studying the formal properties of imagery and
fantasy within psychoanalysis. It was chiefly David Rapaport (1951,
1960) who revived Freud's early concern with these problems of
structure and functional utility of the dream and daydream. Even so,
most practical psychoanalysts, in analyzing dream content and, of
course, examining spontaneously reported daydreams or slips of the
tongue for evidence of transference distortions or clues as to com-

plexes, rarely focused specifically upon imagery or sought to guide or train their patients in its use. Despite the great reliance of Freudian or neo-Freudian therapists on associations, dreams, or daydreams, they rarely published even anecdotal accounts that indicated systematic exploration of the imagery capacity of patients, the origins of imagery, the defensive or stylistic variations in imagery, and possible links of all of these to specific growth experiences. The very important technical restrictions on intervention by the analyst and the emphasis on the "blank screen" and upon primarily transferential interpretation set down in Freud's major papers on technique served unfortunately to block psychoanalysts' experimentation with fantasy approaches.

It is a curious irony of scientific progress that imagery and fantasy as fundamental human processes have been rediscovered only since the 1960s for use in psychotherapy and for general study as important psychological phenomena largely through the influence, not of psychoanalysts, but of their quondam archenemies, the behavior therapists and the behaviorally oriented scientific psychologists studying brain models, computer processing, and simulation models. The influential efforts of Hebb (1949) to systematize behavior in relation to possible neural organization of the brain led to extensive studies of sensory deprivation with the consequence that psychologists became increasingly aware of just how much seems to be going on internally when the impact of stimuli from the external environment is drastically reduced. The extremely important findings of neurophysiology in relation to the sleep cycle (Aserinsky & Kleitman, 1953) opened a tremendously exciting new direction for study of human mentation during sleep and brought the dream out of the limitations of the dyad in the consulting room and into the scientific laboratory. The advances in the use of the computer and the possibility of simulating the great range of human processes by this method also alerted psychologists to the possibilities of systematic study of long-term memories, expectations, and hierarchies of plans (Miller, Galanter, & Pribram, 1960; Tomkins & Messick, 1963). All of these research directions converged to produce the increasingly influential cognitive orientation that is now so important in American psychology.

With specific reference to the field of psychotherapy, however, the greatest influence has been that of the uses of imagery in behavior modification or learning theory approaches to psychological treatment. Introduced chiefly through the efforts of Wolpe (1958), the behavior modification techniques spread like wildfire through the 1960s, and have touched almost every phase of psychotherapy and approaches to social change. A critical feature of a great many behavior modification techniques has been the reliance upon imagery generated by the patient or client, and this at least has forced the behaviorists to look their own private experiences full in the face and once again to welcome man's inner experience back into the realm of science.

To anticipate for just a moment what is discussed at much greater length in this volume, consider the desensitization method for the treatment of phobias which has been popularized by Wolpe and has been the subject of a large number of clinical and experimental studies testifying to its effectiveness. Despite the fact that it is proposed as a behavior modification technique, the crucial feature of this treatment lies in the subject generating images of the frightening places or events that constitute the various components of his phobia. As a matter of fact, the patient once put into a relaxing situation merely lies quietly and runs through in his mind the specific scenes in ascending order of anxiety connected with his fear. The therapist, too, sits silently and intervenes only if the patient raises his hand or otherwise signals that anxiety is too great and is not being reciprocally inhibited by the relaxation method. Here is inference, indeed, about the private experience of the patient, a far cry from the usual behaviorist position with its emphasis on overt responses.

It should be clear, therefore, that the many behavior modification techniques — desensitization, covert reinforcement, and symbolic modeling, as well as the implosive methods — all hinge to a very great degree on the generation of some type of imaginal experience by the patient. Thus, it is critical for the behavior modification therapist to address himself now to the scientific aspects of human imagery if he wishes to continue to maintain that behavior techniques are indeed a natural outgrowth of scientific psychology and theories of learning. In the past, such strictures have not inhibited as extensively the use of imagery by many European mental imagery technique practitioners or, certainly, the encounter group and Gestalt practitioners who have employed some of the mental imagery techniques. The extensive reliance on such private processes requires, I believe, of these practitioners that they, too, explore the scientific bases of their procedures.

A major objective of this book is to look at a whole array of psychotherapeutic uses of imagery and to see if it is possible to relate them to each other on the one hand, and even more important, to some of the basic research in the psychology of imagery and daydreaming. This is perhaps too ambitious an intention, but it seems essential if we are to take seriously the role of clinical psychology and psychiatry as responsible expressions of behavior science. One need not kowtow blindly to "science." Still, we must recognize that there is an implicit contract between practitioners in psychology and psychiatry and the clients who seek their help. This involves the assumption that the techniques of mental health specialists are based on scientific grounds.

There are many people who eschew psychiatric or psychological help for emotional or interpersonal difficulties. They prefer, instead, to turn to traditional religion or its "fringe" varieties, seeking out revivalist preachers and healers who represent themselves as falling within some phase of the major religious groupings. There are, indeed, many others who seek help from quasi-religious or mystical agencies in our society, including practitioners of psychic phenomena, astrologers, palmists, and fortune tellers. But the people who come to psychologists and psychiatrists for help, generally speaking, expect that the help provided is based reasonably upon scientific research. Scientific research, even to the layman, means some type of formal experimentation on the open market of ideas that is subject to further systematic exploration at universities or institutes. Most probably, the layman does not personally ascertain which mental health practitioner is more "scientific" than another: rather, he must rely on the accreditation of the practitioners (psychologists, psychiatrists, and social workers) who have been trained in a university at an advanced level and who have been certified on the basis of an appropriate examination procedures by the states, or their own professional organizations. In this sense, it is a very profound responsibility of the clinical practitioner that he be in position to show some of the ties between what he practices and the background of information and formal theory that makes up the body of knowledge in his field.

We may well ask, then, whether the various practices of imagery techniques by psychotherapists from a great many backgrounds and schools meet these criteria. To make this point even more compelling, it is necessary that we take some time to examine the crisis that has existed in the general field of psychotherapeutic practice. This situation has been further aggravated with the proliferation, within the past decade, of experimental techniques—especially those that resort extensively to the use of imagery and fantasy, phenomena too little studied hitherto in a scientific fashion.

THE TOWER OF BABEL:
THE DILEMMA OF MODERN CLINICAL PRACTICE

The changing fashions of psychiatry or psychology alone may account for the new surge of interest in psychotherapeutic uses of imagery. I would prefer to believe, however, that the emergence of a great variety of uses of imagery in treatment of emotional disorders reflects a genuine increase in the level of sophistication of the behavior sciences, a natural response to the new technology of research, and the need for more cognitive or information-processing models of personality. The exciting new researches and theorizing concerning cognitive processes and role of imagery in learning and memory (Paivio, 1971) reflect an advance in model construction in psychological theory over the S–R or narrowly gauged operant-conditioning models that dominated the field from the 1920s through the mid-1960s. Similarly, if less systematically, the emergence of a diversity of clinical applications of imagery, fantasy, and related "central" or inner processes in the 1960s may reflect a profound dissatisfaction with earlier clinical models, especially those emphasizing hydraulic energy models, displacements of drive pressures, or stimulus–response learning sequences. Some disturbing restlessness about the limitations of classical psychoanalysis or even its neo-Freudian variants has shaken the structure of the psychotherapeutic establishment that became so firmly entrenched during the 1940s and 1950s.

The outcome of this growing uneasiness has been the widespread experimentation with a broad range of methods and new models. Some of these newer approaches have merely been efforts to speed up the slow course of psychoanalysis, but most of the approaches have questioned many of the *technical*, if not always the *theoretical*, assumptions of the "dynamic" points of view. The eagerness of clinicians to plunge into ameliorative efforts without a sufficient basis in scientific research or formal theoretical analysis has led inevitably to a proliferation of methods, schools, and institutes—all with adherents, training programs, and distinctive aptitudes for publicity and self-advertisement.

Just consider what this can lead to. In the New York metropolitan area alone one already finds adherents of the numerous "established" psychotherapy schools, each with its own institute or group and widely differing standards for certification. A mere listing is enough to make one gasp. Classical psychoanalysis is represented by at least three or four separate groups, the most prestigious being the New York Psychoanalytic Institute, which competes with the Institute of Psychoanalytic Training and Research, the Metropolitan Institute for Psychoanalytic Studies, the Freudian Institute, and some others. Neo-Freudian institutes or groups include the Horney School (Association for the Advancement of Psychoanalysis), the William Alanson White Institute (reflecting the influence of Sullivan, Fromm, Fromm-Reichmann, and Thompson, as well as Freud), the Sullivan Institute (a split off from the White Institute), the Columbia Psychoanalytic group, the New York–Flower Medical College group, the Postgraduate Center for Mental

Health, the National Psychological Association of Psychoanalysis (which leans toward classical psychoanalytic theory), and at least three or four others that also combine treatment clinics and training programs. There are, in addition, groups representing the positions of Jung and Adler, the original dissenters from Freud's initial band of followers. The postdoctoral programs affiliated with New York University and Adelphi University tend to be mixes of classical and neo-Freudian approaches, but reflect also the existential and humanist psychotherapy groups. There are, of course, also followers of Melanie Klein or the Fairbairn–Winnecott–Guntrip–Laing object-relations approaches from England—these are largely represented in the White Institute or the university postdoctoral groups. Then there are the Gestalt therapists, the followers of Wilhelm Reich's *Orgone therapy,* now termed the *bioenergetic method,* the various representatives of the Esalen "encounter group" movement, and the various circles of therapists representing group therapy or small-group process approaches. Long established is Moreno's Psychodrama Institute, clearly an ancestor of many humanist, encounter, Esalen, Gestalt, and small-group role-playing orientations.

Most of these approaches may be characterized as being oriented toward "dynamics," the "total personality," or profound personality reorientation as a goal of psychotherapy. But New York, perhaps lagging a bit behind the United States heartland, now also has representatives and training opportunities in various behavior modification and operant-conditioning techniques. Moreover, several training institutes in hypnosis are also in existence; the Morton Price Clinic, for example, is well established.

Thus far, all the groups cited meet at least some criteria as "establishment" enterprises in the sense that their leadership or training cadres include physicians, psychologists, and social workers, who in order to obtain their degrees have been exposed to at least some formal scientific training. There are probably dozens of "fringe groups," self-appointed encounter group specialists, astrologers, therapeutic representatives of various meditation methods, or Oriental quasi-religious sects, psychic healers, and so on. As a long-time New Yorker, I prefer to think such groups are more numerous in Los Angeles.

Had enough? If this situation prevails for more general therapeutic orientations (and I will probably be assailed by some colleagues for having overlooked *their* institutes), consider the problem if we limit ourselves just to the psychotherapeutic uses of imagery and fantasy techniques. Perhaps the reader whose head may already be spinning can be helped if we prepare a small table on which to identify the various imagery approaches along a continuum. Somewhat facetiously, Table I

TABLE I

The Spectrum of Psychotherapeutic Uses of Imagery

Left Wing		Center			Right Wing
Left	Right	Left	Center	Right	
1. Esalen-type imagery games	1. Humanistic group approaches	1. Moreno's psychodrama	1. Izard's affect therapy	1. Lazarus' emotive imagery	1. Hypnosis
2. Drug-focused therapy imagery games	2. Gestalt marathons	2. Gestalt therapy	2. Neo-Freudian groups (Fromm, May, Tauber, Green)	2. Jung's "active imagination"	2. Classical psychoanalysis
3. Mystical or occult fantasy exercises	3. T-group imagery games	3. Psychosynthesis (Assagiodi)	3. European "mental imagery" schools (Desoille, Frétigny, and Virel, Leuner, Rigo)	3. Adlerian uses of early memories	3. Reyher's "emergent uncovering"
	4. Transcendental or Zen meditation therapies	4. Shorr's "psycho-imagination" therapy	4. Gendlin's "focusing"		4. Behavior modification approaches
		5. Berne's "transactional analysis"			a. Systematic densitization (e.g., Wolpe)
		6. Ellis' "rational-emotive therapy"			b. Convert conditioning methods (e.g., Cautela)
					c. Implosive therapy
					5. Symbolic modeling (Bandura)

is modeled on comedian Mort Sahl's method for classifying political parties, issues, and public figures: the Left- (Left–Center–Right), Center- (Left–Center–Right), and Right- (Left–Center–Right) Wing classification system.

In using these ideological polarities as a peg to aid the reader in identifying different methods, I recognize how limited and perhaps downright insulting some of these categorizations may be. My main point is to convey the dilemma that serious behavioral scientists must face if they wish to relate what they or others do in practice and applied psychology to some fundamental scientific principles. Classical psychoanalysts, assigned by me to the Right Wing, certainly can protest that in pure form the orthodox analytic procedure is the most liberating, as well as the most respectful of the individual's growth. The minimal intervention of the "blank screen" psychoanalyst, the premium assigned to endless free association, the slow and painful development of the "transference neurosis," and its careful analysis through cautious interpretation all may be described as reflecting the *least* authoritarian of methods.

Viewed sociologically, however, the direct descendant of Freud's psychoanalysis has for about 25 years dominated the psychiatric establishment in prestige and academic power. Its practitioners are most likely to be physicians well versed in the medical model and most scornful of other schools. They receive the highest fees in the psychotherapeutic field (seeing patients four or five times a week, nevertheless) and, according to some research reports, are the most conservative politically, as well as academically, at least among psychotherapists — who on the whole are inclined toward left-of-center social views. The orthodox Freudians use imagery within the context of the principles of dream and transference fantasy interpretation laid down by Freud some 60 years ago, and the Right Wing assignment seems justified on this basis. Reyher's (1963) application of imagery association, instead of verbal association, represents a technical exploration within this framework that itself harks back to Freud's early efforts at devising a cathartic method beyond hypnosis. Reyher also operates very much within the psychoanalytic drive-cathexis system with much emphasis on symbolism and unconscious fantasy, so his method clearly must be assigned to the Freudian "Right Wing."

Also on the Right Wing, perhaps to the right of psychoanalysis because of their highly academic emphasis and somewhat "dehumanized" style, can be found most of the behavior modification approaches. These methods, although traceable to the early days of Watson's behaviorism, have largely burgeoned within only the past decade. They are "establishment" in psychology, representing as they do an applied flowering of the neo-Hullian and Skinnerian learning theory approaches which have dominated the majority of academic departments in psychology for about 35 years. They also represent very formal methods, on the whole, with rather rigid procedural specifications — much as the classical psychoanalytic procedure.

The uses of imagery in behavior modification that seems especially a part of this Right Wing grouping would include *systematic desensitization, aversive conditioning, counterconditioning* through imagery, and *thought-stopping* methods. Somewhat to the left, one might locate *imaginal modeling* or related symbolic mediation methods of imitation or response elicitation or disinhibition, as well as the *implosive therapy* methods, which combine some psychoanalytic formulations and cathartic ideas with a learning formulation. These methods, as well as *emotive imagery* techniques, would appear to shade over toward the Center because they emphasize somewhat more the social learning or social interaction and affective components of the personality. Hypnosis used purely for symptom removal probably belongs very much to the Right Wing of imagery techniques, but hypnosis cast within a more dynamic approach probably belongs over more toward the Center.

Moving to the Center of our chart, we find on the right end the imagery uses such as Jung's active imagination, part of a well-established analytic technique, more flexible than classical Freudian methods, but still relatively conservative in its control of the amount of therapist activity and in its emphasis on the patient's associations and a fairly structured therapist–client relationship. The Adlerian emphasis on early memories or on the dream as a projective method and the somewhat formalized relationship places it here. More to the Center, one might locate the affect-oriented techniques (Izard, 1971), with their particular emphasis on face-to-face interaction, as well as some neo-Freudian schools which greatly emphasize countertransference reactions as clues to patient communications (Tauber & Green, 1959) or fantasies, and the Sullivan-influenced emphasis on the communication dyad with the focus more on language than on imagery. The kind of symbolic dream analysis used in Fromm's type of confrontation method (Fromm, 1968) or in May's mixture of neo-Freudian and existential approaches (Caligor & May, 1968) are couched in somewhat looser forms than other psychoanalytic procedures, but still remain fairly conservative in the structure of the patient–therapist relationship and in their relationship to traditional psychoanalytic methods.

Very much a part of the Center one must include what are loosely linked together as the European mental imagery techniques. These, of course, owe much to Freud's dream interpretation and Jung's even more elaborate symbolic interpretative methods. Desoille's "guided daydream" technique owes some elements to the conditioning approach, as well, and probably belongs over on the Right of Center, while Leuner's fairly structured system, but freer interpersonal orientation, probably belongs smack in the Center. The somewhat more loosely organized psychosynthesis uses of imagery by Gerard, Assagioli, and Shorr probably belong slightly to the Left of Center, where one might place also Moreno's psychodramatic methods and the more conservative practitioners of Gestalt therapy. Rigo's group use of mental imagery methods probably belongs on this Left of Center location, as well.

Some client-centered therapy techniques such as Gendlin's focusing probably belong very much in the Center, although they are not as widely used. And perhaps some of the more conservative methods of Yoga or Zen meditation belong Left of Center or over on the right edge of the Left Wing.

We come finally to the Left Wing, where we find the most spontaneous — but also least controlled — uses of imagery. On the right edge of this group, one might find humanistic or Gestalt imagery techniques, still cast more or less in a client–therapist mould, but with the distinction often blurred as to who is who and much "acting out" of fantasy and imagery. Uses of rhythmic meditation and imagery games as part of encounter groups or T groups would probably belong to the Left Wing, as well, and over more to the center of Left Wing. Finally, one might find at the extreme left the many Esalen-type loosely structured, sometimes drug-oriented uses of fantasy and imagery in which patients "enter" into each other's imagery and the fantasies of patients and therapists are hard to disentangle. Some of the procedures described by Schutz (1967) range across the whole Left Wing. The group fantasies of the type described by Alexander (1969) seem fairly extreme in their blurring of what is formal therapy and what is a drowsy sense of intimacy, which (as in the case of friends or lovers) can include the sharing of fantasies.

I have led the reader quite purposefully on a "trip" across this chart because it makes especially vivid the great range of imagery approaches, their complexity, and the need ultimately for some kind of integration or establishment of basic principles of imagery. Table I also points up the exciting multitude of possibilities now being explored, as well as the dilemma one faces in trying to make sense of this field. We can return to our earlier question: if the public comes to the psychologist or psychiatrist expecting help based on some systematic scientific knowledge, what can a practitioner say in view of this chart. Are all the methods equally valid or scientifically rooted? Are some of them whimsies off the top of the heads of high-powered "personalities" who are somewhat fuzzy thinkers? Is some of the appeal of newer methods much different from the earlier (and still persisting) attraction that revival meetings, Holy Roller sessions, and Snake-Handling hold for large segments of the population?

While my tone may seem facetious, the issues in this situation are deadly serious. There is a desperate need for a serious and sobering examination of the premises that underlie every facet of psychotherapeutic technique. The Tower of Babel effect in clinical psychiatry and psychology reflects an early and not fully developed scientific discipline. Some openness and exploration can be useful, of course. However, it is critically important that practitioners of a behavioral science not only recognize their limits, but also play an active role in finding a common language and a system that meets at least some reasonable criteria of the scientific method.

OBJECTIVES

Review of Imagery Uses in Psychotherapy

As a first step in attempting to come to grips with the chaotic situation in the field of psychotherapy, specifically in relation to the uses of imagery in psychological treatment, it is necessary to examine in detail at least some of the various types of imagery that have been employed in reasonably consistent and systematic fashion. In presenting this review my intention will also be to include all the possible specific examples of how therapy operates and present references to case material drawn from literature or from references based on my own personal experience in their use. Naturally, the experiences of any individual psychotherapist are limited by the exigencies of his own practice and type of case load. One of the initial motives for development of this book was that there were no reviews available in the literature that examined imagery techniques in psychotherapy. Indeed, some brief articles by myself and others (Singer, 1971b, 1972) and short chapters or sections within other books on imagery (Horowitz, 1970; Richardson, 1969) represented the beginnings of such an effort. Unfortunately, in a field like psychology and psychiatry, subgroups tend to speak largely to each other, and it is surprising how few of the behavior therapists who use imagery are aware of the European mental imagery techniques. It has also seemed to me that many of the practitioners of dynamically oriented approaches to imagery were largely oblivious of the rather dramatic advances in imagery techniques amongst the behavior therapists and some of the nonanalytic groups. If this volume serves no other purpose than to present in reasonable detail the panoply of the techniques to a wider readership, it may open the way for greater communication between groups and also for examination of fundamental similarities and differences that will ultimately lead to systematic research.

Theoretical Basis
for Imagery Research

The second major intention of this volume is to call attention to the explicit or implicit theoretical assumptions underlying the various imagery techniques. By so doing it may be possible to look for common theoretical assumptions or, where these do not exist, to propose some. A possible unifying position may lie in a particular viewpoint temporarily labeled the cognitive–affective position in psychology, which seems to me to be closely tied on the one hand to basic research areas in the psychology of cognition (which includes recent work on imagery) and the interrelations of cognition and emotion, as exemplified in the theoretical position of Tomkins (1962, 1963), for example.

While some aspects of the volume are written in the spirit of proposing a theoretical conception having at least the possibility of encompassing a large number of uses of imagery in psychotherapy, it is also intended to include, wherever possible, relevant theoretical models drawn from basic psychology that may represent either alternatives to the cognitive–affective position, or at least be useful heuristically in fostering integrative research in this area. An important contribution that can be made in this connection is to present in some detail the current status of research on imagery in psychology in close juxtaposition to the applied aspects of imagery in the psychotherapeutic process. This has not yet been done, and it may be that there is too great a gap between what practitioners do and the kind of research evidence available in the field of imagery. On the other hand, it is even more likely that a close look at what actual facts begin to emerge on the nature of human imagery can help us to formulate a more systematic approach to the application of imagery to behavior change of self-understanding. The reader can judge whether this approach is useful as we proceed.

A first step in this direction is to review the changing pattern of approaches to imagery in the scientific literature and to examine some of the methods that have been used by psychologists to measure the effects and special properties of imagery. This will mean that it is necessary to introduce some examples from experimental research, which at first glance may seem a far cry from the applications of imagery to the treatment of various symptoms or personality disorders. Again, the reader can judge as we go along whether such an attempt resembles mixing apples and oranges. It is not intended, however, that this volume substitute for more extensive reviews of the available literature on the psychology of imagery, much of which may not be at all relevant to the psychotherapeutic process. Therefore, the reader is referred to recent books on the subject (see Richardson, 1969; Horowitz, 1970; Segal, 1971; Paivio, 1971; Sheehan, 1972).

Practical Implications
of Imagery Approaches in Psychotherapy

A final major objective is to use this review of theory research and the range of imagery uses to see if it is possible to make some practical suggestions to the psychotherapist. At a time when there is such an abundance of riches in the way of new technology in psychotherapy to choose from, the practitioner may be hard put to know which approaches are useful for particular kinds of patients and which approaches have at least some reasonable basis, in the scientific literature, for application.

In presenting examples of different treatment methods and relating them wherever possible to the formal literature in the field, it is hoped that this volume can give therapists a choice that will increase the effectiveness of their work and also clarify for them the important issue of the relation of their work to the basic knowledge in behavioral science. This is indeed a lofty ambition, but the reader can judge its effectiveness for himself. In addition, the emphasis on practical issues may also lead to a clarification of research possibilities in a variety of studies of applied problems in psychotherapy. The greatest advantage of the behavior modification techniques has been the fact that they have generated within less than a decade far more systematic evaluative research than all other therapeutic efforts of the previous century combined. In this sense, we seem on the threshold of a genuine breakthrough in the knotty problem of evaluating technical features of the psychotherapeutic process.

THE NEED FOR OBJECTIVE STUDY
OF PSYCHOTHERAPY

Set against the need for some effort and integration and enlightenment in the face of the confusion in the field of imagery approaches in psychotherapy, a first step is essentially to review and record the different uses made of imagery in all types of psychotherapy. A glance at Table I will suggest this is no minor task in itself. At the same time, it is also important that one move beyond mere listing to detailed examination of the ways in which these procedures are actually employed, at least on the basis of the descriptions in available literature by their practitioners. Here any single author is bound to be somewhat limited since no one is likely to have had any extended experience with the full range of procedures. There are bound to be in any account of therapeutic procedures with which one is not directly experienced, misunderstandings or limitations of imagination, as well as of specific approaches. Nevertheless, one of the criteria of a scientific field is that its methods are, within reasonable limits, communicable through the medium of professional literature.

To argue that one must have directly experienced a psychotherapeutic technique either as a patient or as a practitioner in order to understand it and to reason about it is an extremely dangerous position to try to maintain from a systematic standpoint. A Freudian might take issue with the criticism of psychoanalytic methods by a Gestalt therapist or by a practitioner of the "rational–emotive" approach of Ellis. These people in many instances have presumably not undergone classical psychoanalysis. On the other hand, the analyst can scarcely be in the position of criticizing other positions in psychotherapy since he is not likely to have experienced their benefits either as patient or therapist.

Albert Ellis, for example, discounts the significance of transference phenomena as a part of the psychotherapeutic technique. This seems absurd to most practitioners who have carried on extensive analytic types of therapy. But how is one ever to know whether significant therapy can be carried out without transference analysis or the development of a transference at all if one limits oneself only to a psychoanalytically oriented treatment procedure? If the direct personal experience of an individual is the critical feature in determining the validity of psychotherapeutic process, then we find ourselves in the dilemma of never being able to resolve the theoretical or technical differences among the various schools of practice.

The argument that certain psychotherapeutic methods have been practiced for nearly a century is not terribly convincing in the face of the fact that astrology has been practiced for thousands of years, but is not yet taken seriously by scientifically trained persons. The fact that certain prestigious and recognizably brilliant individuals are associated with particular schools is also not a satisfactory argument. Although no one would doubt that Freud was an original and highly gifted individual and certainly one of the towering figures of the twentieth century, it would be hard to deny a similar status to Jung. One need not list the names of other major figures in psychiatry in order to make the point that prestige and authority are simply not sufficient bases for accepting the validity of a given theory or approach to practice. Unless one prefers to view different approaches to psychotherapy as essentially quasi-philosophical or moralistic positions, closely akin to religious faiths, the various imagery techniques must ultimately be judged in some common court where appeal is based on reasonably explicit scientific evidence.

If this argument has merit, then it would not seem necessary to be thoroughly experienced in all types of imagery techniques in order to describe and, at least within reason, to evaluate some of them. One of the major principles of science is that those who espouse a particular theoretical position have the burden of proof upon themselves for supporting such a position or encouraging others to do so. The case in point with relevance to the imagery techniques arose with the emergence of behavior modification methods in psychotherapy in the last decade. Wolpe, Eysenck, Lazarus, and other early advocates of behavior modification argued that their major concern was with the relief of symptoms by direct intervention and the use of learning or relearning method. More dynamically oriented psychotherapists argued that it had long been accepted that symptomatic relief was not sufficiently productive of personality change in psychotherapy, and there was general feeling that all that would occur as a result of removal of symptoms by the behavior modification methods would be the displacement of the conflict to another aspect of behavior with the consequence that other symptoms would emerge. Here is a case where a long-believed factor in psychotherapy had never been adequately tested, but actually was accepted on the basis of some incidental observations reported many years ago by the pioneer psychoanalysts.

The behavior therapists reported that they have little evidence that symptom displacement did occur in patients whose phobic or compulsive symptoms they were able to relieve. They were able to present some case data in support of this position (Bandura, 1969), but, again, their position was clearly that it was not relevant to raise the question of displacement unless someone could provide evidence to support it initially.

Indeed, this really seems the case. The psychoanalyst, however personally convinced he might be that symptom displacement should occur on theoretical grounds, bears the burden of proof for demonstrating that it occurs before attacking behavior therapists for simply ignoring the issue of displacement and the "underlying" problem. If a psychotherapist maintains that the symptom of behavior disorder shown by a patient is not itself the problem, but rather a manifestation of the deeper difficulty, then it behooves him to demonstrate this before he challenges the validity of work that is addressed directly to the relief of symptoms.

Here, clearly, is a question that can be resolved by formal investigation. To the extent that psychoanalysts can demonstrate that patients treated by behavior therapists under appropriate conditions and who have shown clear improvement in specific symptoms indeed show later recurrence of the same symptoms or of symptoms that can be systematically related to the original ones, they are in position to criticize the limited value of behavior therapy. Failing such demonstration, they had best keep silent on this point, and, indeed, reexamine their own theoretical formulations.

While one need not, therefore, have experienced or practiced all of the forms of imagery therapy in order to review them, it does help in terms of presentation and expression of some of the characteristics to have attempted at least some. In this sense, although trained in neo-Freudian interpersonal psychoanalysis on the basis of a strong allegiance to psychology as a scientific discipline, I have found myself forced not only to review the literature but, where it seemed feasible, to employ some of the imagery techniques described. As a particular therapist I have perhaps a somewhat broader experience in the use of these techniques than most psychoanalytically oriented clinicians. Nevertheless, it would be folly to insist that I have any practical experience at all, other than attending case conferences or reading appropriate literature in some of the European mental imagery techniques.

It is important in a review of this sort to attempt to present the theoretical basis of the various practices to the extent that they are made sufficiently explicit in the available literature and to relate them to significant historical positions within the behavioral sciences. This I will attempt to do at least in a relatively abbreviated fashion. In addition, it is necessary that one examine examples of specific practice approaches. Fortunately, there is a sufficient number of case examples of most of these methods described with reasonable explicitness in the literature to do so. Where such a case example is not sufficiently explicit, this constitutes a criticism of the practitioners themselves.

An important breakthrough in psychotherapeutic method was made when Carl Rogers began, in the early 1940s, to record complete psychotherapy sessions and to begin to analyze them according to reasonably reliable methods of judgment and rating. Many techniques of psychotherapy are now being subjected to the same detailed scrutiny. Any ongoing treatment process is difficult, indeed, to examine from this standpoint because of the cost of transcribing the tape recordings or videotape material (if this more expensive method is used). Such recordings are primarily employed for teaching purposes, for which they are invaluable. Ideally, one ought to have sets of protocols of patients treated by the different methods under circumstances where the personalities of the patients and of the therapists are systematically varied so that one can evaluate how much of the outcome or differences in process is a function of the characteristics of a patient and/or therapist and how much is indeed a function of a specific technique. Thus far, it is almost impossible to mount so expensive a research program for the kinds of methods described in this volume. The volume by Meltzoff and Kornreich (1970) or the extensive reviews by Strupp and Bergin (1969) demonstrate the range of possible methods for evaluating psychotherapeutic approaches. These reviews are extremely valuable in indicating just what methods are available scientifically for comparing different psychotherapeutic approaches and what criteria must be employed in examining the available research literature in this field.

CHAPTER II

THE HISTORICAL VICISSITUDES
OF IMAGERY

Man consists of body, mind, and imagination. His body is faulty, his mind untrustworthy, but his imagination has made him remarkable. In some centuries, his imagination has made life on this planet an intense practice of all the lovelier energies.

John Masefield (1924, pp. 3–4)

Man's capacity to produce imagery, which has rarely been questioned, has served as an inspiration to writers and artists over the millennia of man's recorded past. There have, of course, been some shifts in the degree of emphasis placed by the literary or cultural traditions of various societies upon the use of imagery and its role in human experience. Perhaps our earliest indications of the power of human imagery, both as a capacity of mankind and also as a symbol of control over the environment, are the famous Lascaux cave paintings, which we still admire so much today. In these haunting works, man's creative powers, as manifested through memory images, are evident in the vividness and clarity of the drawing. Obviously, in many cases the cave painters worked by torch or firelight from memory. In the darkness of the cave they still had the capacity to project, from the mind's eye, impressions of leaping bisons, which they then could trace upon cavern walls.

Given the internal power to span time through the use of his images, it does not seem strange that early man should also believe that his reproductions of the beasts could give man the power to control these animals in fact. Man's imagery thus gives him a sense that he can control his world and determine, to some extent, his own or other's destinies through his image-making capacity. Strangely enough, the power of imagery used in decorating the tombs of Pharaohs may not have served its original purpose of providing a homelike atmosphere for the dead dignitaries in the world beyond, but it has indeed reproduced that world for us to appreciate and understand, and indeed to see that world in action thousands of years after all the living participants disappeared. Reproductive imagery does have the power of transcending time and space.

The more fanciful facets of imagery have also long been recognized for their power and human implications. One need not review the many biblical references to the nature of dreams and visions. The story of Joseph the Dreamer is sufficient example to indicate the important power attributed to this nocturnal imagery by the ancients 3000 years or more before our time. The exact meaning of dreams for different cultures is quite a separate study and need not concern us for the moment, except to call attention to the fact that there have been greatly varying emphases placed on the dream as either a symbol of one's problems or status in life or as an indication of actual events to occur in the future. There is little question, however, that most cultures in both religious and literary expressions have paid considerable attention to man's images whether waking or sleeping and have sought to understand their import.

Complex and contradictory attitudes toward image-making are evident in different religious traditions as well. Consider how important image-making was in the development of Judaism for the notion of an abstract God to be proposed and the use of statues or "graven images" to be condemned. One facet of the Judaic tradition has to do with the internalization of the image of God, and the defeat of "extroverted" idol worship. Recall the quaint Talmudic story of the child Abraham destroying a whole group of idols—leaving only one standing. He defended himself in the morning to the dismayed worshipers by suggesting that the biggest idol had destroyed the others. The legend exemplifies the attempt to scorn the power of external imagery and support the more advanced concept of an abstract monotheism.

Within Christianity itself, as well as in Islam, there are contradictions and doubts concerning the importance of imagery. We are poorer today in the availability of Hellenistic and later Roman art because of the iconoclastic movement within Christianity in the eighth century A.D. Similarly, within Islam, the ban on human imagery had led to great developments in the field of abstract design or nature drawing—the ban exemplifies a widely held fear of the power possessed by drawings of the human image.

By the beginnings of the Renaissance in Europe, there were many indications that imagery, both of human forms and of nature, could be put to powerful literary and artistic use. Consider, for example, the tremendous effect of the vivid images, concrete examples, and metaphors that appear in the writings of Dante and Chaucer. Without question, an important feature of the power and impact of writers such as Chaucer, Spenser, and Shakespeare lies in their extended use of concrete words in combinations likely to evoke fairly vivid auditory, olfactory, tactile, or visual images in their readers. Perhaps the greatest of all image masters was Shakespeare, and he seemed to have a clear psychological sense of how imagery could be used to evoke moods or powerful emotions. Here, for example, is Shakespeare's prologue to Henry V wherein he urges the audience to use their imagination in order to make the drama more vivid than mere players on a limited stage can accomplish:

> O, pardon! since a crooked figure may
> Attest in little place a million
> And let us, ciphers to this great accompt,
> On your imaginary forces work.
> Suppose within the girdle of these walls are now confined two mighty monarchies.
> Whose high up-reared and abutting fronts
> The perilous narrow ocean parts asunder:
> Piece out our imperfections with your thoughts;
> Into a thousand parts divide one man,
> And make imaginary puissance;
> Think, when we talk of horses, that you see them
> Printing their proud hoofs i' the receiving earth;
> For 'tis your thoughts that now must deck our kings,
> Carry them here and there; jumping o'er times,
> Turning the accomplishment of many years
> Into an hourglass . . .   (*Henry V*. Prologue)*

Shakespeare's great capacity for imagery is so evident even in the brief passage just cited; its reference to the "printing . . . [horses]

* Cambridge Edition, W. A. Wright, Ed. Doubleday, 1936. P. 557.

hoofs" into the "receiving earth" has been extensively analyzed by Spurgeon (1935) in a remarkable study of Shakespeare's poetic achievement. Spurgeon contrasted the imagery of Shakespeare as evidenced in his plays with those of contemporary poets and playwrights. By a careful count of the actual occurrences of imagery in the writings of Shakespeare, Marlowe, and Bacon, among others, she was able to show that Shakespeare produced a much greater number and range of images, including many more specific references to what she called "town" imagery, but which we might view as the use of images related to specific sensory modalities, smell, touch, taste, audition, kinesthesis, as well as vision. The power of Shakespeare as poet and playwright lies very much in the use of images from every modality in ways that at once force us, as we listen, to reproduce, at least to some extent, the same image in a comparable modality. Hence, Shakespeare draws us much more actively into the experience of the character or into the scene being described.

In English literature, such an emphasis on imagery was maintained in the writings of Donne and Milton, and persisted at least through part of the seventeenth century. A period of almost 100 years followed, however, in which imagery lost its importance in literature in favor of the emphasis on skillful and clever use of words. This was the more classical era of English literature, where emphasis was largely on wit and rationality. The imagery employed tended to be (at least in the case of poetry) rather stylized—nymphs pursued by shepherds, much in the rather passionless and cloying quality that characterizes so much of the art of the period.

It was only with the onset of the nineteenth century that the Romanticism reemphasized concrete imagery, fantasy, and dreams as central features of literature. There was a recurrence of the strong use of specific modality-oriented images of the type that Shakespeare stressed. The creation of a mood, of a vivid internal experience, rather than the communication of a verbal idea, again became a central goal for poetry. We see this clearly in the sensuous poetry of Keats, in works such as "Ode to the Nightingale" and "St. Agnes' Eve." On the European continent, the forerunner of Romanticism was Goethe, whose plays, novels, and poetry revived and revivified interest in imagery, dreams, and the fantasy realm of human behavior. As Goethe said in one of his *Conversations with Eckerman:*

> It was altogether not my manner as a poet to strive for the embodiment of something *abstract.* I received *impressions*—impressions that were sensuous, vital, lovely, motley, hundredfold—whatever a lively power of imagination offered me; and as a poet I did not have to do anything but round out and form such

visions and impressions artistically, and to present them in such a live manner that others received the same impressions when hearing or reading what I
offered.

Can we surmise that Shakespeare and Goethe are so eminently quot-
able in part because their lines, replete with concrete references, are
more easily remembered by their readers? The experimental research
work of Paivio (1971) has made it very clear that concrete words are
better remembered than abstract ones. I will return to this theme
shortly.

To continue examining the many changes in literary and artistic
views of imagery would carry us too far afield. Rather, it seems sufficient to call the reader's attention to the importance of imagery in
both Western civilization and many Eastern cultures, as well. Nor
should the emphasis on literary representations of imagery limit the
reader's appreciation in this regard. Certainly, the use of music to
evoke emotions of various kinds, as well as images, is part of many cultures. Within Western Europe, the power of music to evoke not only
devotional attitudes, but fairly specific images, is widely recognized.
Today critics are less attracted to music that is specifically "pictorial" in
quality, but there is no doubt that composers as diverse as Bach,
Couperin, Beethoven (the Sixth Symphony), Berlioz, Wagner, Debussy,
and Richard Strauss were especially effective in evoking mood, as most
composers seek to do, and also in conveying striking visual images
through the use of tonal effects. Romantic composers such as Mendel-
sohn and Schumann were masters at producing in the listener, on the
one hand, the sense of the humorous and strange land of elves and
fairies and, on the other hand, the sense of mystery and awe of the
olden times or of the dreamings of the child.

Before we turn to the somewhat drier examination of the scientific
study of man's imagery, it may be worth quoting one more example of
the insight of the artist into man's inner experiences. Scholars such as
Bachélard (1964) and Chateau (1967) have been reviving recently our
awareness that our interior monologues, our memories, our fantasies
are an essential part of our own reality. But listen to Shakespeare:

Our revels now are ended. These our actors,
As I foretold you, were all spirits, and
Are melted into air, into thin air:
And, like the baseless fabric of this vision,
The cloud-capp'd towers, the gorgeous palaces,
The solemn temples, the great globe itself,
Yea, all which it inherit, shall dissolve,
And, like this insubstantial pageant faded,

Leave not a rack behind. We are such stuff
As dreams are made on; And our little life
Is rounded with a sleep.*

EARLY PSYCHOLOGICAL STUDIES OF IMAGERY

Formal research on imagery did not begin until well into the nine-teenth century, but some systematic thinking in this field can be traced back to Hume, the great British philosopher of the eighteenth century. Hume distinguished between what he called *impressions* and by which he meant sensations and emotions or what we would call *percepts* today, and the more *faint images* which characterize thinking and reasoning (Hume, 1912). The criteria Hume employed in making his distinction were the degree of force and liveliness or vividness of the images, ex-ternally derived sensory material being characterized by greater combi-nations of force and vividness when compared with thoughts. The nineteenth century saw a great deal of armchair analysis and specula-tion about the differences between images and percepts, but with very little attempt to move beyond the private experience of the particular investigator. Even with the development of an experimental psychology in the laboratory by Wundt, the emphasis was still upon a distinction based essentially on the personal experience of the subject in any study, and this hinged largely on intensity, vividness, and persistence of the percept in comparison with that of the memory image.

A major problem that psychology faced throughout most of this period was how to obtain some reasonably objective estimate of the presence or absence of imagery and of its relative vividness in relation to the intensity of a percept. Work carried out by Schaub (1911) in-dicated that observers producing imagery and also listening to actual sounds in four different kinds of tasks reported that when both the images and sensations had pretty much the same degree of intensity they could not serve as suitable criteria for differentiating an objectively presented stimulus from an imagined sound.

Still another half century passed before these problems were ad-dressed again by a more specific and advanced technology and method of measurement. To demonstrate more precisely the relationship between an image and an externally derived percept, Sheehan (1966) was able to develop an apparatus by which one could evaluate, through manipulation of color and form, the relative vividness of an individual's

* *The Tempest,* Cambridge Edition, W. A. Wright, Ed. Doubleday, 1936. P. 1319.

simple images. Even more extensive research (described in later sections) by Segal (1971), indicated that individuals projecting imagined scenes on a blank screen could not detect whether an actual, externally projected image was simultaneously appearing on the screen.

Segal's (1971) work in the 1960s was essentially an extension and replication by a study done by Perky (1910) many years before in Titchener's laboratory. There had been raging in psychology considerable controversy during the first part of the twentieth century about the nature of imagery and whether indeed all thinking required some form of visual or auditory imagery in order to be carried on. Titchener himself, a person of apparently acute imagery, argued strongly in favor of this position, while the opposition came from the so-called Würzberg school in Germany led by Külpe and Ach, among others. The issue eventually seemed decided in favor of the Würzberg school because of a series of studies which indicated that attitudinal sets did not require imagery in order to influence thinking or perception. Probably, the emphasis on set and function placed by the Würzberg school also meshed well with the functionalists and beginning behaviorist tendency in American psychology and brought about the downfall of Titchener's hegemony over American psychology.

Along with the defeat of Titchener came the loss of interest in what had been for him a central issue in psychology: the nature of the image. It is said that the brash and vigorous John B. Watson used to make considerable fun of the introspective efforts, characteristic of Titchener's students, to catch hold of sensations and images. In his push toward development of an objective psychology based essentially on precise definitions of stimulus and response, the response often enough being measurable in the maze running of a rat, the founder of behaviorism led American psychologists far away from the study of inner experience. Indeed, Watson on occasion referred to all thinking as subvocal speech. No doubt, implicit vocal responses are a part of our thinking, as McGuigan's studies of muscular responses in the throat have demonstrated (McGuigan, 1966).

Watson's emphasis on thought as behavior and, more specifically, as subvocal speech won some experimental support in a limited sense, but has also been subjected to quite serious theoretical criticism (Lashley, 1929). A similar argument, although not specifically oriented to the issue of the muscular aspects of thought, also has been raised by Skinner (1953) in his attempt to show that basically what psychologists need to study are overt behavioral reactions characterized either by spoken words or by overt movements of the organism.

Neither Watson nor Skinner, whose thought and research emphases have dominated American psychology between 1910 and 1970, were so naive as to deny that people indeed have thoughts, images, and dreams. Yet Watson and Skinner did represent a certain healthy influence on the development of psychological science in the sense that they made it important for psychologists to examine in detail all of their inferences, to demonstrate that these inferences were based on reasonably parsimonious interpretation of a set of facts, and they particularly emphasized that public operations be the basis for scientific discussion. By *public operation* they meant, generally speaking, overt responses or verbalizations that could be quantified.

While it may be argued that an extreme form of this position is naive and self-defeating for psychology, Watson and Skinner did open the way for many ingenious methodologies to be developed to capture the ongoing behavior both of animals and human beings. In addition, they set a limitation on introspective speculation of the kind central to psychoanalysis, where so many "data" depend on the personal experience of individual analysts who report their case material only very sketchily and then proceed to elaborate theoretical formulations. The operational emphasis of the objective behaviorists imposes a difficult, but welcome, standard for what kinds of evidence may be admitted in psychological research. In a certain sense, this is a most democratic system for it means that we rely less upon the authority of powerful figures or teachers and that the lowliest graduate student has the right to question a statement that cannot be supported by observable and replicable data.

Viewed in a historical perspective, Watson's development of behaviorism can be seen as an attack on the then establishment figure of Titchener, who was a strong advocate of introspective research in the study of sensation and perception. Watson, as indicated earlier, is reported to have made fun of Titchener's methods at public meetings much to the delight of the younger psychologists and graduate students in attendance. To some extent this satire was justified because of the extremely arid and nonproductive nature of much of the introspectionism that characterized Titchener's group and also because of its heavy dependence on the authority of the "professor," rather than upon replicable research.

With the rout of introspectionism during the second decade of the twentieth century, there was, however, a movement toward the other extreme. Suffice it to say the valuable aspects of Titchener's emphasis on imagery and some of the interesting research already under way in Titchener's laboratories was forgotten. One example is the Perky effect. Perky, a student of Titchener, demonstrated that if a subject imagined an image projected on a screen while the investigator surreptitiously flashed a slide of that image on the screen, the subject frequently could not tell whether the image he had seen was his own projection or whether an internally generated image could indeed prevent his being able to report the occurrence in the same field of an externally projected stimulus. It is of no use now to complain that psychology may have lost 50 years in research in imagery or to wish that applying sophisticated psychophysical methods of signal detection theory suggested by Segal (1971), had been applied to the imagery problems generated by Titchener's students in the interim.

The fact remains that the serious criticisms of mentalistic concepts advanced in the 1920s through the 1950s by Kantor (1947), Tolman (1932), Skinner (1953), and many others represent a position that requires a much more careful examination of language systems in behavioral science. The criticism may ultimately lead to agreement among investigators in different settings and laboratories and to avoidance of excessive emphasis on private experience as a means of coming to conclusions about significant events in our psychological repertory. While at first it was felt that the strict requirements of operational formulations precluded study of many of the most intriguing aspects of human experience, emotions, wishes, daydreams, nightdreams, aesthetic experiences, and so on, it seems, rather, that this behaviorist criticism has forced greater ingenuity and more profound examination on the part of psychologists of how they can study the processes that are indeed so interesting.

Inevitably, one must be prepared to give up some of the popular language to which we are accustomed and perhaps resort increasingly to fairly precise descriptions of behavior related to internal events that are geared to specific operations in a clinical or an experimental situation. We may have to fall back on terms such as *mediation* or *stimulus-independent thought* (Antrobus, Singer, Goldstein, & Fortgang, 1970). This does not mean that we will not study the glamorous inner life, but rather that we will study it increasingly in a form susceptible to replication and to reasonable experimental control. The dozen or so studies by Segal (1971) on the Perky effect, the extensive research of Paivio (1971) on the learning implications of concrete and abstract words which differ in their capacity to general imagery, the analyses of children's learning by Reese (1970c) and Rohwer (1970), among others, make it clear that we have moved far toward being able to carry out careful and replicable experiments on events hitherto classified as entirely private.

It is important to note that most of the psychologists cited here began with a strong orientation toward behaviorism, but have been forced, in order to do justice to the data and also to their own private experience, to find methods for examining covert events, such as images, through systematic behavioral techniques. A fine example of a symposium in which behaviorist-oriented psychologists examined and proposed many methods to study imagery and other related internal experiences such as affect and self-regulatory responses is available in a volume edited by Jacobs and Sachs (1971). In experimental research, then, we seem today on the threshold of significant new advances in the area that as Holt (1964) noted has been "ostracized" for so many years.

CLINICAL AND PSYCHOANALYTIC ORIENTATIONS TOWARD IMAGERY

The kinds of self-criticism and detailed examination of the technical problems faced in a scientific study of imagery and related internal experiences such as fantasies or dreams have never seriously troubled clinicians who have so often relied on internal experience as the main emphasis in their work. As I noted earlier, Freud and the psycho-analysts stressed, for Western culture, the tremendous significance of these inner experiences during the half century when they had been considered out of the purview of scientific research. At the same time, there was a curious lack of interest within psychoanalysis or related approaches in exploring in detail the structural properties of fantasies, daydreams, and affect. One looks in vain through the vast psycho-analytic literature for careful analyses of the functional role of fantasy material within the overall sensory motor apparatus or, more generally, the personality structure. Fantasy tends to be studied primarily for its content and as a manifestation of conflict or defense. For the psychia-trist, hallucination is accepted simply as a report associated largely with serious mental disturbance or brain pathology: correspondingly, there is little emphasis on its generality of occurrence on the one hand, or on the linguistic and symbolic meaning of a report of hallucination (Sarbin & Juhasz, 1970; Horowitz, 1970).

Although Freud himself, in his long-unpublished *Project for a Scientific Psychology* (Freud, 1966), attempted to develop a careful model of the relationship between neural events and the organization of thinking (discussed also in the seventh chapter of the *Interpretation of Dreams*, Freud, 1962), few of his followers showed much interest in developing conceptual models of the nature of attention, memory, and thought. It remained for Rapaport (1951) and Klein (1967) to attempt, within the classical Freudian tradition, some systematization of the nature of thinking and cognitive organization. Most psychoanalytically oriented clinicians or researchers tended to take too much for granted concerning the structural features of the associations and images with which they dealt and, hence, perhaps also to minimize the significant questions about these phenomenon which were being raised in criticism by the behaviorists. The result of this somewhat arrogant assumption that fantasies and dreams ought to be taken as given led to a kind of sterility in terms of research application and also undoubtedly contributed to the Tower of Babel effect described in Chapter I. Namely, by not specifying precisely the different characteristics of fantasies, images, and dreams, or the conditions in which these were elicited, or examining issues reliability of report, and so on, the clinicians opened the way for tremendous variation in interpretation of these events as a function of different schools. Furthermore, they left no recourse for resolving difficulties except by what amounted to "party discipline" or adherence to a given school or institute.

The structural theorizing that did survive in psychoanalysis was largely built around energy constructs that have now in the main been discredited (Holt, 1967; Klein, 1967; Rubinstein, 1967). In fact, the very assumption that the clinician's judgment and interpretation become the basis for theory proposal and testing led to a limited possibility for change within the psychoanalytic systems. Even the emergence by the 1950s of ego psychology, with its assumption that whole sets of basic functions such as language, cognition, and perhaps even fantasy developed as fundamental human characteristics and thus need not be viewed as means to resolve conflicts between the id and reality (Hartman, 1958), has not really significantly advanced the psychoanalytic model.

In effect, the notion that there is a sphere of behavioral functions that develop free of conflict and generate their own energy system may be viewed as fundamentally subversive to the entire special quality of the psychoanalytic model. If functions such as motor skills, language, and thought development are not part of the libidinal system, then what special role does the traditional body-orifice-oriented theory of psychoanalysis play in personality development? If one argues that the traditional psychosexual developmental schema are really more basic or special, then it is up to the analytic theorists to show what significant structural differences in language, thought, or motor behavior are generated by these schema; they must demonstrate that such variation cannot be explained simply as special cases of the more general cognitive development of the child.

As White (1960) pointed out, is there not good reason to believe that even without the assumption of a psychosexual Oedipal phase, a child might develop a set of competitive and fearful attitudes toward the father, who is physically larger, generally more competent, drives the big family car, and deals out occasionally painful physical punishment? Why do we need assumptions about specific phallic rivalry in order to recognize, simply from the cognitive capacity of the child, the potential for confusion or rivalry? Grey's (1973) fine paper on a comparison of the Oedipal theme in Indian and American students' dreams makes this point most effectively. It may, therefore, be likely that, by incorporating a more general aspect of psychology, the development of language, motor, and cognitive skills, into the framework of psychoanalysis, the ego psychologists have done away with any special contribution that psychoanalysis makes as a theoretical system. Perhaps this may be for the best if there is, consequently, a genuine integration within behavioral science.

A great deal of attention has been paid in psychiatry to illusions and hallucinations as they occur in relation to specific syndromes, but there has also been relatively little attempt at systematic examination of the nature of images, fantasies, and memories. A pioneer in this area was Schilder (1953), who was perhaps one of the first investigators to examine the constructive and functional values of images and fantasies in personality development. It has remained for very recent writers such as Arieti (1967) and Horowitz (1970) to attempt a more formal structural examination of the nature of thought processes and their relationship to pathological organization. Arieti, for example, has reexamined in a systematic way some of the fundamental language, cognitive, and emotional functions and then shown how they lead ultimately, on the one hand, to intrapsychic reality and, on the other hand, to various facets of pathological transformations, as well as creative capacities. Horowitz dealt more specifically with the various manifestations of imagery, both in normal functioning and in psychopathology. His work is especially valuable in providing a much more formal set of definitions and a classification scheme for images which, perhaps for the first time, permits the likelihood of some common language in the description of pathological manifestations of imagery. The publication of both of these volumes within the last five years indicates that perhaps, at last, medical specialists and behavioral scientists are now ready to examine imagery and related internal events in a systematic fashion.

EUROPEAN STUDIES OF IMAGERY

For various reasons, the kinds of restraints on experimentation and on scientific discourse that characterize the American and British orientation toward the study of internal processes (a restraint to some extent also in Pavlov-influenced Russian psychology) did not seem nearly so influential in continental European psychology. Generally speaking, of course, behavioral science as a separate discipline was seriously weakened in the 1930s and 1940s by the Fascist and Nazi influences, as well as by the turmoil of that period. One might indeed take issue with the strong persistence in France and Germany, for example, of theorizing and scholarly research built around the particularly private phenomenological reports and the reliance on introspection as a basis for research. Viewed from an American perspective, the European literature on imagery and fantasy raises extremely intriguing questions, is full of fascinating examples and of problems that require approaches and attempts at solutions, but is lacking in methodological sophistication of a type that would lead to a resolution of any of these differences and to possible systematic action of the varied reports. The early work of Jaensch (1930) on eidetic imagery did, of course, lead to some fairly interesting research, but our understanding of the nature of these highly vivid images that occur in children remained relatively poor until the 1960s with the much more sophisticated technical research of Leask, Haber, and Haber (1968).

An enclave of extremely productive and stimulating studies of imagery has remained in the sphere dominated by Jung at Zurich. Jung's influence on thought in Britain and in the western hemisphere has been mainly upon isolated literary figures. The scholarly and imaginative use that Jung and his followers made of symbolic materials found in dreams, fantasies, myths, and related material had, however, widespread impact on the Continent. While one cannot say specifically that the influence of analytic psychology, which came out of Zurich, was politically significant within psychiatric or psychological circles in France, Germany, or Italy, the fact remains that the spirit of Jung's kind of sweeping symbolic interpretation was woven into the fabric of European thought. This influence is reflected in the view that we carry within us a great range of metaphor and symbolism reflecting the cultural experience of our past and, indeed, perhaps the very culture of our ancestors in relating themselves to the major issues of family experience, masculinity and femininity, and the nature of man within the universe. Such interpretations are compatible with the general spirit of the times and woven quite easily into the fabric of European psychology.

Philosophical influences such as those of Bachelard (1964, 1971) provide a useful background for understanding the seriousness with which many European scholars and psychological or psychiatric investigators approached the private experiences of imagery and reverie, which were contemporaneously so alien to American behavioral scientists. Originally, a distinguished physicist holding the major chair in physics at the Sorbonne, Bachélard moved more and more toward examining the nature of human experience and introducing a phenomenological point of view into his examination of the range of human symbols such as the symbols of air, nature, and fire. Bachélard argued that "the creative imagination" is a fundamental human experience, and that indeed it is as much a part of man's reality as the stored reproductions of external events and stimuli. Bachélard has little to say with respect to the technical problems of psychology or psychotherapy and makes perhaps his greatest contribution to the appreciation of the literary imagination. His beautiful and moving expression of the significance of the imagination and its pervasive role in human experience as a part of the truest reality all men face is basic to many of the more specific developments of mental imagery methods in clinical work.

While there are many other influences besides Jung and Bachélard upon European psychology and psychotherapy, the seriousness with which so many leaders of the intellectual community in Europe have taken the works of these men has undoubtedly colored the point of view of many practitioners and opened the way for a readiness to employ imagery methods not similarly welcomed in the western hemisphere. With specific respect to technique in psychotherapy, Jung (1968) recalled how he early broke with Freud on the approach to dream interpretation. It became clear to him that the associative approach advocated by Freud would lead away from comprehension of the totality of the dream as a phenomenological experience.

In a most enlightening description of Jung's narration to Freud of a dream, Jung pointed out that he realized that the free association method would only lead him away from a true comprehension of his own dream. He was constrained to lie and to give Freud an association and interpretation that complied with Freud's own system, and at the same time it became clear to Jung himself that his dream would have quite a different meaning to him personally and had to be understood within its own structure, rather than by separating out the elements and associating independently to them. This led Jung ultimately to advocate a technique called *active imagination*, which required that the dreamer, in a therapy session, attempt to redream the dream before the therapist and reexperience it imaginally, and then report a kind of more general, overall reaction to the dream in place of the piecemeal analysis characteristic of the Freudian system.

The method of active imagination, a kind of extended phenomenological approach, was a part of the Jungian technique in psychotherapy. Moreover, it was also encouraged for private use by the patient as a means of increasing his own capacity independently to use his dreams, not only to understand current problems, but in a certain sense to protect his own future since many of his tendencies toward creative or self-defeating action were already implicit in his current life situation and were likely to emerge in symbolic form in his dreams. Although there was very little written of a technical nature on this method by Jungian analysts, who concentrated much more on the question of the meaning of symbols and their relation to cultural, religious, and aesthetic experiences, there seems no question that Jung's method underlies the mental imagery movement in psychotherapy.

Two important currents that ultimately led to fairly specific features of the development of mental imagery techniques can be traced somewhat tenuously in France to the thoughtful analysis imagery by Binet (1922). Binet reported a careful series of studies with two young girls that served as a basis for his presentation of an analysis of mental imagery. His approach included a description of a technique for inducing the subject to generate imagery with eyes closed, a forerunner of many of the later mental imagery techniques. Whereas Binet was primarily concerned, as a psychologist, with examining the formal characteristics of imagery, his work established a viewpoint for structuring the processes involved that has been influential for the most scientifically oriented practitioners of imagery methods in psychotherapy (Frétigny & Virel, 1968).

Another pioneer in the development of imagery techniques was Schultz (Schultz & Luthe, 1959) who early in this century began work on an approach to self-control and muscular relaxation that led ultimately to a technique for using relatively fixed imagery as another means of self-control. In many ways, Schultz was probably the originator of the very new and vigorous field of biofeedback, the method of identifying, labeling, and training of one's own autonomic and cognitive responses. There have been active practitioners for more than 50 years in Europe who have followed various aspects of Schultz's work, and reflections of this approach can also be seen in the progressive relaxation methods transmitted via Jacobsen (1938) and Wolpe (1958) as key features of the behavior modification techniques so widely practiced today in the United States. Schultz's techniques are of importance for the mental imagery movement because of one phase of the process in which special attention was paid to carefully controlled generation of imagery under the direction of the therapist. Some of these suggestions for specific images later also were used by Happich (1932), one of the earliest German practitioners of the mental imagery method.

Happich's work and that of another physician in France, Daudet (1926), who also explored the private use of the daydream as a therapeutic device, separate from the therapeutic session itself, did not lead immediately to formal developments in the use of imagery techniques in Europe. It is difficult to be certain as to all of the exact threads of origin, but it seems most likely that the major impetus for the development of mental imagery techniques came from the writings of Desoille (1938, 1945, 1961, 1966). Desoille, an engineer, was exposed to the efforts of a man named Caslant, who had been attempting to develop a mechanism for generating psychic experiences. Caslant had explored the possibility that by using directed imagery, scenes such as climbing mountains or descending to the earth, to break up a subject's reliance on actual memories, the person could be freed to generate a completely creative form of imagery likely to induce some sort of extrasensory experience.

Desoille began by using Caslant's method for exploring the range of conscious and unconscious experiences and then gradually moved into the psychotherapeutic realm, developing the "waking dream" technique, as he called it. Desoille did not have formal training in psychiatry or psychology, and his initial efforts and subsequent training of other "guides" for the exploration via this daydream technique (*le rêve éveillé dirigé*) has seemed to distress some of the more formally trained psychotherapists. Desoille has been criticized for training of laymen in his technique and also for the tendency of his earlier work to ignore the scientific forerunners of the uses of imagery and therapy, as well as to some extent for his own lack of theoretical sophistication (Frétigny & Virel, 1968), but it seems likely that the major thrust of modern mental imagery techniques came from Desoille. It was he who formalized many of the procedures still used, with variations, by practitioners such as Leuner (1955), Frétigny and Virel (1968), Rigo (1962), and Assagioli (1965), all of whom have had formal medical or psychological training. In Chapter IV I review the mental imagery techniques of these European investigators. The main point here is that with adoption and modification of Desoille's methods and their elaboration in a variety of clinical situations by more formally trained scientific investigators, the way has been opened for active research in this field. In Germany, Leuner has stimulated an extensive series of clinical, and indeed some experimental, investigations in this area, and in France, Virel has produced a number of formal researches, in addition to the many clinical reports in association with Frétigny.

RECENT APPLICATIONS OF IMAGERY TECHNIQUES IN THE UNITED STATES

The application of imagery techniques to psychotherapy in the United States and to some extent in Britain has come about much more recently and from two somewhat separate avenues. Nevertheless, it would be fascinating to trace them historically to their original sources. On the one hand, some of the mental imagery techniques developed out of Desoille's work and elaborated by Leuner, Frétigny and Virel, and Assagioli have appeared in the United States in the form of occasional direct individual and group psychotherapeutic use based on exposure to the European methods (see, for example, Gerard, 1964; Hammer, 1967; Johnsgard, 1969). Other applications have appeared in some of the Gestalt therapy techniques employed by Perls (1970) and Schutz (1967). Undoubtedly, many of these usages in encounter and related therapeutic methods are best described as "wild" applications; that is, much of their application is dependent on the intuitive reaction of the therapist and frequently involve group participation in a somewhat uncoordinated fashion.

A separate and quite distinct vein of application of imagery techniques in England and United States has been manifested in the behavior therapy movement. One can trace the origins of this approach in a number of its forms back to some of Watson's early followers. Yet the main impetus came on the arrival of Wolpe (1958) in the 1950s in the United States with his active proselytizing and rather dramatically effective results using particularly the method of desensitization. Despite the insistence of the behavior modification groups that their techniques are closely related to learning theory and are scientifically more objective than the great majority of approaches in psychotherapy, the fact remains that these methods rely to a very great extent on a combination of relaxation and imagery production by the patient. In this sense, there appears a continuity with the European methods. The fact that both groups emphasize relaxation may suggest that they ultimately can be traced back to some of the influences of Schultz (1965). In a strange way, moreover, the recent increased concern with biofeedback seems to justify the early pioneering work of this investigator. It is intriguing also that Desoille has preferred to relate his method, so obviously related to Jung and Freud, and especially the former, also on theoretical level, to Pavlovian conditioning, which of course lies at the heart of the method developed by Wolpe. To explore this point further here would lead us into the admittedly intriguing field of the history and sociology of scientific trends, not the subject of this volume.

Some imagery techniques have grown largely out of the more psychodynamic orientations, as in the case of the work of Shorr (1972) and Ahsen (1968). Other approaches stem primarily from attitudes that focus on the learning experience of the individual, for example, the many techniques described by Bandura (1969) and Lazarus (1971). It is clear that considerably more attention is now being paid to man's capacity to generate imagery and to the possibility of learning to control imagery processes. The insights of Bachélard or Vahinger (1925) and the various clinicians who emphasize the importance of transference, expectancy, and introverted imagery as key aspects of human experience have a place in the current emphasis on cognitive psychology and the role of private experience as a behavioral determinant. Theoretical proposals offered by Miller *et al.* (1960) on the nature of plans in the organization of behavior, or Tomkins (1962, 1963), who emphasizes the organizing function of the image in affect and motivation, again are becoming central concepts for psychology.

In the experimental realm is the work on the psychophysiological study of sleep, which focuses attention upon private experiences occurring throughout the night and upon methods for tapping into the ongoing thread of nocturnal thought. The sensory-deprivation studies and, more recently, the extensive work on imagery by Paivio (1971) and Segal (1971); the continuing research on the psychology of daydreaming and imaginative play (Singer, 1966, 1973); the resurgence of interest in hypnosis as an experimental field (Hilgard, 1965; Barber, 1970); and various works attempting to organize the psychiatric and experimental knowledge on imagery and fantasy (Horowitz, 1970; Klinger, 1970) all attest to the great change in the spirit of the times.

One need not view this new emphasis as a regression in any narrow sense of the term. Rather, it seems more likely that the important gains made in setting criteria for careful observation of behavioral contingencies and for specifying the operational components in research that have grown out of our long experience with behaviorism will continue to provide important critical features in evaluating future research. What seems likely at this time, however, is that we have moved beyond the narrow extroversion of behaviorism to recognizing the tremendous relevance of private experiences of fantasies, marginal thoughts, dreams, and images, and we may greatly increase the power of prediction and control in human behavior through more extensive study of these phenomena via both experiment and psychotherapeutic application. Viewed from this perspective, then, the vicissitudes of the concept of imagery in psychology and the behavioral sciences may be a reflection of an upward curve of increasing scientific capacity to approach the most central of human capacities.

CHAPTER III

IMAGERY AND DAYDREAM METHODS IN PSYCHOANALYSIS

> *The patient misunderstands the present in terms of the past; and, then, instead of remembering the past, he strives, without recognizing the nature of his action, to relive the past and to live it more satisfactory than he did in childhood.*
> O. Fenichel (1945, p. 29)

THE EARLY USE
OF HYPNOSIS AND IMAGERY ASSOCIATION

Sometime in 1887 a young Viennese neurologist named Sigmund Freud began using hypnosis in the treatment of neurotic patients. At first his method was primarily to give suggestions that would lead to the relief of symptoms. Soon, however, he found that he was more inclined to elicit from the patients their images and memories and gradually to lead them back to the past; at this point, the uncovery of certain traumatic incidents, often enough from fairly early in childhood, would lead to a traumatic emotional catharsis and a more permanent relief of symptoms. Freud had been influenced in his development of this technique by his association with an older physician, Joseph Breuer, who, in the early 1880s, had treated a woman by hypnosis and obtained very dramatic effects on the basis of extended emotional catharsis through revival of early images and memories. The story of the collaboration between the proper and reserved Dr. Breuer and the energetic and imaginative Dr. Freud needs no further retelling here; it is a part of the history of modern behavior science and psychiatry. For the purposes of our present emphasis on the uses of imagery in psychotherapy, it suffices to remind the reader that psychoanalysis was indeed an outgrowth of the use of hypnosis, and that the degree to which imagery is a central feature of hypnosis undoubtedly has colored the later development of psychoanalytical technique.

The relation of hypnosis and imagery techniques is complex and indeed merits treatment beyond the scope of this volume. There is some further discussion of the interrelations between hypnosis and imagery techniques in psychotherapy, but the main point to stress in this chapter is that much of the viewpoint that Freud brought to the psychotherapeutic situation reflected his earlier experiences with hypnosis. As Wolstein (1954) has carefully demonstrated, psychoanalysis never fully lost its original connection with hypnosis, preserving some of the mesmerist's paraphernalia, such as the couch, and also, more subtly, by fostering positive transference and establishing a setting of enhanced suggestability.

Freud himself was quite sensitive to the limitations of suggestion as a technique and strove to avoid this in his development of psychoanalysis. Today we may have somewhat different views about suggestion and its importance in hypnosis since much of its mystery has been removed by the important research of Hilgard (1965), Orne (1959), and Barber (1970). Still, as Wolstein has noted, Freud's emphasis on toleration by the analyst of positive transference permitted strong elements of suggestion to persist into the later stages of psychoanalytical technique.

Influenced by Breuer's use of the abreaction of early memories with hypnosis in the case of Anna O., Freud at first emphasized this method in his practice. Gradually he began to give up the formal use of hypnosis, particularly in relation to the use of suggestion, and increasingly as a means of reaching childhood memories. In the case of Elizabeth Von R., Freud (1955) described a technique that he had begun to use to "bring out pictures and ideas by means of pressing on the patient's head . . . [p. 153]." Freud pointed out that with this technique, his patient's behavior sometimes yielded, with great rapidity, different scenes relating to a central problem, which emerged chronologically: "It was as though she were reading a lengthy book of pictures whose pages were being turned over before her eyes [p. 153]."

Freud also gave a brief description of this technique in the case of Lucy R. When the patient indicated that she had no idea how a symptom had begun, he took her head between his hands and told her that as soon as he relaxed the pressure on her head "you will see something in front of you or something will come into your head. Catch hold of it. It will be what we are looking for [p. 110]."

It was in these early efforts that we see Freud explicitly using a mental imagery technique and a series of associated images as the basis for his therapeutic efforts. Freud made use of suggestion in this method to the extent that he insisted to the patient that images would indeed occur when he engaged in this form of "laying on of the hands." As a matter of fact, it was in the course of his work with Elizabeth Von R. that Freud discovered the nature of resistance and referred to it clearly for the first time (Freud, 1955, p. 154).

It is not known for certain when Freud actually abandoned his use of physical touch as a means of stimulating the flow of images from the patient. Apparently, this procedure was discontinued sometime before 1900 since he does not mention physical contact in his description of the method of free association in the second chapter of *The Interpretation of Dreams*. Somewhere in the period between 1896, when Freud appears to have given up the use of hypnosis, and 1900, Freud also began to move from the emphasis on imagery association to a more extended free association technique of the type that has become a cornerstone of psychoanalysis.

In the second chapter of *The Interpretation of Dreams*, Freud specifically referred to the manner in which he encouraged the patient to notice and report whatever came into his head and to adopt an attitude free of criticism so that the associations might emerge almost spontaneously. Freud, by this time, no longer specifically emphasized an imagery association method, although he did, of course, call attention to the fact that the patient's situation was somewhat analogous to that of an individual preparing himself for sleep and who was relaxing to the point where critical evaluation of his own thoughts gave way to a more relaxed awareness of the emerging "visual and acoustic images" (Freud, 1955, 1962, Vol. IV, p. 102). In the famous specimen dream of his own which Freud then analyzed, however, there was much emphasis on verbal association, rather than on pure imagery, in Freud's examination of the dream content.

It is intriguing to note that in this same period, Freud still required the patient to recline in a restful attitude with his *eyes shut*. This injunction, as well as the insistence on the recumbent position of the patient, make it clear not only that Freud was carrying over some of the features of the hypnotic situation, but also point up his strong emphasis on the production of visual imagery. By 1903, when Freud prepared a brief account of the psychoanalytic method for inclusion in a textbook by Lowenfeld (Freud, 1962, Vol. VII, p. 250) on obsessional neurosis, the closing of the eyes had been discontinued. Freud emphasized that the patient recline on the couch, while the therapist sat behind him outside his field of vision, and "the session thus proceeds like a conversation between two people equally awake, but one of whom is spared every muscular exertion and every distracting sensory impression which might divert his attention from his own mental activity [p. 250]." Clearly, Freud had already recognized the cognitive nature of the task and the importance of avoiding irrelevant complex external stimulation, perhaps because of his reduced interest in imagery per se he apparently was willing to allow the patient to keep his eyes open. The shift at this point was clearly toward a more verbal type of free association and, indeed, Freud in this same article referred to the situation as one resembling a rambling and disconnected conversation.

It seems clear that Freud began with much greater concern specifically for evoking vivid imagery and only gradually, in the period between 1896 and 1903, gave up this concern in favor of a more conversational or verbal associative method. This did not mean that imagery was completely excluded from the analytical session—far from it. The reexperiencing of the dream material was central to the analytic enterprise. The examination of daydream material and the ultimate evocation of early memories in the course of analysis of the transference were obviously central features of the process, which necessarily involved some degree of visual or auditory imagery. Nevertheless, there was a turning point here in which the specific focus on imagery as the therapeutic medium was altered. It remains to be seen whether this was an unfortunate step in view of the emphasis placed on imagery in the European imagery approaches or in the development by Reyher (1963) of the "emergent uncovering" method for associative imagery.

Even though Freud began to pay less attention specifically to imagery, the major goal of therapy was the revival and flooding back to consciousness of memories of early childhood, or in lieu of recall of specific events, the reexperiencing of childhood sexual fantasies. Clearly one approach to obtaining this effect, in addition to the development of the transference, which I discuss later, was the establishment of a setting conducive to producing relatively free associations and opportunities to revive early memories and related images. Let us examine the psychological situation of the patient in classical psychoanalysis a little more closely from the standpoint of its relationship to the production of imagery and to circumstances conducive to different types of information processing activity.

THE COGNITIVE IMPLICATIONS OF THE PSYCHOANALYTIC SITUATION

I shall begin with an emphasis on the classical Freudian method, which remains today a central part of the practice of the most prestigious analytic institutes. I am not concerned for the moment with the validity of the general procedure or its place in modern society. The fact remains that it is still being taught and practiced, and it is worth examining how relevant the structural characteristics of the situation are to the task of producing associations, images, and memories.

The situation in formal analysis calls for the patient to be seated in a relaxed position on a couch, the therapist sitting to the side, perhaps slightly to the rear and out of vision of the patient. The patient's obligation is simply to associate freely and to report all thoughts that come to his head without active censorship of any of the material, however irrelevant it may appear. The relaxation and free association were regarded by Freud as methods for outwitting the defense. Keeping the therapist more or less out of sight of the recumbent patient also played a part in this method, although Freud himself confessed that part of his motivation for sitting behind the patient was his own self-consciousness (Freud, 1962, Vol. XII). By reducing the great variety of competing stimuli, the therapist's face and expression, the furnishings of the room, the opportunities to gaze out the window at passers-by, etc., Freud was instinctively establishing for the patient a situation in life achieved only in preparation for sleep. In effect, the patient lies, staring at the ceiling or perhaps at an acute angle at what is generally a blank wall. There is, therefore, relatively little complex external information that he is required to process visually that might interfere with his attending to his own ongoing stream of associations or becoming aware of the visual imagery of a dream or early memory. The recumbent position would appear to have a number of very critical advantages for subjects in enhancing the likelihood of the occurrence of vivid visual or other types of imagery. In fact, one can even find some traces of formal research evidence that suggest the value of Freud's use of this method, at least from the standpoint of his stated purposes.

Viewed first from a purely cognitive standpoint, the subject lying on the couch, out of sight of the therapist's face, has already entered into a situation of mild sensory deprivation. That is, he does not have many new external stimuli presenting themselves to him which would require some movement of the eyes or some degree of processing, filtering, and matching with material from long-term memory in order to eventually encode them. A formal experiment by Antrobus and Singer (1964) found that normal young men in a darkened booth monitoring a blinking light for periods of 90 min with the requirement that they talk continuously during this period produced a great variety of interesting images and remained more alert and comfortable than when they were required to limit their internal activity simply to counting from one to nine continuously. The subjects were in a mild sensory-deprivation situation, and external stimulation of an auditory nature was restricted by having them continuously receive white noise through earphones, thus preventing them from hearing their own verbalizations. Under these conditions, considerable imagery emerged and, in addition, there was ample evidence that the situation was tolerable and did not greatly interfere, in this case, with their ability to perform an external task of vigilant observation of the lights.

Bertini, Lewis, and Witkin (1964), using a similar technique, found an enhancement of imagery in subjects who were required to free associate—indeed, almost a hypnagogiclike situation. There were quite intriguing individual differences in the patient's imagery and capacity to tolerate this situation. A study by Kroth (1970) indicated that subjects reclining on a couch and free associating showed a greater amount of freedom, spontaneity, and general effectiveness of free association compared with subjects who were sitting and engaging in free association. Unfortunately, Kroth did not report data on imagery per se, but the results make it clear that associative fluency in general was considerably greater in the reclining posture. There was no clear evidence in the study, however, that the patients in the supine position produced significantly more evidence of emotional involvement in the material they produced.

More clear-cut evidence on the effectiveness of the reclining position was reported by Morgan and Bakan (1965), who found that subjects in a sensory-deprivation situation produced reports that could be rated as much higher in vividness of imagery than subjects who sat up. This study was followed by another by Berdach and Bakan (1967), who obtained memory material from the subjects in reclining or sitting positions. They also asked the ages of the memory situations from their normal subjects. These investigators found that earlier and more frequent memories occurred when subjects were in a reclining position. Of course, one cannot be certain that the memories reported were actually accurate recollections of events that took place in the subjects' lives at the specified ages. The much greater recall of memories for ages 0–3, when the subjects were reclining rather than sitting, may merely reflect an attitude or set brought on by the more "childish" reclining posture, not a genuine reinstatement of factual events. Nevertheless, it seems clear that imagery was enhanced by the reclining posture, a result attributed by Berdach and Bakan to the decrease of head and neck muscle tension, a condition also found to prevail at the onset of "Rapid Eye Movement sleep."

Even more objective evidence was obtained by Segal and Glicksman (1967). These investigators employed the Perky phenomenon. Subjects were in either sitting or reclining positions and gazing at a blank white screen onto which they were encouraged to project specific images. Unknown to them, the experimenters actually projected comparable images via a slide projector at their focal point. Segal and Glicksman found that the recumbent subjects were much less likely to recognize the fact that an external signal had been flashed on the screen. In other words, their own imagery in the reclining position tended to be sufficiently vivid as to preclude awareness of the actual external signal. It would appear, therefore, that the situation of lying down does have distinct advantages for producing relatively clear images and in generating a fairly untrammeled free associative flow.

It is not clear, however, whether this effect is specifically the result of actually reclining on a couch or of the fact that such a position ordinarily leads to a reduction in complex external stimulation due to what one sees on a blank ceiling or bare wall under these circumstances (Rychlak, 1973). There are other important characteristics that accompany reclining on the couch which need to be mentioned at this point. These characteristics may or may not be valuable therapeutically even though they might indeed generate considerable vivid imagery.

Consider the fact that the patient does not see the analyst's face. This naturally prevents him from observing annoyance or distress or disgust on the part of the analyst and permits greater likelihood of projection of his own distortions onto the analyst, which then become grist for the transference analysis. Recent theoretical and experimental research on the significance of the human face as a key feature of our environmental stimulus complex (Izard, 1971; Tomkins, 1962, 1963) has made it abundantly clear that facing another person provides so much new material to the viewer as to occasion some problem in processing material from long-term memory. This phenomenon account for the fact that subjects frequently look away from the face of an interviewer in order to process material from long-term memory (Meskin & Singer, 1974). The human face, with its likelihood of positive or negative reinforcement, a look of disgust, or smile of pleasure, can inhibit or stimulate the ongoing flow of our own communication patterns. Removing this complex stimulus from the immediate environment of the patient increases the probability that he will be able to generate vivid material from his long-term memory system without interference from the nuances of the therapist's facial expression.

The reclining posture has still another special characteristic. It is the position we assume when we are preparing ourselves for sleep. In this sense, it is already associated in our minds with an extensive upsurge of fantasy material. Most people report that their greatest amount of daydreaming actually takes place at the very point of preparation for sleep (Singer, 1966).

Lying on the couch thus seems to produce a situation in which complex new information from the environment is minimized for the subject. The reclining posture permits more attention to be paid to the material from the long-term memory system and also establishes for the subject a psychological atmosphere similar to that experienced at the onset of sleep. In this sense, the last named of the situations is a reflection of the hypnotic origins of psychoanalysis. It should be kept in mind that hypnosis is basically a self-engendered state, an attitude of extreme concentration on internal experience, and a blocking out of a great deal of external material—except, of course, compliance with the hypnotist's instruction to heed his voice. Since it has been shown that simulators can produce most of the effects usually associated with hypnosis without entering into a trance state and indeed can deceive even an experienced hypnotist (Barber, 1970), it would seem likely that reliance on the couch merely establishes a condition for a mild form of heightened imagery and self-directed attention comparable to a hypnotic situation. It is a separate question whether this situation is desirable in psychotherapy. It has been argued, particularly by various neo-Freudians, that the hypnotic remnants of classical psychoanalysis obstruct a genuine confrontation between patient and therapist and create an artificially authoritarian atmosphere despite the analyst's best intentions (Robertiello, 1969; Wolstein, 1954). There is at least some small experimental evidence available to support the notion that reclining on the couch is more conducive to the production of imagery and early memory material.

The recumbent position has some additional implications which might be stressed here since they also bear ultimately on the conditions conducive to the production of imagery in a therapeutic setting. When an adult lies down on a couch, the situation is one in which he changes the psychological vantage point most typical of his daily interpersonal relationships. The couch position immediately indicates that some special situation is already underway of a quasi-medical nature, and that some relatively novel kinds of experiences may be anticipated. To lie down, generally speaking, before another adult symbolizes a condition of greater passivity. For those who have been ill or hospitalized, it revives memories associated with such experiences. Of course, it also brings into play sexual experiences and attitudes. Finally, the situation of one adult lying down, while another sits up, reflects a more childlike relationship between the two individuals; this position is one that the patient is likely to associate more with childhood situations — being put to bed by his parents, most precisely.

A case can be made from the standpoint of the nature of memory itself in that particular bodily positions or sets of environmental circumstances are stored along with groups of schema and related specific memories so that the recumbent position is more likely to evoke memories of dependent states, of illness, helplessness, sexual involvement, and in addition, many experiences of a more childlike nature as the adult now assumes a childlike position in relation to the analyst. It is often noted clinically that as patients seem more ready to terminate therapy, they are much more likely quite voluntarily to sit up on the couch, and then later to move to a chair facing the analyst. In effect, such behavior would seem to be saying, "I'm getting a little bored with being caught up in my childhood. I'd like to start acting like a full-fledged adult at this point."

The Memory System and Body Posture

The idea that body postures may be associated with fairly encapsulated memories and fantasies was suggested long ago by Reich (1945) in his development of the notion of the "character armor." Such an emphasis on body posture and its relationship to stored memory has also been a part of various practices of Gestalt therapy. A much more formal theory of memory proposed by Tomkins (1970) provides a carefully thought out basis for explaining how early childhood memories might best be revived by the use of the couch.

Without reviewing Tomkin's rather complex theory in detail at this point, it is sufficient to say that Tomkins has proposed that the storage system of the brain operates through discontinuities and that many significant aspects of early childhood are stored reasonably intact, but in "a location" for which the "name" has been partially forgotten or is being systematically avoided. The ability to call forth the specific pattern of behavior that was stored at a period of childhood requires the establishment of a complex set of external circumstances that revive many of the stimuli also a part of this stored schema. Tomkins has called attention to the fact that (as Schactel, 1959, has also noted) many experiences learned in childhood and much of the thinking of childhood is less organized and complex than that of the adult. Early memories are "forgotten," not so much because they are actively repressed, but rather because two different memory systems or two different systems of locating the memory are in operation. Tomkins elaborated on the many kinds of experiences, in addition to those emphasized by traditional psychoanalysis, which are early a part of the child's experience, but which, owing to a variety of social pressures, become separated from adolescent or adult experience and the childhood experience. Many of these behaviors remain encapsulated, emerging occasionally in adult life only when the adult is put into a situation that dramatically revives the early childhood experience. Many facets of childish exploration, curiosity, direct expression of emotions such as shame or helplessness, or even very open expression of joy, may be taboo for various reasons in particular families or cultures. Because the growing adolescent or adult learns to establish a different set of behaviors, there may occur the discontinuity between the adult role and the memories and experiences associated with childhood.

Tomkins himself cited an instance of a middle-aged man who began to experience pain in the eye, tics, and depression when he learned he needed glasses for reading. Focusing attention on his eyes, something that had not occurred for many years, brought back an early childhood memory of an incident in which he had been caught peeping into an aunt's room and had been so severely reprimanded that he thought he would become blind. This incident was not followed by other similar events. Thus, gradually, since there was no further focusing on his eyes, the memory remained lost until middle age, when the set of circumstances of again having to focus on his vision at first brought great discomfort until he was able to relate this fact to the earlier experience.

A patient in my experience described the situation in which her husband would suddenly cry "Mommy, Mommy!" at the point of orgasm during sexual intercourse. While it would be simple to say that this was a galloping Oedipus complex, and that the husband was viewing wife as mother, another possibility was explored. It turned out that the husband had learned early that overt expressions of positive affect or of affect in general were frowned upon and not considered "manly." As a result, many of his early childhood expressions of joy and tenderness had been strongly suppressed, and indeed his own self-image as an adult did not include much of this type of behavior. The intimacy of the sexual act to which he came without any real prior experience and the warmth of his wife's response, as well as her acceptance of his genuine pleasure, led to the return of the joyous shout that had once been a part of his childhood behavioral repertory.

In a somewhat fanciful vein, Tomkins (1970) proposed that if we were to seek to revive through images and memories the dormant traits of childhood, we might adopt the following procedure:

> What are the parameters that are likely to be unique in childhood? The foremost is relative size. The child is smaller than the adult and the objects of his environment are functionally much larger to him than they are to the adult. In order to retrieve childhood memories, we should, therefore, fabricate rooms from two to two and one-half times normal linear size in all dimensions . . . in addition to living in a space that is relatively larger, many types of experiences are peculiar to infancy and childhood, such as being alone in the dark in a crib, nakedness, being fondled, being tweaked on the face, being wet, being hungry and wet, being sated and cuddled, being in a crib, being looked at intently by an adult, smelling urine and feces, talcum powder, the mother's body odor, . . . being read to sleep at night, . . . tickling and teasing, being spanked, being made to write one thousand times, 'I will not pick my nose', being sent to bed without supper, castration threats, and so on [p. 108].*

In summary then, it should be clear that if a major goal of therapy is to increase the likelihood of the patient's producing vivid imagery and if, in addition, this imagery is desired to take the form of experiences that have become discontinuous with adult life, then the use of the couch has distinct advantages. If one were to argue that the establishment of a continuity between childhood and adult experience will not only be satisfying to the individual in a broad sense, but also will preclude sudden discomforts, as in the case of the man with the eyeglasses, then a method of this type has clear merit. This notion has been grasped intuitively by various therapists who tried to get patients to regress actively during group therapy or to emit "primal screams." A critical technical question for psychotherapy is how to integrate these retrieved experiences and associated strong emotions into a current behavioral pattern. This is quite a separate and difficult task, which, unfortunately, cannot be pursued here.

Dream Analysis and Imagery

Other aspects of the classical psychoanalytical method that involve the use of imagery are mentioned briefly in this section, but I return to

* From Silvan Tomkins, A theory of memory. In J. S. Antrobus (Ed.), *Cognition and Affect*, p. 108. Boston: Little, Brown, 1970. Copyright © 1970 by Little, Brown and Company, Inc.

them a little later, after reviewing some of the neo-Freudian approaches to the same issues. Clearly, a central role in Freudian theory is played by the analysis of dreams. The patient who brings in a dream, while in the office of the therapist, must, in effect, reproduce the dream visually, unless it is written down on paper and he reads the words without any serious effort toward reexperiencing the visual or auditory components of the dream itself. In most instances, it seems likely that a serious patient, while on the couch or sitting in the analyst's office, does indeed attempt to reconstitute the actual image of the dream within the limits of his capacity to do so in the waking state. It is at this point that analysis makes perhaps its most extensive use of imagery, but here the different schools diverge in how much attention is paid to the imaginal component and how much to the flow of verbal associations produced by the dream content. As I noted in Chapter II, Jung moved away from Freud's approach to dream interpretation in favor of a very active reexperiencing of the dream image taken as a whole and responded to in a more global fashion. Similarly, Fromm (1951) emphasized a more metaphoric type of interpretation of the dream as a whole, rather than the step-by-step analysis through associations characteristic of Freud's method.

Classical psychoanalysis also places great importance on reports of daydreams and fantasies, some of which occur during the analytic hour itself and others that are remembered from previous days, or, of course, from earlier periods in the patient's life. Again, the emphasis tends to be one of associating to the material as if it were a dream, rather than upon the reexperiencing of the material during the session itself. It is hard to say what actually occurs in the hundreds of types of analyses underway at any time directed by so many different analysts, even if they are of the same general theoretical orientation. Almost certainly, many psychoanalysts as astute clinicians use any opportunity to evoke significant appropriate affective reactions from the patient and will, therefore, rely often enough on the evocation of strong imagery as one means of accomplishing this task. Nevertheless, it does seem likely that frequently the analytic process may lead to a series or chain of verbal associations to the initially imaged content and perhaps less toward a vivid and varied flow of imagery on the part of the patient.

Transference Imagery in Classical Analysis

Finally, a critical feature of classical analysis is the use of transference interpretation as a key element of treatment. In the course of an extended period of association with a therapist under conditions in which his own personality is not strongly in evidence, and indeed in which he may often say almost nothing, it is assumed that the patient will develop a strong transference neurosis to the analyst. In transference reactions, patients repeat the complex attitudes of ambivalent love and hate they may have experienced for a parent or family member. The task of the analyst is to identify these reactions, using criteria such as their inappropriateness to the particular social situation. Then, his task is to help the patient recognize these transference occurrences and their generality. When such identification of transference phenomena takes place in a setting already emotionally charged by the strength of the patient's reaction, the likelihood exists that there may be a vivid retrieval of early memories associated with the parental or sibling relationship in question and that the revival of such experiences may be liberating for the patient.

Hopefully, the positive transference that the patient develops early for the therapist can be used by the analyst to help the patient overcome resistances and doubts and to persist toward a full examination of all transference reactions. Such an effort should lead to the eventual liberation of the patient from these ghosts of his past and restore his ability to see the analyst as simply a helping professional. Perhaps no concept is more unique to classical analysis than the notion that, in the fostering of the transference neurosis, one reconstructs an elaborately imaged miniature life experience. The careful identification of distorted expectations and "working through" carried on by the patient once he has been helped by the therapist to identify transferences and resistances or defenses can be tremendously liberating of the individual personality.

Perhaps no other concept in psychoanalysis has been more generally agreed on by both Freudians and neo-Freudians than the significance of transference. There are certainly differences in the emphasis placed upon the specific proposal that the battleground of the analysis is in the development and then dissection of the transference neurosis, as the classical position maintains. However, viewed from the standpoint of technique and therapeutic efficacy, the genuine nature of transference experiences during psychotherapy and the important contribution such experiences make in our understanding of personality more generally are questioned by psychoanalysts. Let it suffice to say that transference phenomena generally do represent some manifestations of imagery. For example, there are numerous dreams that are interpreted as having transferential qualities. Typical of these is the dream reported by a patient to me in which she had a very clear picture of herself sitting on the couch next to her mother, while I sat on an armchair across the room, in her living room, wagging my finger at the two of them.

The patient's mother was in no way a part of her current life situation, and the home scene was from much earlier period of childhood. Nevertheless, the mother was *there*, depicted in very vivid imagery in the dream along with some additional content not of concern at the moment. This bringing together of the mother and myself was reported by the patient with a sense of immediacy; the dream seemed completely real at the time she woke up in the morning and continued to have some quality of reality about it.

In many instances, transference reactions are represented in attitudinal sets or orientations without a strong element of actual imagery or fantasy. Still, the most likely way in which they will be identified is through some report of a dream or a fantasy. Another patient, for example, described a daydream he had had about my home, which in actuality he had never seen. The daydream described a house, as a matter of fact, that was similar in style to my home and reflected some considerable astuteness on the part of the patient (who was an architect). At the same time, however, the story line also reflected some desire to cast me in the role of a better father than he had had.

The physical arrangement of the classical analytic situation undoubtedly contributes to the development of certain types of transference imagery. The analyst generally sitting somewhat out of sight of the patient creates a perceptual situation of ambiguity so that the patient can project his own anticipations and images onto the facial expressions of the therapist. In addition, the relatively minimal social contact between patient and therapist in formal analysis leaves the patient frequently without a detailed awareness of the analyst's appearance and so more likely to attribute different characteristics, lines in his face, gray streaks in his hair, or even occasionally to think of the analyst as bearded or mustachioed. Indeed, the very lack of information to some extent encourages the patient to generate imagery about the therapist, in addition to which the recumbent position increases the likelihood that the nature of the transference will involve parent–child memories. The absence of communication from the analyst also is likely to provoke an anticipation of particular comments and to create situations in which outside the therapeutic sessions the patient may find himself carrying on interior monologues with the image of the therapist sitting nearby.

In a certain sense one might argue that some of the childhood components built into the analytical situation lead to the revival of the common experience of imaginary companions with the analyst now playing this role for the patient. I discuss some other implications for imagery of the concept of transference later in this chapter in connection with the neo-Freudian orientation toward this ubiquitous phenomenon. On the whole, despite the many occurrences of imagery in psychoanalysis, it does seem likely that the classical method does not concentrate specifically on imagery for its special qualities. If anything, the emphasis is upon the analytic work and the interpretation of the content of fantasy and dream material. Kanzer (1958), in what may be regarded as a fairly typical presentation, emphasized the defensive characteristics of the visual image as it occurs in psychotherapy. Certainly, for many analysts the visual images reported in therapy are reviewed as "screens" which conceal instinctual conflicts and repressed wishes. There are others, however, who see the content and form of the image as reflecting the ego capacities and growth potential of the patient.

Imagery Association Methods in Psychoanalysis

Pierce Clark (1925), an early psychoanalyst, reverted to the imagery association method in an effort to treat the kinds of patients who at that time were felt to be inaccessible in traditional psychoanalysis. Specifically, Clark worked with borderline schizophrenics who fell under the classification, narcissistic neurotics, then in current use, that is, patients who were unlikely to develop a transference. Today we might have serious question about this conception of transference. Indeed, evidence from the work of Sullivan, Fromm-Reichmann, and many others is that the problem of the schizophrenic patient is more likely to be one of being all transference, rather than the lack of the ability to establish such a relationship. Nevertheless, Clark, around 1923, working within the framework of the time, began to use what he called "phantasy method." He applied this technique accepting the then current notion that the emergence of early childhood memories was critical, but feeling that narcissistic patients would be unable to provide these memories in the framework of transference to the therapist.

Clark established conditions for the use of imagery to recover childhood memories. He encouraged the patients to relax on the couch and to shut their eyes, while trying to imagine in detail scenes from their childhood. Clark worked in a much more flexible manner, without definite appointments and with opportunity for the subject to continue in a session for as long as he seemed to be producing significant material; finally the patients were required to report on the protocols of their sessions. It is intriguing to realize that this method is actually employed today by practitioners of the mental imagery methods in Europe. Clark found that patients produced strictly vivid and effective imagery and went from one series of images to the next—generally under the assumption that these were indeed early memories. He was inclined to believe that probably the image contents were not essentially veridical recollections, but that perhaps this was less important than that they essentially evoked the affect appropriate to the childhood experiences and, therefore, had a beneficial effect.

This striking pioneering effort was not integrated, however, into the general trend and was largely unknown for many years. Somewhat later, Kubie (1943) proposed a return to this technique, particularly as a form of catharsis similar to the type employed in the treatment of traumatic neurosis. He felt that imagery methods might actually elicit stronger emotion and have more immediately beneficial psychological effects. Again, the proposal was not actively pursued by other workers, and it was not until well into the 1960s that Reyher (1963) began exploring an approach to imagery association within a classic analytic framework.

Reyher himself began his work with hypnosis and studied various aspects of hypnotically induced conflicts for psychopathologic analogs. While he has continued with this interest, he has also gone on to explore more extensively the properties of what he calls "emergent uncovering," a method for producing profound involvement on the part of the patient in the analytic session and also for establishing conditions that will permit research study of the vicissitudes of the instincts. In brief, the method calls for the patient to produce a set of clear images in sequence and then to describe them for the therapist. The therapist's interventions are chiefly to clarify the meaning of the patient's productions or the nature of the imagery and to encourage the patient to go on with the task. Occasionally, there are reflections of feeling on the part of the therapist or a most gentle kind of interpretation that usually is closely related to the descriptive material of imagery being presented.

It is Reyher's belief that considerable insight will be gained by the patient himself from the ongoing production of the imagery as each image blends into the next, and that active interpretation is not essential for this procedure because of the dramatic impact of the flow of imagery. The therapist does suggest that the patient close his eyes, and frequently makes guiding statements such as, "Images will come into your mind's eye," or, "What's in your mind's eye?" He has described in detail the interpersonal situations, and points out that patients are often afraid to close their eyes at first, but will overcome this anxiety after a few sessions with some analysis and the use of more traditional free association. A typical sequence, as reported by Reyher (1970) for emergent uncovering, begins with the client's visual imagery initially seeming rather static and only gradually taking on a more lively quality. Soon there appear dreamlike images. As a matter of fact, Reyher makes a point of encouraging patients to begin a session by "re-dreaming a dream." This soon leads into a form of Jung's "active imag-ination" method, except that Reyher is more inclined to use the Freud-ian analytic approach and also to emphasize a drive energy system in his explanatory method. The first periods of imagery tend to be largely symbolic and have very much of the dreamlike quality, but gradually, as the defenses weaken, the material of the images becomes more of what Reyher terms "hot." These images, representing strong associated affect are often required to be reexperienced by the patients at the suggestion of the therapist.

As indicated, Reyher's work takes place very much within a classical Freudian framework. He has presented protocols with very elaborate series of subscripts which are intended to describe the various instincts, defenses, and body language transformation that emerge in the course of the ongoing imagery association. Reyher examines each phrase the patient uses and each separate image and relates them to specific sexual drives, symbols of an erect or soft penis, resistances, displacements, variations in intensity of drive, anxiety equivalence of psychosomatic symptoms, birth fantasies or psychosexual transformations, erogenous stimulation, anxiety, symbolism of a father, genital responses of various kinds for both sexes, symbolism of the mother, castration fantasies, etc. While one might quibble about whether Reyher's emphasis on cyclinical drives and sequence of defenses really makes sense or whether his sym-bolism is rather exaggerated, there seems little doubt that from his pro-tocols the emergence of vivid imagery and very powerful associated af-fect is striking indeed.

Here is a brief section of a protocol with the therapist's comments in parentheses:

> I feel tense —— I see, like a man starting to climb a ladder, then I saw a man leaning on a post —— (What do you see now?) Nothing. —— I saw like an an-teater —— I saw like myself doing dishes and something else —— I saw a cream pie and then I was just about ready to say it and then I just stopped. (Just stopped what?) It's like I just stopped thinking or something. I don't recall what happened after that. (You saw a cream pie?) Uh-huh. (Can you get that image again?) —— yes —— I see a hand reaching around; it was one of my boys in my room. (Reaching around in what way?) around the corner, very sly-like; a finger around the corner. I saw a boy like being at the bottom of a shelf full of, or the bottom—like a briefcase or something. And I was trying to, you know, it was like a little compartment, and this thing that he went in changed into a big rag doll and when I saw it, I thought of it. I wondered if that would mean that I wanted to have a son or something. You know, I feel strange now . . . I just feel that I'm somebody else or something . . . I saw like somebody peeking through a small hole. It's like everything was gray. Like looking through a gray mesh cur-tain (Reyher, unpublished manuscript).

This brief excerpt leads to a very extensive analysis by Reyher of both the language and images produced by the patient with indications of sexual drive emerging, defenses, anxiety, and with the reference to reaching around the corner being associated with the subject's desire for a penis and her father on the basis of some previous information that had been obtained. This patient was a sexually frigid female, and a continuation of the images eventually led to much more direct experience of strong emotion, sexual desire, and awareness of sexual confusion and desire for male organs.

Even if one does not accept the specific drive model and symbolic transformation system proposed by Reyher, one cannot deny that the "emergent uncovering" method does yield a greater apparent involvement on the part of the patient. Reyher himself has generated a number of formal research studies which deserve mention here because they represent some of the few efforts within this entire realm of the use of imagery techniques to validate them or at least to explore their ongoing physiological concomitants. Reyher and Smeltzer (1968), for example, asked 21 young men to imagine pictures with eyes closed when presented with specific series of words or, under an alternate condition, to associate to the words presented with eyes open and to verbalize the "first thought that comes into your mind." In other words, Reyher was attempting to test whether the production of an image in association with significant words related to psychological experience, or, from his standpoint, instinctual tendencies would produce differential physiological effects when subjects actually engaged in visual imagery of some kind, or when the subject merely produced a verbal association to the words presented. Three areas of conflict were employed: sex, hostility, and family relationships. The subjects were presented with words such as, "masturbation," "pregnant," "breasts," etc., or, "slaughter," "kill," "maim," or "fatherly advice," "brother," "master of the house." The subjects then were required either to associate verbally or to produce an image. Subjects were hooked up to a polygraph and physiological measurement employed was the level of GSR (galvanic skin response), used here as a measure of anxiety. One need not interpret the data as representing different degrees of remoteness from an aroused drive, as Reyher did in implying that responses, for example, to the sex and aggression words are related to the underlying drives of sex and aggression. The fact remains that the data seem to suggest a greater flexibility and disorganization of verbal response in relation to the imaged material (suggestive of a breakdown of control) and, even more striking, a much slower return to base line of the GSRs after initial arousal when the subjects were producing imagery than when they were producing verbal association.

A subsequent study by Reyher and Morishige (1969) also seemed to support the general notion of a greater arousal of subjects during the production of free imagery and also while recalling dream material. It may not be possible to make a direct relationship between the experimental findings of Reyher and his students and the actual behavior of patients during emergent uncovering, but at least the beginnings of a more systematic exploration of the effects of imagery and their relationships to affective states are implied in these intriguing studies.

Reyher does not by any means claim that emergent uncovering is a substitute for traditional analysis. He is sensitive to the transferential features of the therapeutic relationship and indicates that gradually imagery will drop out of the regular sessions in favor of the more free associative style, or perhaps in the direction of a more genuine interaction and communication between therapist and patient, as the patient no longer needs to circumvent defenses through the medium of imagery. At this point, one might question whether Reyher's approach is partly limited by the assumption of a drive-energy system underlying the patient's products. It is entirely possible that imagery has a valuable function as a form of concrete expression at all phases of human interaction and that it can be effective in many situations not necessarily involving the circumvention of defenses. Certainly, much of our aesthetic experience depends on the concreteness of imagery. Why assume that awareness of a production of imagery reflects a regression to a more primitive level of functioning? The ultimate value of Reyher's approach still remains to be tested, but it does seem clear from his work that even the more traditionally trained psychoanalysts could benefit from paying greater attention to the encouragement of imagery association, rather than the more common type of verbal association as part of the ongoing therapeutic enterprise.

My own experience, undoubtedly shared with many other clinicians, has yielded a number of instances where to a patient who says, "I can't seem to get started," or, "I don't seem to have anything to say," the suggestion that the patient lean back, shut his eyes, and allow an image to appear usually leads to a rather effective breakthrough. In this sense one finds oneself essentially harking back to the original observations so astutely made by Freud in the 1880s in his work with Elizabeth R.

A woman patient with whom I was working at one point, though usually quite verbal, suddenly seemed unable to talk and said, "I just can't find anything I want to talk about but something is sort of nagging at me." A few efforts to elicit more direct associations were unsuccessful. When I suggested that she lean back, shut her eyes, and allow an image to come into her mind, the first thing she reported was a vivid picture of Siamese twins except that one seemed to be an old man and the other a relatively young man. This evoked laughter from both of us at the oddity of the image, but suddenly it struck us both what this may have been about. The patient herself quickly realized that what had been disturbing her was the fact that her husband and her son seemed to have developed in recent years a much closer rapport with each other that often excluded her from the relationship. There had been an incident just a day or so before the therapeutic hour that bore out her feeling, and had been a source of great distress, but she had been unwilling to face fully the implications of this situation. The image dramatically brought the problem into focus and permitted her then to talk quite freely about the situation. This type of image strongly resembled the kind of hypnagogic imagery described in the extremely interesting self-experiment carried out by Silberer (1951) and repeated by myself (Singer, 1966) many years later.

NEO-FREUDIAN PSYCHOANALYTIC APPROACHES TO IMAGERY

In reviewing the many changes in technique and viewpoint introduced by the various schools that were strongly influenced by Freud, but have essentially broken away from the classical analytic model, our intention here is to focus again specifically on the therapeutic relationship to imagery. There are many nuances of method and theory that could be elaborated upon in general as to what the nature of different approaches to long-term intensive therapy may be for the different schools, but this essentially is a separate work. Our emphasis, therefore, is primarily on the different approaches to dream material, taken by groups that have moved away from classical psychoanalysis; particular emphasis is placed on the transference as a key facet of psychotherapy.

I have already mentioned the ways in which Jung moved toward a more phenomenological and broadly symbolic interpretation approach in his method of active imagination. (Since much of Jung's methods has been incorporated into the European mental imagery approaches, I will not deal further with this technique here.) Adler (and some of his followers), while less concerned with analyzing dream and fantasy material or with transference viewed from the standpoint of very early childhood experiences, made extensive use of reports of early childhood memories as clues to the current life style of the individual. The request for the patient to produce early memories is cognitively a rather complex demand and in itself merits more extensive formal research. As indicated in the reference to studies by Berdach and

Bakan (1967), if one wants to obtain genuinely vivid reports of early memories, one would be better off to require that the patient recline or to introduce some situation that aided in redintegration of the early childhood context. This is contrary to the general Adlerian viewpoint, which emphasizes a vis-à-vis therapeutic orientation. An Adlerian might counter this argument by asserting that since it is the current life style and orientation with the patient that is critical in the treatment process, obtaining more veridical memory material is of less consequence and, therefore, the patient might just as well sit up.

For the Adlerian and for many other post-Freudian approaches, the nature of fantasy content or memories does not serve the cathartic purpose that had never really been discarded by Freudians. Rather, such material helps obtain a broader view of the stylistic patterns of the patient in his current behavior, his assumptions and private mythology, and his expectations in relationships to others which might lead to distortions or to frustrations when these expectations are unfulfilled.

After Freud, perhaps the most influential figure on the psychoanalytic community was Harry Stack Sullivan. Sullivan's emphasis on the interaction between therapist and patient and on the communication process involves much more of a direct confrontation and mutual examination and less room for extensive exploration of fantasy and dream material. In general, Sullivan, in his writings, seemed somewhat uncomfortable with dream analysis and was very astute in pointing out how this often can be a diversion from the critical problems of the patient. Of a much more "American" pragmatic or functional background, Sullivan was impatient with many of the elaborate emphases on complex inner experience that characterized the slower-paced European methods. Certainly he turned against the notion of a gradual development of a transference neurosis, but moved much more directly into confronting the patient with his own self-deceptive tendencies.

At the same time, Sullivan was acutely sensitive to different nuances in the use of imagery and fantasy by different styles of personality. For example, in a fine comparison of the hysterical personality with the introverted or schizoid personality (Sullivan, 1956, pp. 210–211), he pointed out that the more introverted person's fantasies are elaborated over and over again and differentiated, becoming increasingly complex, so that the product seen in therapy may have changed greatly from the early childhood fantasy. By contrast, the more hysterical personality, who is less geared toward producing fantasy and also more inclined toward separating fantasy from distressing material, tends to have a fairly circumscribed recurrent daydream that remains largely unchanged. Sullivan warned the therapist working with the hysterical patient to be sensitive to the likelihood that many of the fantasies of such patients are adopted wholesale from books or other communication media, and, while they may to some extent reflect personal problems, the danger is that the therapist who overemphasizes fantasy material in actuality may be spending his time analyzing "somebody else's fantasies," rather than the patient's. Sullivan was particularly concerned lest the kind of imagery technique developed by Pierce Clark be applied to hysterics, who will simply find this a pleasurable but fundamentally irrelevant method of resisting a confrontation with their more basic dilemmas (Sullivan, 1956, p. 225).

In keeping with his general approach, Sullivan is also somewhat critical of the emphasis on the "wish-fulfilling" nature of daydreams. He did not discuss this problem in any great detail, and it is obvious that to some extent he accepts some of the Freudian notions of partial drive reduction through fantasy. He is, however, at pains to urge the therapist to consider daydreams in a different light. In an impressively terse manner he has called attention to the fact that the daydream in many ways may have a rehearsal or constructive planning function that can lead to an important action. Sullivan (1953) advised therapists with respect to such fantasies that "he should carefully study them in order to determine to what extent they are 'mere' partial satisfaction, and to what extent they include elements of foreseeing—in other words to what extent they are prospective revery, tending to improve what one does in the next similar situation [p. 350]." In this respect, Sullivan's position seems much closer to the view that relates daydreaming fantasy and plans characteristic of more recent approaches (Miller *et al.*, 1960; Singer, 1966; Tomkins, 1962).

Perhaps the greatest difference from classical psychoanalysis in the post-Freudian schools is found in the approach to interpretation of the *content* of dreams which characterizes the neo-Freudians. Obviously, Jung had already begun to move far from Freud in his emphasis on the cultural and archaic racial components that intruded into dream material, but the more recent neo-Freudians have placed much greater emphasis on the dream as a metaphor or a symbol taken as a whole, an approach quite different from Freud's analytic viewpoint. The history, changes in technique, and relation particular to the current psychophysiological research information on dreams and dream interpretation in psychoanalysis has been summarized most effectively by Green, Ullman, and Tauber (1968). Fromm's (1951) emphasis on the dream as a "forgotten language," a system of communication that characterized man in a less complex social milieu and which pervades our sleeping life, has been influential. More recently, another approach is presented by two psychoanalysts in an intensive report on a single case (Caligor & May, 1968). Here the emphasis is less upon the "primitive" nature of the dream than the dream as a freer and broader awareness of experiences hidden from the self, so that dream interpretation is viewed, not merely as an understanding of childlike awareness, but as a more open and more complex self-awareness than that ordinarily produced in traditional free association. Again, the emphasis in these approaches, which have been widely respected and employed by neo-Freudians, has been upon how to interpret the content of the material; there has been much less stress upon the general structure of a dream in relation to personality. The neo-Freudians have not demonstrated particular innovation in method of using the dream within the analytic situation. A particularly insightful summarization of many of the experiences of neo-Freudian therapists with the ways in which dreams are used defensively, as part of transference, and many other details of technique for dream interpretation has been effectively presented by Bonime (1962).

Somewhat more innovative in using both the imagery of the patient and of the therapist has been the approach of Tauber and Green (1959). These authors, in advance of other trends, called attention to many of the constructive and creative functions of a variety of types of imagery which could be employed in psychotherapy in the course of an ongoing psychoanalysis. While agreeing that some of the replaying of frightening incidents or potentially distressing events may have a magical drive-reducing property for some people, Tauber and Green (1959) also call attention to the fact that such "correcting situations either in daydreams, dreams or in play . . . imply that something different *might* have occurred. This suggested alternative fosters the hope — and the intention — of playing in any future challenging situation the role in which one has seen oneself in his reveries [p. 51]." They note that "responding to a threatening situation [in the form of a fantasy or a daydream] . . . does not unleash only defensive referential processes but also creative potential [p. 52]."

Perhaps the key to the differences between the neo-Freudian position, emphasized by Tauber and Green, and the more classical analytic position may be found in the concept of communication. Influenced on the one hand by Sullivan, whose concern is greatly with the communication dyad as the key to psychotherapy and, indeed, ultimately to all relationships, and on the other by Fromm, who, after all, called his book on dreams *The Forgotten Language,* the position of Tauber and Green views the dream not so much as a reflection of inner processes struggling for discharge and erupting intrapsychically as compromise formations and symbolic representations of unconscious material. Rather, they refer to view the dream as an attempt at communication, a struggle on the part of the individual to find awareness and also to communicate this awareness to others. They are critical of Sullivan's rather easy dismissal of most dream interpretation. They prefer to regard the dream as a "message." Tauber and Green (1959), State: "In telling the dream, the patient describes his life situation; and he describes not only what he experiences in awareness but much more than he is aware of. The peculiar wisdom of the dream, inscrutable as it may appear, often transcends man's waking knowledge of himself [p. 171]." They go on to emphasize that the dream is an attempted statement about the individual's way of life and self-concept and contrast this with the view of the dream as a resolution of instinctual problems.

This interactionist orientation to the dream image is carried further in their stress on the nature of the therapeutic situation. They note that while free association works best in an atmosphere of minimal external stimulation, Tauber and Green speculate that: "an atmosphere that is not so totally permissive may be more stimulating to the emergence of inner experience [p. 102]." They have warned against the possibility that "the exclusively circumscribed atmosphere that sometimes prevails in analysis may, like the perceptual isolation situation, provoke trance-like phenomena and it certainly fails to prepare the patient for dealing with the problems of living [p. 103]." In keeping with their approach they feel that the dream's message is best clarified by allowing the dream viewed almost as a poem to evoke images in the therapist's mind.

Indeed these authors have pointed out that not only the patient's dreams, but the therapist's dreams, which may often deal in fairly direct form with patients, can themselves be used to communicate significant issues in the therapeutic relationship or significant characteristics about the patient's mode of relating to others through their revelation, under carefully controlled conditions, to the patient. The therapist's willingness to share his dream with the patient may serve first of all to help the patient address a significant problem within himself, but also may serve as a model to the patient of honesty and of the value of attending to inner process and of struggling to find meaning and clues as to the portions of one's own impact upon others that were being denied.

Tauber and Green are cognizant of the importance of imagery both from the patient's and therapist's standpoints. There is much more direct interaction between patient and therapist as part of this approach. In addition, it would seem from their vantage point that the kind of extended silence that certainly characterizes the early phases of many classical analyses or the kind of extended imagery trip that is a part of the European mental imagery techniques would appear beside the point. They would see such approaches to imagery leading the patient perhaps too far from a confrontation with his own humanity in relation to the therapist and also away from a realistic awareness that his basic problems have to do with his day-to-day interaction with the real people around him.

A COGNITIVE–AFFECTIVE APPROACH
TO TRANSFERENCE IMAGERY IN PSYCHOANALYSIS

One of the major distinctions between the neo-Freudian or especially Sullivan-influenced approaches to psychoanalysis relates to the different view of the transference that is held by these practitioners. The most extended effective analysis of this is given by Wolstein (1954), who described more than 20 specific occurrences in psychoanalytical sessions that were indications of a transference. These included such things as the patient expressing an unreasoning dislike for the therapist or an excessive liking beyond any reality possibility in the situation, or such things as persistent misunderstanding of the analyst's interpretations and remarks. From the neo-Freudian vantage point, all transference is essentially a distortion and, in a certain sense, represents the persistence in the psychotherapeutic situation of attitudes and images that are based on earlier experiences and do not take into account the immediate situation on its own terms. Singer (1965) has pointed out that the general trend today is to view the distinction between positive and negative transference as useless on the whole; moreover, all transference must be regarded as negative in the sense that it does violence to the reality of the therapist as an individual and, for example, ascribing "angelic qualities to him" is both disrespectful and indicative of distinct avoidance in perceiving the therapist's individuality. Singer has also called attention to the relationship between transference and Kelly's (1955) notion of personal constructs—long-established organization of experience which the patient uses to guide his view of current situations, often with the likelihood that he will actually evoke the very patterns he seeks to avoid. Singer (1965) carried this point ultimately to the following conclusion: "the patient who engages in massive transference behavior employs the basic operation which makes for a marked diminution of a sense of self. By not experiencing varied reactions he does not experience at all; . . . in this way he may well protect himself, but he pays a horrible price: not being. Transference is the vehicle for self-elimination [p. 285]." In this view, the transference is essentially a kind of very generalized image of what the world is like. It may be regarded as a set of expectations of reactions and fantasies about what interactions do occur between people. These fantasies are continually played out internally. A more disturbed patient sets up actual situations that reveal at least to the patient himself their apparent validity.

For our purposes, the essential point is that transference may be viewed as a more or less organized set of anticipatory images and ongoing daydreams about what the nature of relationships are like. Sometimes the fantasy experience may be so important and so strongly developed in order to avoid the anxiety of a direct interaction that the person misses many of the actual occurrences in the environment in the interest of attending to the fantasy. A clever cartoon by Jules Pfeifer depicted a young woman daydreaming about the arrival of the handsome prince who will love her. She is so immersed in her daydream that when the young prince actually comes and offers her his hand, she doesn't even notice his presence, and so he goes off in disgust, while she continues to dream about the prince who will come and love her.

In actual clinical practice among neo-Freudians, there is a great deal of attention paid to fantasies produced by patients and to patients who dream material or have misunderstandings that may reflect this kind of distorted images at the very beginning of the therapeutic encounter. The neo-Freudian will move to ascertain initially the anticipatory images of the patient about therapy, if there is some suggestion, for example, that the patient overestimates the powers of the therapist.

In keeping with this sensitivity to the distorting characteristics of transferential phenomena and also to the greater focus on the interaction or communication pattern in the therapy session, neo-Freudians are much more willing to examine their own fantasies or fleeting daydreams about patients and indeed to reveal them to the patients (Tauber & Green, 1959) when there seems to be some reason to indicate to the patient how his impact on the therapist is leading to certain consequences which may ultimately be self-defeating.

It is possible to take an even broader view of the nature of transference and perhaps redeem it somewhat from the rather negative presentation emphasized by the Sullivanians. Transference may represent just a special case of a more general pattern of behavior which is necessary for us in order to steer ourselves through our physical and social environment. In order to maximize the efficiency of our physical movements or of our social comfort, we have to rely often on fairly automatic responses. In this sense, anticipation of what we may expect in certain physical surroundings leaves us "channel space" for thinking about other things while we are walking through that physical environment without the fear of bumping into things. In a similar sense, a fairly reasonable set of expectations about certain relatively unimportant social situations may leave us free either to think our own thoughts or to function more creatively once we know the courtesies or conventions of the particular social milieu. What I propose, therefore, is that part of our way of getting around in the world involves setting up hierarchies of anticipatory notions based on our past experience, of course, and our fantasies about what the world is like. To the extent that we are relatively free of gross neurotic distortion, these fantasies, while they may not be completely correct in predicting future events, will serve reasonably well.

Hence, transference as perceived in the therapeutic hour represents an overgeneralized tendency to use childhood experiences, or particularly unpleasant interactions, to determine all kinds of new situations and the failure to modify these early developed anticipations on the basis of actual subsequent experiences. Sometimes the very early developed fantasies are maintained because the patient avoids new kinds of situations which would alter the likelihood of these fantasies' value for the future and, therefore, the patient tends to persist in using outmoded anticipations in the situations when they do occur.

The phenomenon of transference may well represent a special case of the broader use of the central image or "plan" that has been introduced by such cognitive theorists as Tomkins (1962) and Miller, et al. (1960). Image-making is one of man's major activities. In many ways, it is a highly efficient system of organizing experience, and it permits us a kind of leeway to operate with considerable freedom in a physical or social environment. Transference for most of us represents a whole series of well-established expectations of what authorities, men, women, elderly people, or sexual situations are likely to become. Within psychology, special emphasis on the relationship of affect and emotion to these hierarchies of guiding images has been stressed by Tomkins (1962, 1963), and, in relation to psychotherapy, the work of Kelly (1955) has special relevance since he makes the person's construct system the key to all human interaction. Rotter's (1954) social learning theory represents a somewhat more experimentally oriented approach to this general phenomenon.

The question as to whether all of these expectancies are in the form of conscious imagery is very complex. More likely, the position of the Wurzburg school, which argued in favor of attitudinal sets as a key part of human thinking, must still be taken seriously, and it is quite likely that only from time to time do all of these images emerge into consciousness. The question of how much fantasy or imagery is completely unconscious, as would be argued in the traditional psychoanalytic position or in the position of a Kleinian psychoanalyst, is more conjectural. Nevertheless, if one adopts a viewpoint of this general type, then it becomes clear that a major purpose of psychotherapy, particularly one oriented toward extended analysis of ongoing life styles, calls for a gradually teasing out of the fantasies and anticipation and their patterns in the individual.

Whether or not the psychoanalytic schools of various persuasions make use specifically of some form of mental imagery techniques, their work is intrinsically involved with eliciting the images and plans of the patient. The constant work of exposing defenses and the so-called "working through" phase of psychotherapy, in which there is a repetitive pointing out of defenses and of persisting conflict areas, can be regarded as a kind of training of the patient in a more effective sensitivity to his own ongoing imagery. I deal with this issue at length later in this volume, but it is important to note in connection with the psychoanalytical methods that they do involve a kind of formal training of the patient which often is not explicitly recognized by practitioners. If psychoanalysis is effective and leads to freeing the patient from his dependence on the analysis itself to do the work of self-awareness, what happens is something like the following:

> A patient experiences a sudden sense of unrest or annoyance upon entering a room. Under some past conditions he might have hastily left the room or perhaps talked rudely in response to questions raised. His analytic experience now alerts him to the fact that this sudden unease is occasioned by an irrational anticipation or transference in the situation. He replays in his mind the thoughts just previous to entering the room or what he was thinking about immediately prior to this situation. On this mental screen, he "instant replays" the thoughts and perceptions that occurred and suddenly is aware that he had been thinking about some obligation to one of his parents and that on entering the room he noticed across the way an elderly gentleman who rather resembled his father. He now perceives that his distress is a combination of anticipatory image plus the scene occurring in the room and generally is freed of his anxiety and certainly is less likely to engage in an irrational and self-defeating bit of behavior in this new situation.

This example may seem somewhat idealized, but I do not believe this to be the case. It is my experience that effective therapeutic experience, particularly of an analytic type, does indeed provide the patient with this kind of controlled sensitivity over his own imaginativeness and gives him the ability to play through sets of images very quickly so that he can sort out the distorting transference possibilities in a situation.

An effective psychoanalysis, therefore, is indeed very much of a kind of training in imagery control. As Strupp (1970) has very convincingly argued, one of the chief purposes of psychotherapy is the promotion of self-control. By teaching the use of careful attention to ongoing dreams and fantasies and the replaying of associations leading up to these experiences, psychoanalysis, whether classical or neo-Freudian, in effect provides an opportunity for careful training of the patient in self-control and autonomy with respect to his own imagery capacities.

CHAPTER IV

IMAGERY AND GUIDED DAYDREAM TECHNIQUES: THE EUROPEAN SCHOOLS

I dream the world, therefore the world exists as I dream it.
Gaston Bachélard (1969, p. 158)

CULTURAL AND PHILOSOPHICAL BACKGROUND

To understand what brought about the vigorous development of mental imagery techniques in Europe, while they languished in the United States, is an intriguing part of the sociology and history of scientific movements. While Freudian and neo-Freudian theories found a fertile soil even in the behaviorist, empiricist atmosphere of the United States, the Jungian orientation in psychoanalysis gained scarcely a foothold in this country, yet was very much a part of the cultural atmosphere in Europe. Perhaps the more tough-minded experimentalists among American psychologists might argue that the effects of the world wars hindered the scientific development of psychology in Europe and kept it open to the somewhat more speculative, mystical, and quasi-philosophical features that characterized psychology at the turn of the century.

It is certainly true that psychology as a separate discipline failed to develop vigorously in the political structure of various European universities during the 1930s and 1940s. Moreover, the amazing influx of the great minds of European psychology into the United States from Europe during this period was, for obvious reasons, not balanced by an exodus of the more sophisticated American researchers to Europe. Clearly, Europe's loss of Wertheimer, Kohler, Koffka, Lewin, Heider, Brunswik, the Buhlers, Rapaport, Rank, and literally dozens upon dozens of fine investigators and clinicians has enriched psychology in the United States and left Europe impoverished for some time afterwards.

But this view seems altogether too simple. More likely, the development of imagery techniques in Europe, particularly vigorous after the end of World War II, reflected a persisting and profound sensitivity and involvement with the world of imagination and with internal experience that had always been a part of the intellectual atmosphere. The important influence in France of Sartre, with his interest in the philosophical implications of internal experiences — as exemplified in his work on nausea — signaled the power of this interest. I shall not explore all the possible origins of European interest in imagery and private experience. Yet, it may be useful to call attention to the work of Bachélard (1964, 1969, 1971), who may be regarded as a representative of the intellectual leadership in the European community that fostered sensitivity to dreams and reverie. Bachélard perhaps could best be called a kind of poet-philosopher of science. He was a physicist who devoted himself primarily to examining the relationship between the material world and its physical properties and the transformation of the material into imagination by the individual. He also explored the forms that imagination assumed in its own right as part of our phenomenology. Although Bachélard was himself neither a psychotherapist, nor particularly concerned with clinical issues, nor the leader of any school of thought, his example undoubtedly colored much of the approach of the professionals in France and probably in Germany and Italy.

Beginning with an attempt to understand how certain elements — fire, air, or earth — had been interpreted by human experience and formed a part of the broader consciousness of the human being, Bachélard rather soon came to the conclusion that man's reality was not merely a replaying of material perceived in the outside world. He came to recognize that the human imagination had in effect its own properties and ongoing nature that provided man with a reality, perhaps in some respects, even more fundamental than the sense impressions he gained from his environment. While he was at first intrigued by the capacity of Freudian theory to relate symbols which appeared in dreams or fantasies to the basic elements we experience in our daily lives (such as fire and water), Bachélard soon became critical of psychoanalysis. He moved toward Jung's view of the symbol, not merely as representative of sensual desires or sexuality, but as a basic component of the broader range of human experience.

Bachélard did not adopt the notion of the racial archetype in Jung's exact sense, yet he did express considerable interest in the male and female components of human experience, the *animus* and *anima*, which he himself could sense in the difference, for example, between a dream (*rêve*) and a fantasy (*rêverie*). He emphasized not so much the fact that our fantasies and dreams use symbols passed on through man's history, but rather that they represent our own current experience, the metaphors and symbols of our culture so intertwined with the actual experience of our sense that we cannot disentangle them. These symbols endlessly reverberate and intermingle as part of human experience so that our vision of the world is in part a vision of our own ongoing imagery. What Bachélard called the "function of the unreal" is as critical a part of the human condition as the reality principle, which was so emphasized by the psychoanalysts. In discussing, for example, the dream of flying, he (Bachélard, 1971) called attention to the fact that while the psychoanalyst might propose that it relates to sexual experience, this would overlook the intrinsically aesthetic quality of the flight movement itself. The fact that so many myths and legends create different images of flight would argue against them simply representing only one underlying trend since each image of flight has its own *special* qualities.

Again and again, Bachélard writes with great eloquence and with a convincing quality that goes beyond traditional logic. In a sense he speaks to our own imagery tendencies so that we experience what he is driving at by reviewing our own fantasies as he presents his. This view of the human condition is one that lies at the root of the widespread use of mental imagery techniques which are the subject of this and the following chapter. Even if one does not make explicit connections between specific techniques such as those of Leuner, Desoille, Virel and Frétigny, or Assagioli, there is no doubt that their faith in the ongoing unfolding of imagery as intrinsically therapeutic reflects the same serious view that imagery is an essential part of man's reality which is so eloquently fostered by Bachélard.

It seems easy to dismiss this emphasis on reverie as the worst kind of armchair speculation. Certainly, it represents a type of poetic elaboration which often has been used in place of formal scientific inquiry.

Nevertheless, a careful examination of Bachelard's position (Kaplan, 1972) makes it clear that there is a powerful intellectual impulse behind this notion of the central role of imagery in human psychology. It has been in the past too easy for psychologists to dismiss fantasies, thoughts, and reveries as epiphenomena that have little true meaning for an accurate description of human behavior. It is all too clear from recent developments in cognition and in research that such a view does have more relevance to human thought.

I shall now look at some examples of imagery techniques that have been developed in Europe and consider some of their general clinical characteristics and broader implications. The intention is not to cover each of the techniques in detail, but to highlight certain of the special qualities of the major methods and to indicate how these may have implications for some of the psychotherapeutic techniques now in use in the United States. A particularly useful volume which presents the most thorough and scientifically oriented description of mental imagery techniques is by Frétigny and Virel (1968).

THE GUIDED WAKING DREAM
OF ROBERT DESOILLE

There seems little doubt that the major impetus to the development of mental imagery techniques in Europe came from the work of Desoille (1938, 1945, 1961, 1966). This method developed over a period of almost 30 years, and it is somewhat difficult at times to reconcile its earlier statements, which were largely based on the personal experiences of Desoille with very few indications of awareness of the literature of psychology or psychiatry, with the most recent statements by Desoille, which reflect a strong antipathy to psychoanalysis and an affinity with the Pavlovian conditioning, as well as with some of the behavior modification techniques, although this latter similarity is not explicitly recognized by Desoille. Since Desoille's strong point is not psychological theory, it may be best not to dwell on his efforts in this direction, but to focus on the method itself and some of its clinical applications.

The directed daydream technique is presented to a patient by a fairly simple explanation. Then, almost without anamnesis, the patient is initiated into a relaxed state using a procedure approximating the Jacobson *progressive relaxation* method. Reclining on a couch in semidarkness with eyes shut, he is encouraged to imagine a specific image, a sword or a seashore, and then to locate himself in an environment and begin moving about in this imagined setting. He is reminded that anything can happen in a dream and is encouraged to produce a series of continuous images. Generally speaking, the emphasis is on ascent in the vertical dimension; the therapist (or *guide,* as Desoille prefers to call him) directs the client's movements initially and later encourages him to allow the images to unfold with their own momentum. There are two main directions of movement, either ascending or descending, with the former generally producing images associated with positive affect, joy, striving, and so on, while the downward movement is more often likely to evoke frightening negative images or fearful scenes.

Over the years, Desoille has gradually systematized the initiating images assigned to the patient. Now these images have been developed around six themes, which he feels cover the major problem areas in human experience. The first has to do with confronting one's own personality characteristics and these are stimulated by beginning the patient with an image of a sword (if male) or a vessel or container (if female). Clearly, the Freudian influence is evident in Desoille's emphasis on the sexual component, but it is also broadened into the use of symbols that reflect Jung's influence.

A second situation—confronting suppressed characteristics—is created by encouraging an imagined descent into the depths of the ocean or through moving underground. The third area is coming to terms with the opposite sex parent. To this end, the male patient is encouraged to descend into a cave and find a witch or a sorceress, whereas the woman is encouraged to find a wizard or a magician in a cave. The fourth phase involves a relationship with the same-sex parent: cave descent takes place, except that a male figure is involved for the man and a female witch or sorceress for the woman.

The fifth major theme centers on the constraints of society on the individual and here the image that Desoille emphasizes is a descent into a cave to confront a legendary dragon or monster. Finally, Desoille, in his sixth situation, focuses on the Oedipal conflict and for both sexes suggests the image of the castle of Sleeping Beauty located deep in a forest.

The typical directed daydream session begins with the relaxation and is followed by the specific image suggested by the guide. There is next an imagined trip with a variety of images occurring and with considerable concomitant affective expression. At the end of a session, which often may have involved considerable variability in emotional reaction, the therapist may encourage the patient to rest and enjoy the view of a scene and experience the satisfaction of having accomplished the journey. For homework, the patient is encouraged to write out a full account of his experience and to bring it to the next session so that it can be discussed in detail. This discussion may occasionally involve free association, but primarily makes use of further imagery and also the taking of some case history material.

The initial use of the climbing image or the sword indicates to the therapist to some extent the degree to which the patient is capable of imagery and is responsive to the therapist's suggestions. When moments of inhibition occur, the therapist may use his judgment to intervene and indicate that perhaps there is some help available or some magical opportunity to increase one's strength. At what seems to be a natural end of the journey, the guide may encourage the patient to hold the sword up to the sunlight and then to report what happens, or in the case of a woman, to hold up her vessel and see what fills it from the heavens.

The descent imagery generally calls for the therapist to prepare the patient for the possibility that quite frightening images may indeed occur. The patient is encouraged to confront these and to show a certain amount of bravery. The guide also provides appropriate assistance by suggesting different implements or techniques the patient may use to continue his journey or to deal with frightening monsters. Desoille gives an example of a patient who meets a monster in an underwater grotto. The guide encourages the patient to ask the monster to give him a tour of the grotto and then to bring the monster back onto the beach with him. At this point he encourages the patient to tap the monster with a magic wand with which he has been provided—this turns the monster into an octopus and his true identity can then be revealed. Desoille indicates that on these occasions the image of the actual person in the patient's life whom the monster had symbolized is likely to occur. Desoille (1966) reports: "The dream then goes into its final stages with the subject's ascension of the mountain overlooking the sea in the company of the person into whom the octopus has changed [p. 6]."

Reading specific accounts of some of the guided daydream trips in this literature is most intriguing. Certainly, the vividness of the imagery, the elaborateness of the scenery generated by the patient, is impressive indeed. At the same time, it is hard to avoid the feeling that some of these people are already highly gifted fantasizers and perhaps rather talented individuals. The quality of vocabulary, the subtlety and complexity of the "story line" in the case that Desoille presents in his most recent series of lectures (Desoille, 1966), makes one wonder whether this technique is especially appealing to individuals already strongly inclined toward fantasy.

Without attempting to summarize the major points that Desoille makes in justifying his therapeutic approach, suffice it to say that he calls attention to the diagnostic value of the procedure since the imagery allows relatively undisguised expression of fundamental problems without active resistance by the patient. The imagery serves also a desensitization function since the patient must confront, from time to time, frightening figures or frightening persons and is encouraged to remain in their presence while in the relaxed state and with the awareness that the therapist is at his side. Finally, there is a reeducation aspect in which under the relaxed conditions the patient can begin to develop new patterns of responses.

Desoille's efforts to relate the guided daydream technique to Pavlov and the second signaling system are not convincing because they seem so general as to preclude detailed application to his case material. Obviously, employing some aspects of Jungian and Freudian symbolism, Desoille also describes quite clearly methods that closely approximate desensitization techniques or variants of what Lazarus (1971) called *emotive imagery*. This is exemplified in the case of a woman with a fear of driving on the highway who was treated by the directed daydream method. Desoille (1966), after ascertaining to his own satisfaction that there was no gross psychogenic involvement, indicated that probably on the basis of her physical history the woman had a momentary blackout once while driving. This experience led her to be quite frightened, and the problem was now to decondition this associated fear. Desoille began by having her imagine herself driving with the therapist at her side, talking in a relaxed fashion, and describing the scenery as they drove along. He also instructed her to employ some of the thoughts while driving and to follow these up by regular reports to the therapist. Desoille insists that dynamic aspects are irrelevant at this point and indeed sounds very much like Wolpe as he presents the case.

Still another example of the use of the technique is in the case of a patient who was climbing a mountain in imagery and suddenly became frightened, could not go on, and opened her eyes. This reaction was connected to an early experience of having been traumatized by being caught in an animal trap and being separated from her mother subsequently because of her response to this accident. Desoille (1966) firmly encouraged the patient to shut her eyes again and then helped her reestablish a pleasant, positive image and gave her the suggestion that her own daughter would appear to her and serve as her guide. This technique worked, and the woman with her daughter's hand in hers was able to resume her fantasy upward climb.

From Desoille's point of view, while he is aware of transference and reports occasionally having to deal with it, basically the method is one of having the patient go in sequence through the six situations, several times in each situation, depending on the clinician's judgment. There is no extended discussion or interaction of a more traditional psychotherapeutic type, and most of the treatment genuinely consists of a series of trips that, from Desoille's standpoint, are intrinsically curative. The ability of the patient to undertake these conditions and to follow through elaborate trips is impressive indeed on the basis of the many case reports in the European literature. While some of the situations are typically European and would seem inapplicable if introduced to American patients (certainly the Sleeping Beauty daydream seems an unlikely choice), Desoille's work demonstrates the great richness of human imagery capacity and wide applicability to a great variety of patients. Some examples of different types of patients treated with mental imagery techniques are presented subsequently in this chapter.

THE ONIROTHERAPY OF FRÉTIGNY AND VIREL

Although Desoille must be credited with the major influence upon the development of the mental imagery techniques for psychotherapy in recent times, he generally has remained somewhat on the outside of the mental health establishment in Europe, in part owing to the fact that his training was in engineering. Indeed, Desoille shows little evidence of formal background in psychology or psychiatry. Roger Frétigny and André Virel, by contrast, make up a team of a psychiatrist and psychologist, both with extensive scientific training; they have explored a number of the dimensions of mental imagery techniques experimentally and theoretically, as well as in actual practice. While there is no question that Frétigny and Virel have largely made use of Desoille's techniques, their general approach has been more one of systematic inquiry into the parameters of the process and also has embedded the method into a more general psychotherapeutic orientation. Their book *L'Imagerie Mentale* (Frétigny & Virel, 1968) is at this time perhaps the most scholarly and definitive statement available on the mental imagery techniques, particularly as practiced in France and, to some extent, Italy.

Frétigny and Virel have made the most extensive efforts to relate what they prefer to call *onirotherapy* to current research on electrophysiological functions of the brain, night dreaming, and the sleep cycle, and to relate their theoretical thinking to psychoanalysis and Jungian theory. Frétigny and Virel began their collaboration shortly

TABLE II

Relationships between Psychological States, Levels of Arousal, and Patterns of Consciousness[a]

Psychological states	Levels of arousal	Electroencephalography	Clinical and subjective characteristics	Types and expressions of awareness
Emotional states	Hyperaroused	Rapid-frequency trace (30 cycles per second), low amplitude.	Anger, abreaction, etc.; lysergic mental imagery, poor or uncontrolled motor behavior.	Disturbed
States of attention or alert	Aroused	Rapid-frequency trace (30 cycles per second), low amplitude.	Thoughts and behavior well integrated; maximum adjustment.	Predominance of thoughtful or pragmatic awareness.
Hypnotic-like states	Hypoaroused	Typical alpha rhythm trace (9–12 cycles per second) in spurts, with back spiking.	Attention wavering, allowing the association of ideas or images to take place freely. Rapid eye movement during the duration of mental imagery. Reflexes normal.	Detachment of dream-like awareness; mental imagery (dialectical) or dreaming (solitary).
Hypnagogic states	Quasi-aroused	Diminution of the amplitude and number of alpha rhythm spurts.	Drowsiness. Disconnection from self and from reality. Reactions mechanical and badly coordinated.	Passive awareness during imaging. Disconnected imagery.
Sleep states	Hypoaroused	Different phases of sleep corresponding to hypoaroused level.	During one phase, self-contradictory speech, rapid eye movements, indicating dramatic visual dreams that will be remembered	In the phases of sleep, periods of detachment of dreamlike awareness.
Comatose states	Unaroused	Very slow waves, flattened out and near the zero-potential line.	Cessation of reaction to stimuli.	?

[a] From Frétigny and Virel (1968, p. 26).

after World War II ended. Frétigny was then established as a psychiatrist and was engaged in direct practice using various imagery techniques; Virel worked more in anthropology and then began to move into the area of psychophysiology, eventually obtaining his doctorate in psychology with work in that area. Virel spent two years working extensively under the supervision of Desoille as part of his effort to gain further experience in this field.

By employing the term onirotherapy, these authors sought to distinguish between the very specific guided daydream method of Desoille and techniques oriented around the use of states intermediate between wakefulness and sleep. Table II gives their classification of various types of mental imagery in relation to different levels of consciousness, which is based to some extent on the available literature and on some research carried out by Virel and reported in their book.

Basically, the method proposed by Frétigny and Virel has evolved out of fairly extensive experimentation on their part and, indeed, they claim to have influenced Desoille in his use of some of the formal imagery situations cited earlier. They generally begin treatment with a rather complete case history and are concerned with the details of family background and orientation, psychosocial factors in the case, as well as significant features of physiological and psychological development. They then encourage the patient to relax deeply and to begin with imagery—much in the fashion of Desoille, imagining a sword, climbing a mountain, etc. They also require the preparation of a detailed account by the patient of the imagery he produced during the previous session which then becomes a subject for discussion in a subsequent session. They also are alert to obtaining relevant dream material from the patient. In this sense, their approach is more within the general therapeutic tradition than that of Desoille.

Frétigny and Virel pay considerable attention to evidence of resistance on the part of patients and, in general, are concerned in analytic terms about the emergence of transference of behavior or fantasies, which they treat in a manner similar to that of the neo-Freudian psychoanalysts. Although it is clear that they are active in the therapeutic endeavor, in the sense that they intervene at moments of great panic on the part of the patient or make suggestions for magical devices to move through difficult moments in the imagery or to overcome monsters, etc., they tend to prefer to allow the imagery to unroll as freely as possible once they have suggested a particular direction. Rather than *guide*, the term used by Desoille, they prefer the term *operator*. Operator suggests someone who starts a process in motion and is available to monitor its unfolding, but who is not himself actively involved at each stage of the process, thus allowing more freedom of action to the patient. This term also seems to them more in keeping with the information-processing quality of much of the mental imagery produced.

Frétigny and Virel presented a fairly detailed case study of a 40-year-old store manager troubled for five months by insomnia and periods of anxiety, nightmares, and depressive thoughts during the day. The clinicians obtained a case history, which indicated that on the whole the patient, who was married for 15 years and had two children, was not grossly disturbed, nor had he had any previous indications of serious mental illness or severe neurosis. The patient could indeed relax rather well and began his first imagery explorations in a fairly unresistant manner, but without evidencing particular originality in the quality of his images. In the course of the first session, which was not especially remarkable, there were indications that as he engaged in climbing imagery and experienced himself as being bathed in light from the sky, he noticed a strong desire for sleep. This relationship of the desire to sleep and the consequences of the imagery recurred a number of times in later therapy and indicated that the patient might indeed benefit from imagery techniques in relation to his recent insomniac condition. It turned out, for example, that he had suppressed describing some scenes of a sexual nature and had, for example, imagined a naked woman in a sylvan setting. Within two or three sessions there was already in evidence a reduction in sleeping difficulty on the part of the patient and actually forgetfulness on his part to take the sleeping pills he had been accustomed to use.

Many of the sessions made it clear that there was considerable preoccupation with sexuality and with attempting to relate to attractive women, as well as a great deal of fear of a dominant father. Indeed, in some respects the case, as the authors noted, had all the signs of a classical Oedipus complex.

Here is an example of the way in which Frétigny and Virel set up an imagery session, taking into account the particular psychological characteristics of the patient, but also in keeping with the more general psychoanalytic position they embrace. The patient was assigned the following theme: "You are at home with your parents. You are leaving them to find the castle of Sleeping Beauty." There follows the patient's account of the imagery he produced following this therapeutic requirement by the operator:

> I had to leave my parents in order to look for a Sleeping Beauty. I try in vain to explain the situation to them. They don't understand it at all and I leave my parents' home without their consent. I say especially my paternal home because the refusal comes above all from my father.

I travel in two stages into the woods, spending the night under the open stars. At the approach of noon, I finally see a thick forest, almost an impenetrable one. In order to go on, I have to force my way through branches, vines, and high grasses. I discover eventually, deep in the forest, a towered castle guarded by sentinels. I succeed in getting through the first door and then into the entrance hall up a staircase and across another vestibule which is quite vast and finally, guide myself toward the place where I know I will find the beautiful maiden asleep.

I hasten to see her to waken her and to lead her away with me. At the moment when she awakens and arises, all the furnishings of the castle disappear and Sleeping Beauty becomes my wife to confront the outside world. We unite and I feel myself full of courage in order to face the new life which has opened before me. It's as if at last I have carried to conclusion a task without my parents, alone, and that I have succeeded without them and despite them [Frétigny & Virel, 1968, pp. 156–157; author's translation].

After the twentieth session with this young man, the therapist received a letter from the patient in which he outlined in detail a series of early childhood experiences, including some occasions of being touched on his buttocks playfully by his grandmother and also later spanked there by an older cousin under circumstances that led him to develop a mixture of excitement and guilt in relationship to this area of his body. Although in many respects his later sexual development was normal, he was never free of a tremendous burden of guilt, and the anal involvement persisted as a special pocket of distress and guilt even into his adult years after he had married and fathered several children.

In a careful summary of the case, Frétigny and Virel pointed out the step-by-step development of the guilt in this young man, who had been dominated by a strong father and a very restrictive religious education that evoked guilt for almost any type of sensual experience. Despite this great sense of guilt, he managed to live a reasonably normal life until his own son reached the age of adolescence and began to show the glimmerings of interest in sexuality. This development revived in the patient, Gilbert, his own terrible fears lest his son experience the guilt he himself had. Unable to face consciously the implications of his identification with his son, he became increasingly frightened of his own fantasy processes and experienced periods of free-floating anxiety, as well as the attacks of insomnia.

Frétigny and Virel pointed out how the step-by-step exploration, in symbolic form, of the forbidden pleasures on the one hand, and on the other, the religious and paternal inhibitions transposed into images which the patient had to confront again and again led to significant abreactions and, in addition, opportunity for reintegration of these experiences into his adult role. The authors stated that a large number of individuals even less touched by early accidental conditionings (such as Gilbert's experiences with the grandmother and cousin) may have persisting inhibitions from childhood or adolescence that are translated frequently into some metaphoric or symbolic form and can be relieved only to the extent that an opportunity for expression of them in *oniric*, or quasi-dreamlike, form is possible.

For Frétigny and Virel, the central feature of the mental imagery technique is the so-called *onirodrama*, the vivid and dramatic confrontation through imagery of the critical problems of the subject. The following is an example of another case. This patient had spent a year in a Jungian analysis, but the therapy appeared to be at a stagnant point. Thus, he was referred to one of the authors for mental imagery technique. After a period of relaxation, the patient was able quite quickly to enter fully into the situation. The details of the case need not concern us here except to indicate that it involved a young man with problems in relation to his orientation to women. His father had been interned during the war from the time the patient was 3 years old and he had been raised by his mother and grandmother, having very little contact with young boys his age. He had not the slightest experience with girls and felt considerably inferior to them.

The following example is from the onirodrama in which the patient spontaneously reinvents what might be considered a rite of initiation and where, at least in symbolic form, he resolves some of his sexual difficulties:

> I am on a plain. I'm walking along and I arrive at the entrance of a tropical rain forest with very high trees and vines which block the road. I move ahead into the forest and arrive about sundown before a clearing set within the rocks and surrounded by the forest. Natives dance around a great fire. Meanwhile, night falls. Suddenly a sorcerer appears. The tom-tom stops, the natives seat themselves in rows on one side of the clearing. The sorcerer has a caldron brought before him. He puts in various ingredients and at the moment when the face of the moon arrives just above the clearing, an enormous snake comes out of the caldron and balances itself lightly. The sorcerer gives me the sign to approach; I leave the rows of the natives and approach. The sorcerer now leads me up to a platform near the rocks. I have the impression of climbing for a very long time; finally, I come to a platform suspended on the cliff. I see the clearing far below and I leap into the void. I fall very slowly and for a very long time. I land on the ground quite gently. Then the serpent approaches me, winds around me and I feel myself becoming this serpent. Preceded by the witch doctor and the delighted natives, I direct my steps toward the house, toward the other end of the clearing, in the interior of which a young woman lies on the ground. I approach her; I wind around her body; finally I penetrate into her and roll myself up into a ball. Within her body there reigns a gentle warmth and a great calm [Frétigny & Virel, 1968, pp. 174–175; author's translation].

Frétigny and Virel stated that within this imagery sequence are all of the major elements of the onirodrama. They called special attention to the sensation of warmth that the patient reported experiencing inside the body of the woman in the final fantasy. They compared this image with an earlier one (from previous sessions) where the patient had seen himself in the condition of being a fetus in the chest of a statue, whereas now he has progressed to experiencing the warmth of the body of a real woman. While Frétigny and Virel did not devote considerable space to the development of any elaborate theoretical structure, toward the end of the volume, they attempted at least a sketch of some possible theoretical implications and suggested that they were basing much of what they said on fundamental aspects of normal development and on the neurological necessity of growth.

Frétigny and Virel (1968) propose a formulation of the spatial–temporal environment of the individual. In this outline, temporal and spatial experience are integrated by the ego, which has two poles, a psychic and body-oriented pole, the latter known as the *body ego* and former, as the *psychic ego*. What they call the world of imagination is revealed only when there is a break in level of activation under conditions in which the imagery ego is freed from the excitations of the external world. The body ego is expressed ultimately through imagery, as well.

Frétigny and Virel attempted to compare the development of mankind in general and of the caveman with the development of the child and with the different impact of each stage on the sense of self and individuality, as well as on the ability to organize experience into images and symbolic forms. In keeping with their position, so close to the ethnological and anthropological concepts of their culture, the authors stressed the intertwining of symbolism at the cultural level with the early organization of experience of the child which accounts in great part for the complexity of imagery, its vividness, and its relationship to private experience.

While perhaps not completely committed to a notion of universal symbolism, Frétigny and Virel indeed take symbols extremely seriously. They recognize that the very basic kinds of human experiences that have a wide generality and can be relied upon to describe many of the kinds of ongoing experiences that people do have occur again and again. For example, they reported that such recurring images include caverns that can reveal very many strange things and settings within old chests, which whether closed or open frequently contain jewelry or gold, wise men, monsters, black men, veiled women, witches, and so on. These authors take seriously many kinds of symbolic materials that, in the United States, are largely relegated to children's books and even there are treated in a light vein—dragons, Sleeping Beauty, Snow White. In general, the imagery reflects a kind of cultural richness which, in the United States, could perhaps be compared to the extensive knowledge that young people brought up on television would have of cartoon figures and frequently used commercial scenes, as well as figures from situation comedies or adventure stories. Extensive exploration of this imagery world for the American has yet to be carried out.

An important feature of the work of Frétigny and Virel has been their serious attempt to generate some types of experimental work in relation to the mental imagery technique. Their tabular representation of the relationships between psychological states and levels of arousal, as well as what they call modalities of consciousness, has already been cited (see Table II).

Something must also be said about the brief reference to a psychophysiological study undertaken by Frétigny and Virel (1967) with a small number of subjects as an effort to get more closely at the psychophysiological concomitants of ongoing mental imagery. They reported a number of formal experimental studies of responsiveness to internal and external stimulation while subjects were hooked up to a polygraph. For nine particular subjects there was an attempt to carry out therapeutic sessions while their physiological responses were measured. The findings were reported as extremely consistent. During an onirotherapy session there is the emergence of ample evidence of alpha rhythm and a much-modified overt reactivity characterized by minimal response or orientation to external noises or to any other stimulation except for the voice of the therapist. No evidence of actual sleep rhythms was found, the vigilance level being generally quite stable and related mainly to the production of alpha waves without any movement to any of the many forms generally associated with somnolence. In keeping with Table II, the authors claimed that, while the electrophysiological characteristics of ongoing mental imagery resemble those of hypnosis or Schultz's autogenic training, the conscious manifestation appears quite different from the latter two methods. This conclusion reflects the fact that there is much richer and more colorful imagery with fairly immediate description of this fantasy process and the maintenance of close rapport with the psychotherapist of a rather active nature in contrast to the more passive role observed in hypnosis.

Frétigny and Virel (1968) reported a few instances in which small doses of LSD-25 were employed to increase the likelihood of vivid imagery. They used a formula of between 10 and 30 micrograms of LSD − 1 microgram per 2 or 3 kilograms of the subject's weight. Here again they found the situation quite similar to that with mental imagery, that is, regular appearance of stability with alpha rhythm. They reported that, with such small doses, the sessions stayed quite manageable, giving no evidence that the patient or psychotherapist experienced a loss of control in the situation. In one instance they also measured ocular motility and found steady eye movement throughout the sequence of mental imagery. They related this to the findings of rapid eye movements (REM) reported for sleep. They also noted the fact that the psychotherapist's voice did not lead to any gross interruption in the ongoing story or change in the EEG, except in instances where there seemed to be a discordant interpretation.

A study like this is perhaps somewhat primitive from the standpoint of the electrophysiological research now under way in various sleep laboratories, but it does point up the fact that the mental imagery approach can be studied more formally and also suggests that very likely the level of relaxation produced is one below a more generally activated state of most individuals, yet clearly not one that can be called either a hypnotic trance state or a hypnagogic reverie state immediately prior to sleep. As yet, it is obvious that we have studied far too few subjects in a variety of situations under these conditions to provide any adequate generalization about the so-called levels of consciousness that takes into account tremendous individual differences, not only in individual electrophysiological performances, but also in the awareness and capacity to describe ongoing internal processes. (This issue is discussed later in the volume.)

An important contribution of Frétigny and Virel has been their leadership in the organization of the International Society for Mental Imagery Techniques, which holds biennial conferences on technical, theoretical, and therapeutic problems in the field. They have managed to bring together the somewhat diverse group of European practitioners of mental imagery techniques, and their association is one of the relatively few in which Jungians, Freudians, and neo-Freudians among psychoanalysts, as well as various nonanalytically oriented practitioners of the mental imagery techniques, come together to discuss important questions. Thus far, at these meetings much of the level of presentation and discussion has involved case reports of various detail and sophistication, and there has been only minimal attention paid to the relationship of this material to the more general psychological questions of imagery and attention. Similarly, very little experimental work has been discussed or presented. It remains to be seen whether the group will eventually become a more general part of the scientific world or will remain a somewhat circumscribed group whose major interest is in imagery in psychotherapy; in other words, will only little attention be paid to precise definitions and to adequate operational criteria in their work.

THE GUIDED AFFECTIVE IMAGERY METHOD
OF HANSCARL LEUNER

Closely related to the methods of Desoille and Frétigny and Virel, as well as the other European practitioners of mental imagery, is the so-called *guided affective imagery technique* of Hanscarl Leuner (1954, 1955, 1969) of the University of Göttingen, West Germany. Leuner traces his method to Freud's original use of imagery. Leuner has been employing this technique for more than 20 years with a variety of patients, primarily neurotics, and has incorporated his approach within a broader framework that includes the influence of Freudian and Jungian psychoanalysis. Leuner himself was trained as a psychoanalyst and does not see his method as in any way contradictory to the basic aims of dynamic psychotherapy. He has cited some evidence that "guided affective imagery" can indeed reduce the length of time required for treatment of acute neurosis, and it has proven successful, as well, with chronic cases. An important feature of the method is that it is considerably shorter than traditional psychoanalysis—the average psychotherapeutic program lasts only 40 hours, the upper limit thus far found to be 160 hours of psychotherapy required for a given case. Leuner reported evidence of follow-ups of at least 6 years to indicate the long-term value of personality changes and relief from symptoms produced by the method. Leuner has been careful to note that he has not had any special success with the method for psychotic patients or for addicts.

Essentially, the method is closely related to the technique of Desoille, but is far more systematized. The patient reclines on a couch, and is encouraged to relax with Schultz's autogenic training imagery taken as the starting point. It is interesting that Leuner feels it is important that external stimulation be reduced and that the room be quiet and dimly lit. An initial session may begin by imagining a meadow, much as in the French approach. This technique of visualizing a scene of this kind has also been explored extensively by Happich (1932) as an outgrowth of Schultz's earlier autogenic method.

Leuner's initial effort is partly diagnostic and partly a form of training for the patient to help him experience what will be expected of him in the course of psychotherapy. It also alerts him to the fact that he is indeed capable of rather vivid imagery. The general method involves what Leuner calls *different tools* within the approach. There are first of all ten standard imagery themes presented by the therapist to the patient and which lead to the development of specific daydream trips.

There is also a series of five major techniques for evoking the fantasy material and also for interpreting it. These include the training method, the diagnostic method, the method of associated imagery, the symbol dramatic method, and the psychoanalytic method.

Within the symbol dramatic method, which is perhaps the heart of Leuner's approach, there are six particular techniques employed which have special therapeutic value. These Leuner has termed:

1. the intropsychic pacemaker (a method for giving the subject control over the onset of his own fantasies and associated affect);
2. confrontation (a form of systematic desensitization or implosive technique);
3. feeding (a method for helping the patient mollify frightening monsters which appear in his imagery);
4. reconciliation;
5. exhausting and killing;
6. the magic fluids.

(These techniques are described further subsequently.) Leuner's psychoanalytic method is, of course, more in the tradition of free association and transference analysis. In this sense, Leuner comes closer than any of the other major practitioners of imagery technique in Europe to the Freudian or neo-Freudian schools, particularly the latter, in his orientation.

Let us examine in a little more detail the ten standard imaginary situations Leuner employs as a formal method of approaching the patient in the course of psychotherapy. Each of these methods is designed to move the course of therapy along systematically and also to provide a basis for full exploration of major dimensions of potential conflict and possible personality growth.

The Meadow

Leuner generally begins his work with the image of the meadow. The meadow is part of a group comprising the first three techniques which are also employed in the training of the patient to produce imagery (an interesting point to which I return later in this volume in considering the question of enhancing imagery skills as a goal of psychotherapy). From Leuner's standpoint, the imagery may represent something like a new beginning or a representation of the Garden of Eden or may also be closely related to the nature of the mother–child relationship.

The Mountain

The next image is that of ascent, much as in other imagery techniques, and involves climbing a mountain and providing a view of the landscape. This method, Leuner believes to be relevant to obtaining information about the patient's feelings about his own competence and opportunities for success, as well as his level of aspiration. A brief study by Kornadt (1960) attempted to show that there is indeed a relationship between level of aspiration as measured experimentally and the height of the mountain scene in the imagery method. Leuner is also likely to assign psychoanalytic interpretation to material of this sort and, in the case of the mountain, he says it can sometimes represent a phallic image or the introjected image of the father. A frequent finding, not only in Leuner's work, but in most of the mental imagery techniques, is that clouded or disturbed landscapes become clearer and more peaceful toward the end of a successful course of psychotherapy.

The Stream

The third imagery situation requires the patient, in fantasy, to follow a brook upstream to its source or down to the ocean. The brook may be regarded as representing an experience of energy. Leuner makes much of the meaning of fresh, cool water as a reviving experience for the weary traveler. He has reported that water also relates to relief, at least temporarily, of psychosomatic symptoms. And, he has cited examples of subjects rubbing imaginary waters on various ailing parts. The search for the source also suggests an imaginary symbolic visit or a return to the mother–child relationship. The analgesic effect of the cool water image suggests some comparable findings with hypnotic imagery or positive imagery discussed later in the chapter. These first three images—meadow, mountain, and stream—are viewed as basic; considerable training in guided affective imagery may be necessary through these techniques to help the patient move into the other areas.

The House

The fourth image employed by Leuner is that of a house, which is explored as a symbol of the individual personality. The patient may visualize a castle or he may see only a small hut. The location of food storage areas or toilet facilities may indicate body imagery. The remarkable anecdote by Jung (1964) about his own dream of a house which led him to grasp the direction he would be taking in splitting from Freud exemplifies this image of the house as a key to personality structure.

Relationship

The fifth directed image is to visualize a close relative. Sometimes, the images that emerge with this instruction take on a symbolic form. Leuner described a patient whose fantasy involved an imaginary elephant which stomped toward the patient and put a big foot on her breast. The patient responded with terror and shortness of breath. The therapist indicated that he was there to aid her and encouraged her to see the situation through. This fantasy evoked the memory of a distressing event from the patient's thirteenth year. One evening as the patient lay in her bedroom feigning sleep, her father approached her, touched her breast, and commented on her developing body to the mother. An important technical feature in this example is that the therapist encouraged the patient to confront the frightening image, a method that bears comparison with some of the behavior modification techniques.

Sexual Scene

The patient is next asked to visualize situations designed to provoke patterns of sexual feeling and behavior. A female patient is encouraged to begin by imagining herself on a lonely road looking for a ride because her car has broken down. A driver approaches and offers a lift. For male patients, the symbol of a rose bush is employed. Leuner refers to a famous song by Schubert, "Die Heidenröslein," based on a poem by Goethe about a little boy who touches the rose bush and gets pricked on his finger for his pain. American men may not be quite so likely to produce sexual imagery to the rose bush, although Kosbab (1972), employing this technique with medical students in Virginia, reported comparable sexually oriented fantasies.

Fierce Beast

The seventh situation is to imagine a fierce beast such as a lion. This image is useful in getting the patient to confront his own aggressive tendencies. Leuner described the case of a salesman who had developed psychogenic heart and digestive difficulties which appeared particularly after a much disliked customer had actually struck him lightly on the stomach. A year after these symptoms emerged, he was still unable to work. Leuner began by suggesting that the imaginary lion confront the patient's opponent, but the animal refused to be fierce; it reacted like a shy dog. It became smaller and smaller and finally simply lay down at the patient's feet. By the end of the therapy, however, the lion was ready to attack and swallow the patient's enemy without the patient offering any resistance. The patient had developed a much stronger feeling about his own rights and no longer felt himself to be an underdog. According to this report, the therapy lasted only 25 hours, and a six-year follow-up revealed no recurrence of the symptoms. This is a rather good result compared with some of the long, drawn out classical analyses.

Ego Ideal

The eighth situation is an imaginary manifestation of the patient's ego ideal of a very much admired person. The interaction with this person, the setting in which he or she is encountered, his approachability are all indicative of the self-esteem and identification patterns of the patient.

Dark Forest

The ninth imaginary situation involves the appearance of symbolic figures representing more frightening or deeply repressed material. The patient is encouraged to fantasize looking into a dark forest or looking into the dark opening of a cave. Witches, giants, or other frightening figures may emerge. Leuner here again emphasizes the technique of confrontation. The patient is encouraged to persevere in facing the frightening figure. He may either appease it by some means such as offering it candy or cookies or else simply outface it—a technique not unlike implosive therapy.

Swamp

In the tenth standard situation the patient is called upon to picture a swamp. The therapist suggests a figure will emerge from its waters and this may turn out to be a frog, snake, human figure, or other creature often relating to archaic instinctual material of a sexual or extremely anxiety-provoking nature.

Discussion and Applications

These situations are used again and again in connection with various specific techniques Leuner employs as therapeutic media. Leuner's methods seem to bear close comparison with some of the American behavior therapy techniques. Giving the patient responsibility for the pace of the movement, the pacemaker has elements of training in control and assertiveness. The confrontation is a method that seems to have elements of implosive therapy or, occasionally, of desensitization.

Feeding is used to appease frightening imaginary animals. It has elements of desensitization and perhaps also by a kind of wry humor plays the role of rendering them ridiculous. Reconciliation seems to involve more an establishment of rapport in fantasy or playing out in fantasy of more effective ways of relating—a method not unlike the behavior modification method of symbolic modeling. Exhausting and killing involve techniques of imagined aggression. The magic fluid technique seems to represent a combination of a kind of hypnotic analgesic effect with certain implications of the fluids being related to very basic experiences associated with maternal love and dependence.

An important feature of the Leuner technique is that it has generated perhaps more than 30 articles that involve some careful clinical observation, scholarship, and, in a few instances, formal research. The variety of patients treated is quite broad, ranging from relatively mild problems such as examination phobia through severe obsessional neuroses, alcoholism, and somnambulism (Beck 1968; Koch, 1962, 1968; Leuner, 1969). Leuner (1959) has also described the application of guided affective imagery to children. He noted that it resembles play therapy, but is especially suitable for children in the age periods when play therapy no longer seems appropriate and more verbally oriented therapies are not effective; for example, later childhood and early puberty.

Some examples of more formal research with variations of Leuner's method may be cited. Kornadt (1960) measured achievement motivation and aspiration levels in 30 adult subjects. He found significant positive correlations between these projective test measures of striving and the height of mountains described in the "mountain-climbing" scene. Other measures of aspiration derived from the subjects' imagery also were correlated with the test data.

Two studies (Nerenz, 1965, 1969; Plaum, 1968) employed systematically varied classical music selections as background for generating imagery in both individual and group-therapy sessions with rather heterogeneous neurotic patient samples. Both investigators reported that, while at a superficial level, the associations were influenced by the obvious qualities of the music, for example, vigorous, joyful, sad, mysterious, etc., there was consistent evidence that the images produced eventually moved in the direction of profound "catathymic" imagery. Personal, profound conflict situations emerged in various symbolic forms, and the unfolding sequences of imagery stimulated by the music were therapeutically significant.

Nerenz (1969), for example, described a patient whose initial reaction to an organ selection was to imagine himself in a church meditating on man's transcendant unity. Later on, however, his response to organ music yielded an image of his father performing on the organ and then the picture of his mother in a state of terrible distress. Indeed, the patient's father had been a village schoolmaster who did play the organ. A specific memory dating to age 4 then occurred to the patient, a frightening scene of a violent quarrel between his parents in which the father struck the mother.

While Nerenz's study primarily reported clinical data on improvement of the patients, Plaum's (1968) continuation of this approach with psychotherapy groups tested before and after guided affective imagery provided psychometric indications of improvement on measures of rigidity, extroversion, neuroticism, and anxiety. Although the study lacked some important controls that could pin the positive response down specifically to the interaction of the music and guided imagery, it pointed up the possibilities for further evaluative research in the problem. This is clearly a methodological advance in an area where reliance has been primarily on the anecdotal reports of individual psychotherapists. Leuner (1959) and Barolin (1961) used patients' drawings of their imagery as further clues to the unfolding of symbolism [see also the method described by Horowitz (1970) for evaluating imagery through drawings], but such procedures, however persuasive in the individual case, do not meet the requirements of more sophisticated psychometric requirements.

An interesting application of Leuner's guided affective imagery has been described by Kosbab (1972). Working with psychiatric residents in an American medical school Kosbab employed the mental imagery method to provide his students with a form of self-analysis that has both personal therapeutic, as well as didactic, implications. After some brief training in Schultz's autogenic method as a form of induction of a mild hypnoid state, the students were encouraged in one extended individual session with the instructor to go through all of the Leuner standard images. This "panoramic" view of their imagery capacities was usually tape recorded and could be the subject of some brief discussion with the supervisor. At this point, the student proceeded to a series of about a dozen weekly sessions on his own, employing in each session one of the standard images as a starting point. Carried out in privacy, but tape recorded for further self-analysis, these individual sessions provided a unique opportunity for an extended examination of the individual's range of symbolism and imagery capacity and the major threads of fantasy and motivation. On rare occasions, a meeting with the supervisor might be desirable to deal with excessive anxiety or other difficulties. After the trial working period, a summary of the experience was prepared by the student for review with the supervisor. Some individuals with considerable ego strength might be encouraged to continue on their own for extended periods beyond this point. Kosbab presented some interesting case examples which pointed up useful opportunities for personal growth developing out of the imagery sequences.

Since Kosbab's (1972) work is being carried out at Virginia Commonwealth School of Medicine, his results indicate that the imagery techniques and, indeed, the specific starting points for each session provided by Leuner are not quite as culture bound as might at first appear. Kosbob has added an image such as "the old family album," which is especially effective, but he also states that the scenes developed originally by Leuner work well. Perhaps most dubious for an American male audience is the use of the "rose bush" image to generate sexual fantasies. Generally when I have lectured to professional audiences and described these techniques, the "rose bush" image has drawn snickers and laughter, but Kosbab insists that his Virginia students do indeed produce sexual imagery to this specific scene.

Leuner's approach to mental imagery would appear to be the best organized and systematic of the current methods. It provides a standard group of 10 or 12 "motives," or, perhaps more precisely, areas of involvement and potential conflict, which encompass a great range of our experiences. These may or may not have the universality attributed to them, but their explication by Leuner and his group provides the starting point for further research. Indeed, it seems quite feasible to carry out a series of studies to ascertain to what extent subjects from different subcultural groups or socioeconomic levels will indeed show a commonality of symbolic treatment of these guiding images. One could apply the same types of normative and reliable judging or rating procedures to sequences of images reported with common starting points that have been employed in studies with projective techniques (Singer, 1968) or in scoring of dreams or fantasy material (Foulkes, 1966; Hall & Lind, 1970). At the very least, however, the Leuner's approach suggests valuable diagnostic training possibilities. It remains to be seen whether the reports of specific successes in treatment of a variety of neurotic symptoms and personality difficulties will be matched as the method is more widely used outside Germany.

Since Leuner has had psychoanalytic training, he is more aware than most practitioners of the various mental imagery techniques to the subtleties of the interpersonal transaction in psychotherapy and the nature of transference phenomena. Nevertheless, he has argued that in his experience the use of the standard images and the imagery "trip" has decided advantages for use in psychoanalytic sessions. As Leuner (1969) has stated, the method combines "couchwork" with "dream-work." The patient's involvement with his own imagery becomes so potent and exciting that the elaborate complexity of a transference neurosis, which must then be analyzed (as in classical psychoanalysis), is avoided. Leuner feels, in general, that the analysis of transference, which is regarded by most psychoanalysts of Freudian or neo-Freudian persuasion as the touchstone of the method, is rendered largely superfluous by the method of guided affective imagery. On the basis of personal communication, as well as his articles, Leuner's position might be summarized by stating that the imagery method relies less upon the analyst for interpretation. Defenses and resistances, exposure to different levels of consciousness, and the juxtaposition of "regressive modes of ego functioning with the mature ego" through their interaction—all of these emerge directly under the sway of the patient's own imagery trip. While the therapist clearly is there as a benevolent guide, who occasionally suggests feeding an imagined monster a cookie or provides a magic key to unlock a fantasied cell, the patient experiences most of the therapy as his own trip indeed. The confrontation with the real people in the patient's life takes place in the ongoing symbolic drama and is worked out there, rather than in fantasies about the therapist which are the key to transference analysis. Transference analysis essentially involves the explication of the patient's attribution of childhood unresolved involvements to the therapist, but in Leuner's method, these are approached more directly through the ongoing symbolism of meadow, house, swamp, picture album, etc., where there is less necessity for development or examination of transference.

Although this lack of interest in transferential phenomena may seem utterly incomprehensible to most psychoanalysts, it is the case that most mental imagery practitioners would appear to take a position similar to that of Leuner. They follow Jung's (1928) dictum that the "psychological machinery which transmutes energy is the symbol." Transference analysis can be viewed from this position as a special case of symbolic imagery analysis. Perhaps because so much of ordinary analysis occurs at the verbal level, the patients are less deeply involved in their own imagery and symbolism and so the fantasies about the therapist may become the best *in vivo* source of the symbolic stream of mentation. When patients are trained in relaxation, imagery concentration, and in vividness of experiencing varied levels of consciousness, however, the therapist is less likely to become a focal point of fantasy. This indeed might account for the briefer periods of therapy reported with less complex dependency upon the therapist occurring in the mental imagery methods. Ultimately, differences in points of view such as these must be resolved by careful empirical research. As the argument continues today, it is at best a clash of intelligent opinions.

ADDITIONAL EXAMPLES
OF MENTAL IMAGERY METHODS

The main emphasis in this chapter has been upon the work of French and German practitioners of mental imagery methods, yet it is important to stress that such procedures are widely used in European psychotherapy. The International Congresses of the Society for Mental Imagery Techniques, which take place biennially, are likely to draw practitioners from every major country on the continent. Although interesting technical innovations and experimental research possibilities have been suggested by many of the participants in these meetings, no really major differences from either the French or German schools seem to have emerged in the past decade. The theoretical superstructure proposed by Roberto Assagioli of Italy has probably been more influential in the United States, where his work is available in English and is increasingly read, than in Europe. (I discuss Assagioli's approach, therefore, in Chapter V on American applications of mental imagery methods.)

Perhaps more directly influential in Italy has been the work of Leopoldo Rigo (1962, 1966, 1970), who has been active in this area for 20 years and has published at least a dozen papers on technique. Rigo has had psychoanalytic and psychological training and moves easily between psychoanalytic, Jungian, and the mental imagery formulations of Desoille. He has expanded his procedures through extensive work with adolescents and has pioneered in the application of imagery techniques to group psychotherapy, an approach now widely incorporated into the encounter and Esalen-type groups in the United States.

There follows a brief example of a group therapy session conducted by Rigo (1970):

Patients recline in a star pattern and engage in relaxation. The therapist is seated outside the star. One patient is then encouraged to generate an image. She describes a huge mushroom surrounded by green grass. Another patient is encouraged to produce the same image. The therapist encourages the first patient to move closer to the mushroom and the patient reports herself as touching it. There follows a series of imagined explorations in which the two patients, one leading the way, report on their experiences and images, while the rest of the group empathizes. The therapist occasionally intercedes by suggesting further exploration of sights described or by indicating that they take hands in imagery and move together into a new area in the imagined landscape.

Rigo takes into account typological differences along Jungian lines and is sensitive to psychoanalytic transference issues in the course of his work. He believes that some of the fundamental symbolism shared collectively permits greater rapport between the patients who "journey" together in imagery. In other situations with groups he may suggest that the entire group imagine a peaceful countryside, the sun shining, a clearing in some woods in the center of which there is a giant tree, well rooted and solid with branches stretched toward the sun and waving in the breeze. Each group member imagines himself before the tree, touching it, moving around it, and identifying himself with it. In this technique, there is apparently some feeling that the actual imagery shared by all of strength and closeness to a powerful yet benign symbol affords a psychological strength to the subjects.

A case presented by Rigo's wife, Serenella Rigo-Uberto (1970), demonstrated use of some of these techniques with an 11-year-old girl suffering from a severe obsessional neurosis with attendant phobias, including fears that Jesus was demanding that she hang herself. After some clinical exploration, reassurance, and fostering of a benevolent "maternal-oral transference," the child was encouraged to draw a picture. This drawing served as the beginning of an imaginary journey in which the therapist encouraged more and more exploration of the route and scenery and occasionally suggested touching frightening objects or climbing onto an imagined eagle, which then took the child toward a snow-capped mountain. The eagle found a warm niche among the crags, and the child experienced a great sense of peace as she looked at the wide expanse before her. At the end of the session, the child felt more peaceful and was smiling.

Rigo-Uberto has described a series of these sessions with the child and interpreted them partly within a Freudian framework involving the psychosexual stages of development, but also has drawn upon some examples of a Jungian collective symbolism. There was evidence in the course of the various imaginary adventures of the working through of castration and sibling rivalry problems and of the failures of the girl's mother in regard to many questions about sex and body development. Within about 15 sessions, the girl showed a remarkable improvement both in symptom disappearance and in social maturity and improved schoolwork.

An intriguing feature of the therapeutic application of the mental imagery technique is their apparent utility in cases of psychosomatic involvement. At first one is startled by the use of such purely psychological approaches to dealing with problems that have definite physiolog-ical symptomatology. Careful medical checks on patients are often employed, however, as may be noted in a case Donnars reported (outlined shortly). Yet, it is especially intriguing that we see here the close intertwining of the imagery system and the autonomic feedback system of the nervous system. Indeed, the mental imagery methods provide clues to the entire question of the nature of our body imagery, the biofeedback mechanisms that may lead ultimately to mental con-trols over heart rate and ulcer development. The techniques developed in Gestalt therapy, which emphasizes body attitudes and imagery such as "crawling into one's heart," may be the outgrowths of European mental imagery trips and also may foreshadow much more systematic uses in the future of self-regulatory imagery methods.

Donnars (1970) has been especially active in treating individual cases with psychosomatic symptoms. He described one case in which a pa-tient was encouraged to engage in climbing imagery. Feeling a terrible sense of heaviness and resistance at going further, the patient was en-couraged to lighten himself by removing some of his clothing. This led to further blocking. Eventually, the patient was able to move on to the revelation of a fear of anal bleeding. This fear, once reported, eventu-ally led to a revelation of a period of involuntary anal intercourse to which the patient was subjected by an older relative during ages 11–14. The patient felt that a lump of semen was still lodged in his anus. Much of this fantasy was associated with imagery of blocked entry to a cave. It persisted despite this revelation because the patient had never dared to reveal to anyone the pain in his rectum lest he be forced to confess the events from childhood. The therapist convinced the patient at this point that surgical exploration might be desirable. Indeed, a noncan-cerous polyp was discovered and removed. The imagery subsequently produced reflected the disappearance of the blocked cave symbol and the appearance of a window facing an attractive landscape. Important changes in personality and social effectiveness on the patient's part were reported after a two-year follow-up.

Another example reported by Donnars involved a case of enuresis in a young man about to be married. The patient was so terrified that this symptom would have to be revealed to his new bride that his behavior became extremely labile with rages, anxiety attacks, kleptomania, and fits of depression. The revelation concerning the enuresis emerged only after a period of imaginary climbing within his body, which he experienced as enjoyable; however, as he reached a waterfall, he was overcome by panic. Considerable material about early childhood expe-riences associated with the enuresis, and a frightening nursemaid now emerged. In the course of many imaginary journeys, the patient became more accepting of his body and eventually was able to tell his fiancée of his problem. Her acceptance of him and their subsequent marriage led to complete disappearance of the enuresis at the same time when in his imagery the patient killed a huge dragon that bore the features of his old nursemaid.

Donnar's cases just hint at the increasingly rich accumulation of anecdotal literature on mental imagery methods. The interested reader is encouraged to review the proceedings of the International Society for Mental Imagery Techniques or the bibliographies prepared by Frétigny and Virel and Leuner in these areas. Suffice it to say that the application of imagery in psychotherapy is a vigorous, growing movement in Europe—an approach that perhaps represents the European counterpart to the vitality of the behavior modification groups in North America. Viewed from the perspective of a typically empiricist-psychological orientation, these mental imagery techniques are based as yet too much on individual practitioners' reports, with too little systematic research, few controls, and almost no experimentation. Nonetheless, reports of positive therapeutic benefit cannot easily be ignored. Even more striking are the indications of the powerful potential of our imagery capacities reflected in these numerous reports. Clearly, the time is ripe again to return to a deeper analysis of the image, which indeed was once so central a concept in psychology.

CHAPTER V

AMERICAN APPLICATIONS
OF IMAGERY TECHNIQUES

> *The sources of psychodrama are to be found in my childhood games . . . One Sunday afternoon, . . . I and some of the neighbor's children decided to play at "God" . . . the first thing was to build our HEAVEN . . . we collected every available chair and piled them up . . . until they reached to the ceiling. I now mounted my heavenly throne—mine "the kingdom, the power, and the glory"—while my angels "flew" round me singing. Suddenly one of the children called out "why don't you fly too?" Whereupon I stretched out my arms—and one second later lay on the floor with a broken arm. So ended my first psychodrama. . . .*
>
> J. L. Moreno (1967, p. 131)*

We have thus far tracked some of the usage of imagery in psychotherapy through the psychoanalytic approaches that have been introduced, and are widely used, in the United States and the western hemisphere, generally. Techniques in psychotherapy not specifically psychoanalytic in orientation have been incorporated into various American treatment methods in what appears as two separate waves of

* Reprinted by Permission of the Publishers, Lieber Atherton, Inc. Copyright © 1967 Aldine-Atherton Inc. All rights reserved.

influence. Both of the separate influences have ultimately converged to have a major impact upon the vigorous, if perhaps somewhat "faddist" or "revivalist," kinds of group and individual psychotherapeutic approaches that burst forth in the 1960s and continue to thrive at this time. These methods, which may loosely be termed part of a "humanist" orientation in the mental health movement, now make extensive use of imagery methods deriving from both the original influences, which are traceable almost 50 years in the United States, and to a more recent set of importations more directly influenced by the European mental imagery techniques. Documenting various strains of influence would be a study in itself, a fascinating exploration in the sociology of professional roles and of help-seeking behavior in various segments of a relatively affluent society.

PSYCHODRAMA AND SMALL-GROUP APPROACHES

The first wave of influence on the nonpsychoanalytic psychotherapeutic uses of imagery in the United States can probably be best viewed as indigenous, despite the fact that its progenitor, the psychiatrist J. L. Moreno, was reared and trained in Europe. The origins of psychodrama and of the other methods developed by Moreno undoubtedly reflect, as he often notes, his own specific childhood experiences and personality development, but may as well reflect his exposure in the Vienna of the pre- and immediate post-World War I to Freud and to various dynamic approaches then being generated. Nevertheless, Moreno has been in the United States for almost 50 years at this writing, and his techniques have, in a relatively gradual way, become incorporated into the research and psychotherapeutic set of many American psychologists and psychiatrists who may not even be aware of their origin.

Except perhaps in the area of group psychotherapy, Moreno has never been at the center of "establishment" developments in the mental health movement, and his name is not often cited in textbooks on psychiatry, the psychology of personality, or social psychology. Yet there seems little question that a large number of the significant techniques employed in research on social structure and affiliative behavior in children and adults, and methods of evaluation of organizational behavior in military or industrial fantasy procedures, are almost certainly traceable directly to his innovations. Indeed, many of the concepts of community-oriented psychiatry or psychology are fairly clearly prefigured in Moreno's emphasis on an initial analysis of the social structure of institutional or organizational relationships in order to pick out sociometric patternings as a basis for modifying the organization of, for example, a girls' cottage in a residential treatment center. Moreno's use of large groups, both as participant-observers in an ongoing psychodrama and as "auxiliary" egos in the unfolding drama, is clearly a precursor to many of the milieu-therapy techniques increasingly employed in mental hospitals and day-treatment centers in place of more traditional psychotherapies. With the characteristic freedom from modesty that seems a part of his life style, Moreno (1967) reported that when he was a young student in prewar Vienna he told Freud: "you see patients in the unnatural surroundings of your consulting-room. I meet them in the streets, in their homes, in their natural environment [p. 132]." Certainly, in concept this was a prefiguring of the community-oriented approach to which in many subtle ways Moreno has contributed, perhaps without sufficient recognition by the profession.

We need not be concerned here with why Moreno's influence has not received the kind of widespread praise and attention attributed to other leaders in the psychotherapeutic realm such as Freud and Jung. Probably something of Moreno's personal style has irritated many people, and his extensive use of the psychodramatic performance as a form of show business, which attracts large lay audiences and has developed many off-beat nonprofessional therapists, has contributed to the tendency to overlook his actual influence. Moreno's flamboyant manner and his physical appearance, both at his psychodramatic demonstrations and at professional meetings, have often led people to view him as a prototype of the movie style "mad psychiatrist." His writings have lacked the breadth of scholarship and theoretical and stylistic impressiveness of other theorists in the field of psychotherapy.

Nevertheless, in his active exploration of sociometric patterns and relationship, the emphasis on group interaction in the therapeutic process, and the concept of therapeutic effects of role playing and role reversal, Moreno has affected psychotherapeutic techniques as disparate as George Kelly's psychology of personal constructs, the T-group techniques now so widely used in industry and community health settings, the encounter group methods, in which fantasies are acted out in detail before the group and then roles reversed as part of the process. Many psychotherapists include attempts to influence directly their patients' attitude by "paradigmatic" techniques in which they play the part of a parent and seek to provide increasingly blatant resentments on the part of the patient so that these can finally become clear to the patient. There is little question in my mind on reviewing techniques ranging from *transactional game-playing* to Gestalt psychological efforts at empathizing with elements in one's dreams or fantasies, either in individual or group therapy, that they have by now probably incorporated Moreno's methods without acknowledging him as a source.

For our purposes in focusing specifically on the use of fantasy techniques in psychotherapy, we need not be concerned with all of the ramifications of the psychodramatic method. It is instructive, however, that Moreno (1967) himself traced the later development of his approach to his own "extremely fertile poetic imagination." He described his early experience in entertaining children and subsequently, he claimed even larger groups of adults in parts of Vienna by his capacity for storytelling. Referring to himself as a Pied Piper, again with the same refreshing lack of modesty, he described his storytelling beneath a tree in the park, where "as if lured on by a magic flute—the children would flock toward me, sit down in a circle and listen with rapt attention." He made the point that not only was the content of the stories of interest to the children, but perhaps more important was the manner in which for them what was unreal could become real, vital, actual experience. In this sense we see that the psychodrama takes its origin from the ongoing fantasy activity of the individual. Moreover, it is clear that Moreno's specific gift has been the transposition of fantasy from the realm of private experience (the fantasy is perhaps disclosed in privacy to a therapist) to a public situation. That is, the fantasy is revealed to a group and acted out before the patient's eyes by his own participation with "auxiliary egos" so that this fantasy can now be exposed in the light of reality and examined from many sides.

In the psychodramatic method, after some initial discussion between patient and therapist before an observing group, the patient is encouraged to select a specific interaction he is describing: it may be the memory of an event, a feared future event, or a fantasy of some kind. With the help of members of the audience or trained co-therapists, the patient enacts the situation as realistically as possible. At a crucial point there occurs the famous technique of *role reversal.* The method forces each actor to examine the situation from the vantage point of his opponent in a situation and to try to empathize with the experience of the other. Moreno makes a great point of the *catharsis* experienced both by the individuals specifically in acting roles, as well as the audience observing the situation since so many of the scenes are of situations or fantasies they themselves have experienced.

In describing what seems to take place, Moreno presents what may be a prototype of a combination of a desensitization therapy and a subsequent cognitive reorganization of the experience. For example, as he puts it, when one is playing out an actual frightening event or fantasy on the stage, there is a sense that everything that was done before is now being repeated. In Moreno's (1967) words: "But the self same pain is no longer sensed as pain by audience and actors, the same desire is no longer desire, the same thought is no longer thought—all are painless, unconscious, thoughtless, deathless. Each figure from reality is extinguished through itself in make-believe, and reality and make-believe dissolve in laughter [p. 137]."* Following this situation, for a moment the drama ends; however, this experience of desensitization may be repeated quite a number of times for a particular patient. Next, the patient must face the group without the benefit of an ongoing drama; at this point, there may take place more of what might be called a cognitive reorientation in which the members of the group and the patient reexamine the situation, look at it from different angles, try to integrate it into the current situation of the patient. Although Moreno himself emphasizes the *cathartic* aspects of this process, it seems more likely to actually represent some type of cognitive restructuring.

In effect, Moreno's psychodramatic method follows reasonably on the very nature of the theater itself. The creative writer unquestionably begins with private experiences of his own and some of the fantasies engendered in relation to these experiences. These form a basis for the characters and unusual encounters that make for an interesting drama. Moreno has assumed that all of us are constantly carrying on internal monologues full on anticipated encounters, wished-for adventures, and changes in our current life situation, as well as many horrible and frightening potential occurrences that flash across our minds and may influence our behavior in many ways without others being aware that these internal cognitions are so potent. By encouraging the patient through dramatic interplay to make these very private fantasies public and then, by actually playing in them to reexperience them in a relatively benign setting and with considerable warmth and support from the group, the patient can come to terms—at least in some fashion—with his ongoing inner experience. At the same time, through role reversal, the patient is given a chance to practice seeing what others must experience in an interchange with him and this undoubtedly broadens his behavioral repertoire. Although unquestionably influenced by psychoanalytic conceptions of the family romance, Moreno puts his primary emphasis on the immediacy of the patient's experience and is less concerned with analyzing all the origins of the situation. He does, however, emphasize the degree to which parental characteristics and conflicting messages are interwoven in the fantasies of the subject and, therefore, splits these off by the use of auxiliary egos,

---

* See footnote on page 95.

some of whom may play several sides of the same patient or the parents of the patient.

A dramatic example presented by Moreno is that of a 15-year-old boy who had been arrested for bursting into the White House in army uniform, fully armed, in an attempt to either advise or threaten President Truman. Exposed to a psychodramatic presentation, the young man, by this time declared insane, was largely mute and withdrawn, but finally, after some of the "warming up process" which precedes an involvement in psychodrama, he delivered before the group a reenactment of his trip to Washington and his approach to the White House. Some members of the group then participated in enacting the events that frustrated his efforts at approaching the President and led to his being put in a detention home until a psychiatric ruling was made. With the end of the drama, to the boy's surprise, he was greeted not by just a return to what he thought of as the bitter reality of a mental hospital, but by considerable warmth and feelings of sympathy for what he had attempted to do as he understood it and for the degree of disillusionment he must be feeling. Subsequently, it was observed that he acted as if he were definitely a part of the group; he was later encouraged to reenact some of his experiences with his own family. This led to some very vigorous interchanges with an auxiliary ego playing his stepmother and, subsequently, with role reversal in which the young man himself played his stepmother in the interaction. It became clear to what extent much of his efforts had grown out of frustrating experiences in real life, as well as in fantasy, but there in a more modest fashion. Johnny was given a chance to act out different fantasies of a more realistic nature about jobs he could obtain or training opportunities that would liberate him from his family, but at the same time give him scope for his own adventurous drives. The story terminated with Johnny showing no abnormal psychiatric manifestations for a year and launched into training as a commercial pilot.

Moreno's method emphasizes the subtle interplay between what is real and what is fantasy. He encourages auxiliary egos to engage in physical contact with patients, put their arms around as appropriate, and walk about the stage or setting to engage in acts that create a sense of reality even though they themselves playing characters from the patient's fantasy, rather than themselves. By observing his own fantasies reenacted for him by real people, the patient confronts these experiences and can perhaps see them in a new perspective. Moreno (1967) has written:

> The auxiliary egos are in fact real persons, but enter the *psyche* of the disintegrated patient rather like some good fairy with a magic spell. Like good or evil

spirits, they startle the patient, rouse him, surprise him, console him, as the case may be. He finds himself caught in a world half real, half unreal as if in a trap. He sees himself act, he hears himself speak, but his thoughts and actions, his feelings and perceptions, derive not from himself, but strange though it may seem, from some other person, from the reflected therapeutic images of his mind [p. 141].*

Probably the psychodramatic experience is not nearly as effective as Moreno proposed, partly because many people are much less capable of throwing themselves into the role, and partly because auxiliary egos are not always quite as effective as they might be. Nevertheless, the likelihood of a strong emotional involvement and, at the same time, the capacity for distance from the experience, which is no longer hidden, private, taboo, fantasy, or secret, permits some reduction in the degree of negative attitude associated with the material and generates considerable positive emotion. Moreno is one of the leading clinicians to emphasize the importance of spontaneity, and his focus on the more creative capacities of individuals also identifies him as prefiguring the humanist group and Maslow's emphasis on "peak experiences" and man's capacity for creative expression. Although much of Moreno's description of process and its presumed workings remains at too general a level to be entirely satisfactory to a scientist concerned about a careful analysis of process itself, there seems little doubt that the psychodrama technique and its application to group psychotherapy, as introduced by Moreno, reflect significant contributions to the use of imagery in psychotherapy. Indeed, the use of role-playing as a means of preparing young people for job interviews and for facing a variety of crises has greater applicability than hitherto realized.

It is very likely that our own daydreams and fantasies, so internalized and private as they seem, originally were acted out in the form of overt verbalization, the egocentric speech referred to long ago by Piaget (1932) and the sociodramatic play, which is so characteristic of spontaneous activity of children between 2 years and school age (Singer, 1973). Somewhere between the ages of 6 and 13 or 14, much make-believe play is very subtly miniaturized and internalized in the form of ongoing images and interior monologues. Indeed, we almost appear to train ourselves not to notice the continuous nature of these experiences and are struck with them as part of ourselves primarily when we remember our night dreams, wherein such activities appear with greater vividness and apparent reality.

Moreno's great insight was that these fantasies could be acted out in

* See footnote on page 95.

the open: his psychodrama is, in effect, a license to the individual to re-turn to his enjoyment of the sociodramatic play of childhood. With the advantage of an adult perspective and, presumably, the support from a therapist or other group members, one's fantasies can be examined from different perspectives and the degree to which they are realizable made even more clear; similarly, their association with impossible goals or with irrational negative affect may be thus elucidated. The fantasy also can be practiced from different vantage points through role re-versal and through repeated interchanges, and the spontaneous events of the action can be used to arouse positive affects of surprise, interest, and joy, and also presumably to desensitize a person against some of the pain and negative affects associated in the past with these fantasies. New, alternative behavior patterns that might bring some fantasies to fruition can also be practiced. This, of course, is what many individuals do through private planning and fantasy. Many people use thought ef-fectively in this fashion, but for others, imaginal practice is not at-tempted consistently or is perhaps not sufficiently vivid to be effective. Practice in a variety of role-taking procedures in an actual psychodra-matic group setting, therefore, may be beneficial to many people and may serve the same effect as the private use of fantasy.

It seems important to note that for the psychodramatic approach, there is much less interest in the ongoing flow of private symbolism and, indeed, in the unconscious as such. In many ways, it appears to me that psychodrama is really closer to many of the behavior modifica-tion methods in its orientation.

TRANSACTIONAL ANALYSIS, GESTALT THERAPY, AND RELATED METHODS

There are additional techniques that may be viewed as essentially indigenous to this country and reflect an interest in imagery that predates the introduction of European mental imagery techniques. Among these are uses of fantasy and game-playing that stem from a number of variations in group and individual psychotherapy derived from Eric Berne's *transactional analysis*, Frederick Perls's *Gestalt psycho-therapy*, and the variety of group psychotherapeutic approaches that are in part traceable to the influence of Kurt Lewin upon social psychology and the study of small-group processes in American psychology.

Although Kurt Lewin might today be recognized as the most influen-tial figure in the development of experimental social psychology and has been called one of psychology's few geniuses by Tolman and Allport, it may not be widely recognized that his conception of field theory and of the nature of group interaction, which he introduced to the United States in the 1930s, has led to many of the developments of small-group techniques, the methods of the national training laboratories still widely employed in industry and government, and a whole series of other small-group methods that might also be said to be the "rage" in many colleges and high schools. Lewin was himself one of psychology's subtlest theoreticians, yet he had a strong interest in practical issues. For example, his examination of such problems as the nature of authoritarian and democratic atmospheres in the classroom led, through a number of students, to significant applications of group interaction methods to psychotherapy and a variety of human relations training procedures. Bion's (1948) integration of psychoanalytic concepts with Lewinian field theory represents one important link in the step which led eventually to the development of the so-called Tavistock group procedure, now so very much a part of many educational and mental health activities.

An important early presentation of the process of intensive group psychotherapy by Bach (1954), and the even earlier work on group psychotherapy by Powdermaker and Frank (the latter, like Bach, a student of Lewin) exemplify the way in which this method took shape in the early 1950s. Bach's fine presentation of group psychotherapy was dedicated to Lewin. Bach has traced many of the origins of the techniques used in group psychotherapy, including various types of game-playing and role-taking activities, to some of his own research, influenced by Lewin, on children's responses to frustration in the course of play. Bach described a great variety of role-taking techniques that can be used in psychotherapy, and he has made extensive use of exemplification of private fantasies through dramatic enactment, and shown the continuity between children's play and the kind of play that can occur in group psychotherapy. Bach also called attention to the desensitization possibilities of role-playing, relating this to Hullian theory and, intriguingly, anticipating the work of Wolpe on phobias, which appeared shortly afterward and initiated the current behavior modification movement.

Many of the techniques described by Bach are now so much a part of most group psychotherapy methods that they need not be reviewed here. In effect, they involve such techniques as patients' sharing of dream material with others and attempts at group analysis of the dreams, or the group empathically experiencing the dream protocols and sharing their experiences with each other. Bach has cited numerous examples of dream material that patients enact around the dream experience, try themselves to experience what the dream was like, and also offer, for better or worse, a variety of interpretations. Bach associates himself somewhat more with Fromm, who emphasized the dream as a communication. He also makes extensive use of individual and group drawings as a way of expressing dream content in a variety of forms; moreover, the group perhaps is instructed to improve and comment on each other's drawings as part of an ongoing therapeutic session, the drawings presumably representing both private fantasies, as well as fantasies about the nature of the group itself. Bach cited, for example, the experimental research of Lewin to the effect that an individual may learn to shift well-established emotional attitudes, goals, and conflicting tendencies into new paths that are really required by the current situation of his life if he feels that this shift is a part of a group's decision, that is, a group to which he feels he now belongs. In this sense, Bach pointed to the potential link between the exposure of private fantasy in the group and the reenactment of the fantasies or memories in role playing and the subsequent modification of attitudes around these acts as functions of the additional group identification and pressure.

Since the primary focus of this volume is not upon group techniques, I shall not elaborate further on Bach's work, but it seems sufficient to stress the continuity between, on the one hand, the Lewinian emphasis on field theory and the individual's cognition of his relationship to group forces and the presumably beneficial effects on a variety of methods for exposing private fantasy in the group setting. The continuity between the early techniques of Moreno, the perhaps more formally and systematically developed group theory of Lewin and Heider, among the influential figures of experimental social psychology, and the psychoanalytic emphases on the significance of parent–child interrelations as major socializing influences are all brought together in the type of group therapy proposed by Bach. Inevitably, therefore, private fantasies and images become a part of the group process and are reenacted in more or less systematic fashion within this setting. One would hope that practitioners of the many encounter and group psychotherapy approaches had the sense of continuity with broader aspects of psychological processes that Bach reflects in his own volume. We might then see less of a "religious revivalist" quality about group therapy and perhaps more systematically effective use of the method.

A specific technique that has attained considerable popularity is Berne's (1964) "transactional" method, which has been used both in individual and group psychotherapy. Essentially, it seems to be an elaboration of psychoanalytic theory into an interpersonal framework. Yet, Berne's method is a gross oversimplification in its emphasis on the notion that each individual represents three selves or communication media: the child, the adult, and the parent. Clearly, these selves correspond to the id, ego, and superego, but in a way that is perhaps deceptively simple for the patient or lay audience.

Berne's approach is widely known and need not be pursued in this context as a method of therapy except insofar as it makes the assumption that there is a more or less ongoing "script" that the individual carries around with him and which leads him to engage in a variety of self-defeating games that he lures others into playing with him. The goal of therapy is to identify these games and have them played out actively by the group so they can be clearly identified as games and distinguished from the effective behavior of the adult. The script, often enough a reasonably conscious one on the part of the individual, represents a set of expectations and wishes for particular satisfactions or securities that persist from early childhood. The patient may attempt to get the members of a group to participate in the game he is playing, just as he attempted to do so with parents, friends, wife, perhaps his own children. Examples of games are such things as "How am I doing?," "Schlemiel," or "Alcoholic." The game of Schlemiel, for example, involves an individual who entertains the fantasy that he can get away with all types of egocentric behavior provided only that he has enough sense to say "I'm sorry" or, in effect, to play the clown.

Therapeutic techniques involve much repetition of this pattern until it can be made clear to the actors to what extent they are colluding with the patient in this fantasy. A common tragic script may involve a rescue fantasy in the woman who marries one alcoholic after another. The disruption of her script leads her to despair. Failing therapy, the woman is likely to find still another man whom she hopes she can rescue. From Berne's standpoint, the goal of a transactional analysis is indeed the analysis of these scripts, that is, analysis of the hierarchy of plans and programs of the individual, to introduce a bit of information terminology. In this sense, Berne's analysis of the script as the basis for the goals, destiny, and identity of the specific patient is not really different from the approach of many of the European mental imagery therapists. The major difference seems again to be the emphasis upon the material as presented in relation to other people and not on the assumption of an ongoing intersymbolic realm or symbolic language in which the script is carried. Hence, a major difference, perhaps, is in method and viewpoint, but it remains to be seen whether it is a crucial one. Clearly, however, in transactional analysis, the focus of treatment is not on the mere unfolding of the symbolic system, but on its identification and its systematic modification through a variety of forms of role playing either between therapist and patient or between members of the group.

THE USE OF IMAGERY
IN GESTALT THERAPY

Gestalt therapy probably represents more a social movement than a formal or systematic theory of personality translated into a mode of psychotherapy. Like psychodrama, it stems chiefly from the influence of a dominant personality, the late Frederick Perls (known widely as Fritz). A German-trained psychoanalyst who had worked with the great neurologist Kurt Goldstein, Perls, by 1936, had become disenchanted with the strictures of the *libido* theory then dominant in psychoanalytic thought. *Ego, Hunger and Aggression,* written when Perls was still within the original psychoanalytic group, incorporated some important notions of Wilhelm Reich's emphasis on body tension and "character armor" and broadens the notion of self to bodily awareness, rather than to satisfaction specifically of body-orifice-derived sexual expressions. By 1951, six years after his arrival in the United States, Perls had published, with the collaboration of Paul Goodman (the literary critic) and Ralph Hefferline (an experimental psychologist and pioneer in biofeedback research), his best-known work on Gestalt therapy. This somewhat loosely organized work is notable because it introduced a series of self-awareness exercises and attempted to criticize Freud's theories—substituting a more holistic and perhaps more "humanistic" position. Only modestly effective on the conservative East coast, Perls moved to California, where he emerged in the late 1950s and in the 1960s as perhaps the dominant figure in psychotherapy. Eschewing individual psychotherapy in favor of "workshops," "marathons," and communal living, a founder and the resident "guru" of Esalen at Big Sur, Perls touched the lives of hundreds of professionals and "seekers" and he remains two years after his death a significant force on the fringe of the mental health establishment.

To the extent that it can be classified, Gestalt therapy seems to represent an approach that incorporates elements of Goldstein's (1940) emphasis on "self-actualization," Goldstein's examination of pathology as representing a distortion in the normal part–whole integration of smooth functioning, Reich's (1945) emphasis on body tensions as expressions of inhibitions or suppressed rage, and of course many of the insights of psychoanalysis. It is often considered an existentialist approach because it emphasizes the "new" experience, not a reliving or examination of the past, and, indeed, the 1960 youth emphasis on direct experience, sexual freedom, openness to sensual gratification may all be reflections of the influence of Perls and Goodman, among others.

Perhaps most relevant to our concern with imagery techniques is the significance attributed to body-oriented imagery in the Gestalt techniques. With the body–mind wholeness viewpoint that pervades Perls' and his collaborators' orientation, it is natural that Gestalt therapists would emphasize the possibility that bodily tensions, cramps, facial attitudes, and postural orientations represent not only the communication modes widely popularized as "body language," but represent encapsulated fantasies or memories.

Gestalt therapy was one of the earliest approaches to move the patient off the couch and to ask him to "act" before the therapist, shifting positions, exaggerating or engaging in completely opposite postures. Often such bodily activity yielded significant memories or catharticlike releases of emotion. Related to this orientation was a view of the body image [a notion originated by Schilder (1953)] as subject to therapeutic manipulation through fantasy. Just as patients were encouraged to shift or try opposing postures, they were also encouraged to try seemingly wild fantasies. The "inside the body" trip vividly described by Schutz (1967) is a natural consequence of this position. Gestaltists also use the opposite daydream method, actually a form of Moreno's role reversal. Here the patient contemplates some forthcoming event with positive anticipation and then is asked to imagine it with dread. Often in the course of this reversal, the awareness of some very real misgivings about the situation may emerge. Or, if such strong negative images do not arise, the person may experience a sense of confidence that his positive anticipation is well founded, his whole self genuinely desires the occurrence.

The Gestalt notions of wholeness and splitting of selves are also utilized extensively in interpreting dreams. In numerous examples presented in accounts of Perls' workshops (Perls, 1970) the dream is dealt with not by analysis, but by a form of Jung's active imagination or Moreno's role-playing. The dreamer is encouraged to identify with a character or even an animal or object that appears in a dream, for example, "Imagine you are that rusty old license plate you saw in the dream lying in the pond." In some instances, the dream analysis leads to extended role-taking and role reversal that moves into an active therapeutic exercise far removed from any effort just at understanding "what the dream really meant." The kind of extensive step-by-step examination of each element and the reconstructive efforts so characteristic of traditional psychoanalysis were characterized often by Perls as mere "mind-fucking."

Many of the imagery techniques of Gestalt therapy have been incorporated into the games played in encounter groups and in the "touchy-feely" Esalen groups or marathons. Many of these have also become part of what may be termed the "human potential movement" (Lewis & Streitfeld, 1971), a complex mixture of new forms of socialization, self-help, and party games. Perls, for example, proposed the method of shuttling between reality and fantasy. The subject imagines a place where he feels secure and safe. Then he returns to his present situation and compares the two experiences. The therapist asks what was different about the two situations. There follows a rapid shuttling back and forth until eventually the difference between the two situations is clarified and the *here* situation feels as good as the *there*. For Perls, the fantasy experience was not merely an escape from an unpleasant or conflictual here; it suggested important ways in which the person could sense his own potential happiness. The goal of therapy is not the relinquishing of fantasy for reality but rather the gradual movement of the self toward the possibilities one has dared to envision.

In summary, the influence of Gestalt therapy has been pervasive in opening the way for an expansion of possibilities in psychotherapy. Some might claim that the general effect has been one of chaotic license and a kind of polysensuality in the "now"—momentarily exciting and implying more that it can deliver. Even Perls (1972) had many doubts about the genuine effects produced in his workshops. He realized that often the spontaneous weeping and dramatic catharses seemed like playacting and little related to the long-term realities of the individual's daily life. There is little doubt, however, that the popularity of Gestalt treatment methods, however unsystematic, reflects a popular hunger on the part of both psychotherapists and their clients and on the part of young people generally for more direct encounters with their body and imaginative capacities and freedom from the strictures of logical thought and careful analysis. Since there has been almost no concern in this area with establishing ground rules for scientific verification or evaluation of results, one cannot say whether these methods are especially effective in relief of symptoms or in personality change. Perhaps their main function is to pioneer new ways of socialization and point to many interesting new possibilities for self-experience.

PSYCHOSYNTHESIS AND HUMANIST APPROACHES

Another influence on imagery approaches in psychotherapy in the western hemisphere may be traced to the work of an Italian psychiatrist, Roberto Assagioli (1959, 1965, 1969). The term *psychosynthesis* was deliberately chosen to contrast with the analytic approaches of Freud and Jung. It represents a comprehensive effort at viewing man in a holistic fashion, to include a sense of his spiritual capacities, as well as the more animal or instinctual qualities particularly emphasized in the Freudian orientation. Assagioli has had only a relatively small influence in and outside Europe, although institutes of psychosynthesis have gradually sprung up in Rome, Florence, Buenos Aires, and Athens. In conjunction with Robert Gerard, an American psychologist, Assagioli has had somewhat greater impact on psychotherapists in the United States and Canada. Assagioli and Gerard have particularly influenced psychotherapists seeking a broader and more constructive view of the nature of man and who have formed the vanguard groups for the so-called humanist movement in psychotherapy.

It is beyond the scope of this volume to examine all of the theoretical issues involved in attempt to present a comprehensive view of man, such as proposed by Gerard and Assagioli. Of special interest, however, is the extensive use made of imagery techniques and the original and inventive manner in which these techniques are related to the tenets of their theoretical position. Assagioli, for example, has proposed that the human personality be viewed in terms of seven layers of experience. There is the lower unconscious, which includes drives, urges, bodily functions, primitive dreams and fantasies, and pathological manifestations such as phobias or delusions. There is a middle unconscious, which corresponds more closely to ordinary consciousness. There is, moreover, a super conscious, which involves ethical "imperatives," altruistic attitudes, and artistic or scientific concerns; a field of consciousness, which might be roughly equivalent to what William James called the stream of consciousness, a conscious self or awareness of what I want and what I do, and then a higher self that represents perhaps a fundamental spiritual core of the personality, one ordinarily attained or only through unusual or remarkable efforts at self-examination or significant revelatory experiences. Finally, there is a collective unconscious, which involves the shared human experiences of perhaps the loftiest type with all mankind.

For Assagioli and for Gerard (1964) the goal of psychosynthesis is not only the explication of these various levels of awareness and the relief of personal difficulties. Rather, its goal is a thorough reconstruction of the total personality, exploration of the various levels of personality, and eventually the shift of personality to a new center through exploration of its fundamental core.

At first this approach may seem vague, indeed, and perhaps quasi-religious, rather than scientific. However, these authors take great pains to point out that they are not arguing in favor of the viewpoint that focuses on any of the usual types of organized religious orientations nor, indeed, are they interested in experiences that involve a soul that transcends human life. Rather, they would argue, I believe, that in human evolution an important feature that developed was the need to transcend the limitations of self, thereby to experience the greatest of human capacities—a sense of oneness with mankind as well as a place in the universe. Assagioli (1969) has sought to gather together what he has called 14 categories of symbols which represent man's transpersonal experiences or capacities. These go from introversion, deepening–descent, elevation–ascent, through awakenings, light–illumination, fire, development, strengthening–intensification, love, way–path–pilgrimage, mutation–sublimation, rebirth–regeneration, and liberation. This orientation moves perhaps even beyond Jung in attempting to bring together, without excessive reductionism, major symbols. They form the basis for some of the practical techniques employed in psychosynthesis psychotherapy.

Clearly, one can see a relationship between the experiences of descent or ascent and Desoille's use of climbing and descending techniques in imagery and, indeed, these are explored in psychosynthesis. Assagioli has given examples of the various "psychospiritual" exercises or meditation subjects which can be based on these concepts. He cited, for example, the elaborate visualization of a rose blossoming. Such an experience, if entered into fully and actively by the subject, can foster an "inner flowering" and a sense of growth and development which is a key to human self-expression in its fullest sense.

The exercise itself calls for a subject first to imagine looking at the rose, visualizing it in detail, noticing carefully the color, then noticing the rose itself opening, and, finally, the rose growing full and specific. Gradually, the subject is encouraged to use other senses, smell and touch, in experiencing the rose and finally to move to internalizing the rose, making it indeed a part of himself and himself a part of the rose. According to Assagioli (1969), the exercise ends with statements such as, "The same life that animates the universe and has created the miracle of the rose is producing in us . . . the awakening and development of our spiritual being . . . [p. 15]."

The technique next employed by Assagioli, Gerard, and by others influenced by these authors may be termed *symbolic visualization*. Symbolic visualization has both diagnostic and therapeutic implications and ranges from the controlled imagining of specific symbols to a rather unstructured, spontaneous visualization much like the associated imagery techniques of Desoille or even Reyher's method based on Freud's early imagery association technique. In the category of controlled symbolic visualization, Gerard (1964) lists visualizations of specific dynamic symbols: the attempt is to conjure up an image of a very definite form, such as a white dot within a white circle or a mathematical design, to demonstrate thus to the subject how difficult the maintenance of such an experience is without intruding, extraneous thoughts. There also are symbols of positive human relationships, for example, two hands clasping, or symbols of masculinity and femininity such as the sword and the vase.

Gerard also introduced a novel concept—the visualization of affective states—influenced initially by his own research involving Rorschach methods, as well as the visualization of different color patterns and exposure to different color pattern experiences. Gerard encourages the patient to carry out imagery tasks such as seeing himself at the center of a sphere of a particular color. Indeed, for Gerard, the important differences among colors such as the blue-greens and reds and yellows are quite significant in a variety of experiences. The final exercise of this type includes the patient's attempt to visualize living things which may change and to experience the direction the change takes autonomously once the image begins. Examples include visualizing a seed or a transformation of a caterpillar to chrysalis to butterfly.

The second general category of controlled visualization in the psychosynthesis approach calls for scenes of a more extended symbolic nature suggested by the therapist. Here, of course, there is considerable similarity to the intention of Leuner, but the symbols employed are somewhat different. Some examples are those such as imagining the taming of a wild horse, the rebuilding of a home or temple that has been allowed to become dilapidated, or exploring the origin and unifying center of the personality by means of symbols such as reaching the safety of a lighthouse after a dangerous swim through the waves, climbing to the top and eventually looking for the core of one's being. The more spontaneous symbolic visualization techniques basically represent the use of the Desoille or Leuner methods. Here the role of the therapist as guide and helper who prevents avoidance of frightening situations and at the same time encourages desensitization of the experiences is critical.

Some of the methods used by Gerard (1964) are quite ingenious indeed. Subjects enduring psychophysiological tensions may be encouraged to visualize these in imagery form and produce kinds of sequential fantasies similar to those described by Gestalt therapists. Patients may also attempt to visualize their emotional states, as in the case of a young man encouraged to "contact his own anxiety." This young man soon reported that he pictured a lump of soft dough or unbaked bread. Growth process was then encouraged by having the patient imagine the bread put into the oven and baked. As Gerard pointed out, the therapeutic effort becomes one of producing an experience of growth entirely through the visualization. One need not analyze the explicit meaning of what happens to the bread after it is baked and how this in itself becomes a symbol for the personality. The very process of imaging the puttylike initial image transformed through the baking process is sufficient to help the patient develop a greater sense of potential toughness of his personality through growth.

Gerard also makes use of rather specific techniques to help patients through visualization of the emotional state by imagining a door which opens onto an interior court or by imagining such things as a giant heart which can be explored by the patient. Gerard also encourages symbolic visualization based on elaborations of ongoing dreams or material derived from projected techniques and finally attempts to imagine, through concrete imagery, such notions as one's own "reflected self-image." In keeping with the psychosynthesis view, one must ultimately reach a kind of central core of the personality that might indeed be called the *spiritual* center of the personality. Gerard, therefore, extensively uses not only guided daydream trips involving ascent and descent, but also greatly emphasizes imagining different types of light and color and, finally, complex inner dialogues of the self.

A dramatic tape recording presented by Gerard (1964, pp. 34–37) centers upon a patient who begins an imaginary trip into the sea and goes deeper and deeper into the ocean and then, in a burst of tremendous excitement, eventually seems to penetrate what may well be the very spiritual core of his being as he sees it; the patient then attains a kind of peak experience. For example, the patient at one point confronted with an image of "profound yellow-white incandescence" became terrified and said: "[T]his one is the (deep breathing) – (gives a couples of cries) – I am afraid – my life will be consumed, it will be taken back. It's the thing that is life!" The therapist here responded by saying, "You can experience it and keep your identity. You can know that you are part of that light, and yet are being in your right." The patient, breathing heavily, said: "[T]his is the source of the spiritual things," and followed with a deep sigh. The experiencing of this image with tremendous anguish and drama is certainly an impressive expression of a deeply meaningful encounter for the patient, although it is difficult to be certain what the experience ultimately represents for him and whether it does have any lasting effect. Certainly, this question points up a major difficulty that the more scientifically oriented psychologist will raise in reading many of the reports and protocols of humanist and psychosynthetic therapists. To what extent do we see here quasi-revivalist experiences partly induced by the very cues initially provided by therapists, a kind of role-playing, in effect, that may please the therapist and convince the patient that he is doing what is expected, but what will not necessarily lead to any significant changes in subsequent human relationships. Pending careful evaluative studies of the consequences of these experiences, we must maintain some skepticism, yet not deny that important human interactions indeed occur in the course of extended imagery and visualization.

A word may be said briefly about some of the differences in conceptualization and implementation between the imagery technique as employed by Leuner and by Assagioli and Gerard. Although Leuner was clearly influenced in some of his symbolism by the more mystical Jung, most of his approach — with its emphasis on a group of major conflict areas and relationships among striving, ego, ideals, and parental figures — is quite close to the observational level. Leuner focuses on the role of parental figures in generating particular types of reactions and minimizes attempts to get at spiritual experience. In this sense, his approach is closer to Freudian and neo-Freudian psychoanalytic models. While he clearly believes that the ongoing playing out of imagery and symbolism has its own therapeutic effect, Leuner seems to be arguing this mainly in terms of the repressed experiences in childhood and in interpersonal transactions. By contrast, Assagioli and Gerard seem to have a more profoundly philosophical approach to the nature of human personality and experience. They are less concerned with elaboration in imagery in interpersonal distortions and fears and more interested in penetrating to the core of the experience of self. In this sense, what they propose comes, as I am sure Gerard would admit, closer to a mystical or significant spiritual experience and less like the medical or behaviorally oriented goals or symptom relief and improved day-to-day adjustment.

Confronted with differences in interpretation and orientation of this kind, we again are compelled to assert that formal research is the only method that can resolve such differences. As long as Assagioli and Gerard propose that what they are providing is psychotherapy and continue to talk in terms of these methods as applications of psychiatric or psychological science, then it behooves them to provide systematic evidence in support of their theory or some evaluation of actual outcomes in a series of reasonably well-described and controlled cases. Needless to say, the same requirement holds for Leuner, or for any of the other mental imagery therapists. As noted in Chapter IV, however,

Leuner and his followers seem, at least to some extent, to be making a beginning in an empirical evaluation of the method.

RECENT APPLICATIONS
OF MENTAL IMAGERY TECHNIQUES

Even as this volume was in preparation, a proliferation of clinical reports employing variants of imagery techniques in psychotherapy occurred. I shall choose some examples of how therapists in the past four or five years, have begun to apply the imagery techniques within a variety of settings and to call attention to particular points that may be of interest theoretically or in terms of potential research. Since only a small portion of what is actually practiced by psychotherapists gets into the literature, it is likely that much more use is being made of these techniques than the 20 or so recent journal articles would imply. Indeed, we are at the point where compendia of techniques, many of which involve imagery, are now being published—for example, Lewis and Streitfeld's (1971) *Growth Games* and Masters and Houston's (1972) *Mind Games*. Each of these volumes reflects many of the techniques developed initially in the European mental imagery group and, in addition, some of the role-playing and Gestalt therapy methods cited earlier in this chapter. Furthermore, they add to these methods, methods derived from various oriental meditation approaches. Perhaps it is best that both volumes do indeed use the word *games* in their titles so that they avoid the onus of scientific validation of their proposals.

An early example of the employment of a variant of a European mental imagery technique was reported by Hammer (1967). Hammer was one of the first American psychotherapists to relate himself to the European mental imagery school and has presented a concise description of the methods of Desoille and Leuner, amongst others. His own psychotherapeutic approach is a direct reflection of the guided affective imagery method of Leuner, much as it is described in this volume. Hammer has reported tape-recording examples of sessions using the technique with patients who undoubtedly presented serious therapeutic problems.

For example, in working with a 30-year-old homosexual woman who was imprisoned, Hammer began with the meadow scene for a particular therapeutic session. Following relaxation, the patient was encouraged to visualize herself in a field and then was asked to describe it. The patient described a rather pathetic field with "yellowed grass . . . a black, rather sad, tree . . . [p. 177]." Soon a horse appeared, and the patient attempted in vain to pour out some of her affection on this animal. There was an attempt to mount the horse, but this was not successful. The therapist then intervened with a suggestion that the patient offer some sugar; interestingly enough, the patient herself quickly rejected this as a "bribe." The therapist played a supportive role at this point by suggesting that at least the patient continue to touch or pet the horse, that probably the horse was friendly. The patient was indeed encouraged to the point where she finally could mount the horse, and she moved on to the next phase of the scene. Fairly frequently the therapist intervened in this particular approach, suggesting images such as the mounting as part of the journey and eliciting more detailed descriptions of particular scenes to which the patient alluded.

In another session, while the therapist was inclined to begin the session with the trip of the previous session, the patient herself made clear that she would rather go in a different direction because of her current discomfort. The therapist quickly gave her the opportunity to focus on her present experience in the form of an image and this led to the picture of a "fish." The image then generated a sequence of images built around fish and fishing and then eventually, after a good deal of interaction between patient and therapist, the patient herself launched an extended monologue describing in great detail with much vividness her trip through the water and to a houseboat and eventually into a family of fishermen. The story developed quite dramatically into one in which the mother of the house was dealing with the small fish "daughter," and the patient experienced a vivid and passionate reliving and reexamining of her relationship with her mother and its effect on her self-concept.

It is noteworthy that Hammer encouraged the patient to emerge slowly from the scene and gradually to open her eyes from the vivid imagining sequence. He thus avoided a dramatic transition from this extremely profound cognitive and emotional experience to once again the situation of being in the therapist's office. At the close, the patient said that she somehow felt: "whole, more whole . . . more mature. I feel that I know that was me out there [Hammer, 1967, p. 181]."

An application of the European mental imagery techniques to therapeutic efforts to deal with recurrent nightmares has been described in a rather dramatic paper by Johnsgard (1969). This method includes some elements of Jung's active imagination technique, but carries it further into an elaborate symbolic voyage. In Johnsgard's use, the therapist, too, plays the role of the helpful guide. In one instance, for example, the patient who has had a recurrent toilet nightmare was describing himself as sitting bare-legged on the toilet when he was suddenly faced by a scorpion. The room turned upside down and he was left hanging onto the rickety toilet just out of reach of the scorpion. The therapist intervened by suggesting that in imagination he bring the room back into its proper position; at this point the patient could imagine leaving the room. Later he was able to return to the room, feed the scorpion some dead flies, and thus make possible a series of changes in imagery, which were experienced as breakthroughs.

Johnsgard (1969) generally begins a session with the relaxation procedure and indicates to the patient that he also will go through some of the same relaxing procedures. Following the progressive relaxation, an attempt is made to revive the very vivid nightmare that has been recurrent. After a vivid account of the nightmare, the therapist encourages a whole sequence of images using the original nightmare materials. This leads to a rather extended journey in which the patient eventually finds himself at the top of Mount Everest. There then follows a trip down into the village, some interaction with the people in the village, as well as with objects such as fountains, and a bathing experience that has some of the same positive affect associated with it that has been described by Leuner.

Johnsgard's patients frequently will then go on to associations of a more traditional psychoanalytic type. Thus, the patient who had recurrent nightmares of a frightening, faceless human figure which destroyed others in its attempt to reach him was able to perceive that this destructiveness was not just the representation of his own father, but perhaps of his own angry side. He could feel as a result of the trip, subsequent to imagining the nightmare, that he was now ready to incorporate this anger and accept responsibility for it. Indeed, as a consequence of the extended therapeutic trips, there was a gross behavior change so that the patient began to feel himself more of a complete individual and that his anger, which he had always feared because of its potential destructiveness, was not in actuality dangerous, but a genuine part of normal assertive behavior. There was as a consequence of this symbolic transaction a marked personality and behavioral change, rather like the kind reported in the European literature.

Johnsgard noted that even in cases where there are no clear long-term behavioral changes, the technique has an immediate anxiety-relieving effect; he has cited examples of this. Considerable use is made also of feeding or nurturing frightening objects and occasionally, with careful control by the therapist, of attacking them, although generally the effort is made to use alternatives to violence. In one instance, the patient had started or had discovered a fire in a small cabin. When he began to put it out, the therapist, acting on the basis of previous work, encouraged the patient to allow the fire to develop. The patient made sure that all the things were out of the cabin and then, despite great feelings of anxiety, gradually increased the feeding of the fire to the point where the cabin eventually was vividly burned down in his imagination. A giant molten bird emerged from the cinders and eventually, when confronted by the patient in imagery, it turned into a symbolic human figure; this led to further important confrontation for the patient.

Johnsgard's conclusion was that this symbolic method has the advantage of reducing treatment time. This occurs through both the reduction of excessive anxiety and also through the symbolic formations themselves. In this sense, he is accepting the notion of Leuner and Desoille that it is the trip itself, with its unfolding of images and transformations of symbolism, that is essentially a curative factor, and that the analytic or intellectual work of more traditional therapy is not essential.

A most intriguing recent application of the guided imagery method has been reported by Scheidler (1972) in a treatment program with mixed-sex groups of 10- and 12-year-olds. Children in both groups had unhappy family histories with considerable rejection or family breakup and to some extent they had exhibited predelinquent behavior. Scheidler introduced relaxation exercises as a means of also providing children with imagery training. For example, the children imagined themselves on an extremely cold day with snow blowing and ice forming on their hair and eyebrows. They were encouraged to experience this great cold as vividly as possible (this work was in Maine) and then finally to race to a cabin in which they found a great fireplace with much heat, strip off their heavy coats and boots, and then sit down to drink cups of steaming hot chocolate. In the warmer times of the year, imagery involving working very hard under a hot sun and then leaping into a pleasantly cool lake were used to obtain a similar effect. Following Desoille, Scheidler encouraged the boys to visualize a sword, and the girls, a vase. He asked each member of the group to elaborate as vividly as possible on his own image and allowed the image to follow itself to reasonable ending.

Scheidler, in contrast to other investigators, does not believe that the symbolic manipulations alone are sufficient. His experience has been that this method opens the way for further, more directed discussions about, for example, the children's own experiences in relationship to parents or family life. In general, he has found this technique, along with role-playing, to be especially useful in breaking down periods of blockage or redundancy. Follow-up contacts with the children in both groups indicated considerable improvement after only seven sessions. Both school principals and parents were requested to give behavioral instances of change. For Scheidler, a critical factor in this method was the sharing of the fantasy by the group. The symbolic quality of the imagery prevented the conflict from being too obvious and, therefore, from exposing the child to "psychological nudity."

There is, indeed, a whole host of similar techniques that can be cited—some are employed in groups and others in work with individuals. Especially popular through the influence of the Gestalt therapists and the humanistic approaches are the methods that employ "going into the body" or variants of the "who am I?" imagery (Crampton, 1968; Schutz, 1967). Schutz's book, *Joy*, contains many examples of the use of guided imagery, particularly in group settings. The application of the technique often enough is somewhat haphazard and very much at the whim of the therapist or often of the group itself without a leader (Alexander, 1969).

Crampton (1968), working in the framework of psychosynthesis, presented a recording of a young woman who was encouraged to "take a journey inward in imagination" in order to make contact with her inner self. She was encouraged to begin by imagining the external layer of her personality, describing it as vividly as possible, and then moving inward from that point. In this instance, the patient began by visualizing a grin which she associated with the Cheshire Cat. But then she was aware of two faces to it, one warm and one hostile or smug. She proceeded to imagine herself going inside her own mouth found herself making "wisecracks," and then became aware of how busy her tongue was. She imagined her tongue as a snake and then experienced herself going into her nose and became aware that she actually enjoyed the idea of being "snotty." Eventually she got inside her brain, where there was an encounter with a curious little man who seemed very much like a Freudian censor. Subsequently, she appeared to be going deeper and deeper into her body and the imagery became increasingly symbolic and medievel or ancient. As she proceeded even further into her body, the image took on a more mystical quality and seemed to be reflecting some experiences she had with Buddhism. When she seemed lost in the dark, the therapist suggested that she had a light to guide her through the dark. This led to a very vivid image from early adolescence. This image was quite real and evoked strong emotion. At the conclusion of the session, the young woman, who incidently was not herself a patient, but simply a volunteer for demonstration, reported: "It is kind of hard to come down to earth . . . this room is much less real to me than the light and all the other things I experienced [Crampton, 1968, p. 28]."

As might be expected, many of the images that occur in these expanded voyages are memories and, indeed, the quality of many of the symbolic trips is indeed a "regressive one." I have already discussed the possibility that the very act of lying on a couch or engaging in relaxation in a more or less supine position, while other adults are sitting up, may create the psychological situation of being a child again and, therefore, may make it easier to evoke memories associated with childhood. To the extent that most psychodynamic theories emphasize the fixations and blockings of various stages of childhood which are interfering with effective adult functioning, the importance of reexperiencing consciously these childhood attitudes supports the value of the regressive attitude. While some existential therapists would argue against the advantages of focusing on the child within the adult, the more common trend in psychotherapy is to attempt to communicate directly with "the child" or with the incorporated parent in the adult by means of some type of regressive imagery format. This has, of course, led to dramatic practices such as Janov's "primal scream" technique, which if it spreads more rapidly may seriously increase the problem of noise pollution.

A relatively controlled technique that involves a combination of imagery and psychodrama built around this type of regressive experience has been offered by Allen (1969). Working from a theoretical position that combines a Lewinian orientation with that of Moreno, Allen has proposed that a systematic experience through imagery and role-playing of being an infant can help the patient experience the combination of physical and emotional relaxation which will break down the separate "boundary systems" between different age levels that have probably become too rigid and impermeable. Such a method permits a freeing of repressed material, greater accessibility to the sense of self, and also leads to an awareness of fundamental potentialities that have been ignored during the growth process. Moreover, Allen's method encourages experiences of spontaneity and expressivity and presents an opportunity to make up for deficiencies in maternal nurturance.

In this exercise, the focal point becomes the experience of being an infant in the crib. Somewhat like a hypnotic age regression, the session takes place with the subject being encouraged to go back to age 6, next to age 3, age 2, eventually to being an infant of somewhere between 3 weeks and 3 months and lying in a crib and sleeping. Sound effects such as lullabies are frequently employed along with a soothing maternal-like voice. The subjects are relaxed on a floor or couch and hear the therapist saying things such as, "So the baby sleeps, warm and quiet. And the mother . . . comes and cares for the baby. Pats the baby. Covers the baby. Keeps the baby warm. Gives it milk . . . [Allen, 1969, p. 207]."

This very vivid imagery experience is one in which the patient is not encouraged to talk or respond, but merely to internally experience the imagery and report it only later; in the meantime, the therapist goes on talking about caring for the baby.

Just on the basis of a theory of memory, the results described by Allen are intriguing in their own right. The vivid images often lead to recall of relatives of family friends or toys that had not been consciously thought of for many, many years. [See Tomkins (1970), for a discussion of a theory of memory that deals with these issues.] The vast majority of reactions to the experience is very positive, and, in most cases, the technique seems to have lasting effects. Unfortunately, as in many clinical reports, Allen does not provide any systematic data on the effects of this method, which he says he has used for 17 years.

A very recent and well thought out approach to the use of imagery in psychotherapy has been presented by Shorr (1967, 1972). Shorr seems to consider himself an existential–phenomenological psychotherapist and relates his theoretical position, especially to Laing and May, among others. A reading of his approach to interpretation and to the nature of psychopathology suggests that probably Shorr may best be viewed as representing the interpersonal school of psychoanalysis stemming from the work of Sullivan. A great deal of his emphasis in the therapeutic interaction itself has to do with the question of one's identifying oneself and separating one's own view of oneself from the attributed self as defined by the significant others in one's childhood. Shorr's position seems to present a healthy confluence of the influences of social psychology, neo-Freudian psychoanalysis, and an existential philosophic position. It seems much closer in orientation to observable psychological phenomena than many of the imagery techniques and does not seem to reflect any great interest in the spiritual penetration of the innermost self that characterizes psychosynthesis and a number of the other imagery orientations. The method involves the use of a fairly organized approach that has some of the qualities of Leuner's systematic method, although it makes use of different types of questions and images.

One important method that Shorr has proposed is what he calls the "existential question." This consists of, perhaps, 30 specific questions that may be used as a regular format for diagnostic purposes or else can be brought in as appropriate into an ongoing interaction. These questions are mentioned only briefly here since they do not specifically relate to the use of imagery techniques. Thus, the patient may be asked for an example of a phrase in which one can "call you anything, but never refer to you as what?" Here a patient may say, "You can call me anything but never refer to me as a weak sister." Another question is, "Do you ever make a difference to anyone?" This forces hopefully profound examination of the patient's significance in the lives of parents, relatives, friends, society, etc. Some questions are of ideals or long-term goals, others are very much related to body image. Others attempt to get at experiences of the parents, such as, "What was your mother's fantasy about you?" Sometimes they involve defense mechanisms that are predominant: "How would you drive someone out of his mind?" Some of the existential questions include fantasies about future goals, specifically: "What is your fantasy about marriage, work, fun, etc.?" It should be obvious that confrontation with questions of this kind in a reasonably intelligent and cooperative patient is likely to lead very quickly into significant material.

More important for our purposes in this volume is the extensive use made by Shorr of the imaginative dimension. For Shorr (1972), "imagination lies at the central kernel of our consciousness . . . [p. 11]." Shorr places great emphasis on the ubiquitous nature of daydreaming and employs this to demonstrate to patients their own capacities for imagery and fantasy. Gradually, Shorr has evolved a method for putting the individual in his own imagery into a particular situation which would evoke a set of interactions that would be useful not only in revealing major problems in the areas of significance in the patient's life, but which would also permit him to relive experiences. These methods are not used in an exact form, but are introduced from time to time within specific individual or group therapy sessions as they seem appropriate. Some examples given by Shorr are: "Imagine yourself taking a shower with your father. How would you feel? What would you say to him? What would he say to you?" Another one involves a crib image much like that used by Allen: "Imagine yourself waking up as a baby. How would you feel? What would you do?" Shorr uses an almost infinite variety of images geared very much to the specific characteristics of the patient and to specific developments in therapy.

Examples of some of his *imaginative situations* (IS) include: "Imagine that you have a power machine in front of you and that, by pressing a button, you can get anyone in the world, past or present to appear in front of you. Who would it be? Now have a dialogue with him or her

[Shorr, 1967, p. 454]." In confronting conflict situations, he described using images such as suggesting two parts of the personality in combat, or: "Imagine two large boxes. What person do you imagine in each box [Shorr, 1972, p. 32]?" These techniques are also employed in relation to focusing methods, the use of the existential questions previously cited, the use of incomplete sentences that must be finished by the patient, and the use of a method that requires the patient to imagine the most or least frightening or most and least dangerous experiences, etc.

A particular value of the imagery technique as presented by Shorr is in the case of patients who seem relatively resistant and at an impasse in therapeutic progress. He presented a case of one such patient and he included an extensive tape recording, as well as an annotation of comments by the patient's original therapist who referred him to Shorr to see if a breakthrough could be occasioned through the use of psychoimagination therapy. Upon careful examination of this tape, it is obvious that Shorr's use of imaginative situations is quite different from that of the European mental imagery therapists. While some of the situations he employs are similar, he employs them in a much more "rapid fire" method, with a great deal of interaction between therapist and patient and with the ultimate focus being one of essentially psychodynamic insight therapy. Shorr does not minimize the significance of imagination and, he cites, a profound comment of William James (1890) to the effect that, "each world *whilst it is attended to* is real after its own fashion . . . [p. 293]." At the same time, he emphasizes much more Sullivanian notions of the "participant-observer" in which the interaction between patient and therapist is vivid and active with the imagery, and other techniques such as the various existential questions play a key role in the communication process.

To conclude our review of American applications of imagery techniques, it may be said that the last decade has witnessed a sharp rise in the clinical uses of fantasy. A goodly portion of this trend has been a part of a loosely organized, somewhat faddist "humanist" trend. The parlor game imagery methods may have relatively little long-range effects. What seems more likely is that the daring experimentation with imagery methods will open the way to a much more intensive examination of private processes by psychotherapists more systematically oriented.

CHAPTER VI

BEHAVIOR MODIFICATION
USES OF IMAGERY:
DESENSITIZATION
AND AVERSIVE TECHNIQUES

We believe it is far-fetched at this time to deny that people think, that as you read this page you are not thinking about it, evaluating it, etc. We believe that it is unscientific to deny a priori, that covert responses are by their nature unable to be studied, or do not behave in lawful ways. In fact, the evidence . . . gives further support to the proposition that covert events operate as if they are amenable to some of the same learning processes and manipulations as other classes or responses; that is to say that thoughts and feelings may be shaped, reinforced, or extinguished.

A. Jacobs and L. B. Sachs (1971, p. 2)

From the "Never Never" land of Dionysian mental imagery therapists, I turn now to the "square," straightforward, and "scientifically rigorous" imagery uses of the behavior modification schools. The contrast between the approaches described in Chapters III, IV, and V and the varied techniques of behavior modification, which also employs man's capacity for imagery, is profound. These differences raise fundamental questions about the nature of the scientific endeavor, sociological and historical issues concerning the development of theories and methods in psychology, and perhaps significant questions about the politics of psychotherapy. The contrast between the origins and approaches of the two groups of therapeutic procedures confronts us also with different views of the nature of human experience and also presents questions about the ethics of psychotherapeutic intervention.

At this writing, I know of no one systematically exploring the cultural, cognitive, and personality differences between psychologists or psychiatrists who have moved toward the more psychodynamic approaches to psychotherapy or to the uses of mental imagery methods (as described in this volume) and those who have devoted themselves largely to behavior modification techniques. It would be presumptuous indeed to propose that personal factors alone can account for their striking differences in orientation.

One obvious factor does emerge in a review of the large body of literature in both fields, however. The psychologist or (numerically less frequent) psychiatrist who has been emphasizing behavior modification approaches is likely to have a much closer orientation to experimental methods and to systematic research appraisal of these methods. The practitioners of the various mental imagery techniques or the psychoanalytic approaches, while often well trained scientifically, have relied far more heavily upon anecdotal case history material or very gross types of formal research to support their positions. Whatever criticisms one may have of the intent, sophistication, or personalities of practitioners of behavior modification, there can be little question that they have in their work generated a tremendous body of formal research evaluating each of the parameters of the psychotherapeutic techniques employed. In this sense, the behavior modification movement in the last 15 years has represented a major advance in the scientific study of the psychotherapeutic process.

For psychodynamic psychotherapists to ignore the body of literature that has emerged on behavior modification and to overlook the care with which both case material and formal research are described in these articles seems arrogant and almost unethical. To denounce various behavior modification techniques, as some psychotherapists have done, as mechanistic or dehumanizing of the patient seems to me to be a form of lazy labeling, and renders gross disservice to a clientele seeking psychological help. In my opinion, Bandura (1969) has presented a powerful and penetrating analysis of the ethics and social responsibility inherent in the behavior modification approach. Although he perhaps underestimates the degree to which some ultimate value systems about the nature of society may underlie any therapeutic method, I believe he makes it clear that the behavior modification approach can significantly serve the needs of its clients. It also keeps the client fully informed in a way that contrasts often enough with the somewhat more magical expectations that tend to develop around the psychodynamic approaches to personality change.

Historically, behavior modification can be traced in a fairly direct line to the influence upon John B. Watson of the Pavlovian experiments on conditioning. Whereas habit-training methods of various kinds have been certainly employed for centuries as techniques of modifying behavior and also emotional distress, most current behavior modification techniques take their origin from the influence of Watson's behaviorism as distilled through such significant theoretical leaders in the United States as Clark Hull and B. F. Skinner. It can, of course, be shown that there was some European recognition of forms of desensitization, especially in the treatment of phobias, but the use of a formal learning approach in the treatment of irrational fears probably is largely an American product and is traceable to Watson's demonstration of how a little boy named Albert could be conditioned to become afraid of rabbits. Shortly thereafter, Jones (1924) was able to treat a 3-year-old child to eliminate his fear of rabbits by a desensitization technique.

Although there were a few persons, for example, Salter (1949), practicing conditioned reflex therapy during the thirties and forties, the impetus for the development of behavior therapy as a movement must certainly be credited to Joseph Wolpe (1954, 1958, 1961, 1969). Wolpe himself is a South African, yet he was strongly influenced in his thinking by the learning theory of Clark Hull, and Wolpe has contributed to the experimental research in this field. Behavior therapy in the broadest sense can also be traced to the influence of Skinner and various co-workers who began dealing with operant conditioning techniques in schizophrenics in the 1950s. However, the focus in this chapter is specifically upon methods that employ imagery and related phenomena. Since operant techniques, on the whole, depend upon an overt response, usually motor or vocal, I shall not particularly deal with this branch of development in the behavior modification movement.

Wolpe's initial influence was through his development of the method of *systematic desensitization* — also sometimes regarded as a method of counterconditioning or as a method to treat phobias or anxiety through reciprocal inhibition. Encouraged by the good results that Wolpe seemed to be achieving through desensitization, and encouraged by the fact that the method itself was sufficiently precise and repeatable so that it lent itself to experimental investigation, American and British psychologists who were oriented toward various forms of learning theory and behaviorism began to explore the different methods. Most notable among the early pioneers in this area were Lazarus, Eysenck, and Rachman. In not many years, systematic desensitization became the most widely employed therapeutic technique, and it remains to this day perhaps the most thoroughly studied of all methods of psychotherapy. I shall shortly move to a discussion of the approach and its relevance for imagery. What is especially noteworthy, however, is the fact that despite the focus of the behaviorists upon objective responses, the most widely used and most thoroughly studied method depends upon a private image.

IMAGERY IN SYSTEMATIC DESENSITIZATION

The Basic Method

The popularity of Wolpe's systematic desensitization undoubtedly stems from the fact that it is extremely simple to learn, seems a straightforward approach to dealing with a problem that is widespread, and appears to make a good deal of sense. Part of its initial appeal to psychologists with backgrounds in learning theory was its apparent relationship to Hullian notions and to learning theory more broadly. Even if one has serious questions about the underlying theory of recip- rocal inhibition proposed by Wolpe and indeed about the very rela- tionship of this approach to learning theory (Breger & McGaugh, 1965), the method has the clinical value of engendering a precision in inquiry about symptomotology that had become a forgotten art in the emphases on "spontaneity" or "expression of feelings," which charac- terized so many of the dynamic or relationship approaches to therapy.

The construction of a hierarchy is a key feature of Wolpe's method. It requires a patient who has reported an irrational fear of closed spaces, for example, to describe as precisely as possible a whole range of settings in which this fear is likely to occur. This activity of attention to contingent events linked to symptom occurrence has tended to be overlooked by therapists whose assumption was that the phobia was merely a symbolic representation of an underlying conflict. As a result, it seemed unnecessary in many cases to explore the behavior of the pa- tient in a variety of settings and the range of intensities of anxiety as- sociated with the settings. Wolpe's approach, therefore, was exciting, not only for its theoretical implications, but because, in effect, it in- troduced a degree of systematic inquiry that seemed much more thoughtful and responsible than the kind of rather loose interaction that often characterizes psychotherapeutic sessions. [My concern here is not so much with detailing all aspects of systematic desensitization, nor reviewing all of the relevant literature. The reader is referred to Wolpe (1958), Rachman (1959, 1965, 1968), Paul (1966), and Wolpe and Lazarus (1966) for treatments of this technique and for some of the relevant research.]

Essentially, the method is designed primarily for patients with phobias, but it has also been extended to a large variety of interpersonal difficulties by viewing the components of these difficulties as often involving phobias of some kind. Thus, for example, systematic desensitization can be applied to a person who is essentially shy and feels inadequate in social relations if one indeed views the shyness as representing a series of phobias in relation to attendance at social events, asking members of the opposite sex to join in social activities, irrational fears of social sexual limitations, etc. As Lazarus (1971) pointed out, to the extent that one attempts to broaden the use of desensitization to a much greater variety of conditions—Wolpe (1969) has suggested this is possible—one runs into danger of constructing tremendous numbers of hierarchies and of almost making trivial the process of treating interpersonal difficulty.

If we for the moment limit ourselves to viewing desensitization in relation to phobias, the process involves initially interviewing the patient in detail about the nature of the irrational fears and then very carefully constructing a hierarchy of the occurrence of the phobic response, ranging from the least frightening situation to the most frightening. These situations are labeled for generating a visual image that the subjects can produce more or less at will in the course of the treatment process. There follow exercises in deep muscle relaxation, essentially the Jacobson method. Here we see a historical tie, through Jacobson, probably back to Schultz's autogenic training of the turn of the century. This is perhaps the one common historical point between mental imagery techniques and the behavior modification uses of imagery.

Following relaxation training and indications that the patient feels considerably relaxed, he is encouraged to bring to mind as vividly as possible the lowest item on the hierarchy. This is envisioned as fully as possible under conditions of deep relaxation, which are presumably to yield a counterconditioning effect for the anxiety associated with the image. If, at any point, the anxiety in association with a scene is too great, the patient is to signal the therapist. At this point, deeper relaxation exercises are undertaken before that image is again generated. As the individual works his way up the hierarchy, from least to most feared situations, he is likely to experience a reduction in the general amount of anxiety he experiences in contemplating the phobic situation. To the extent that there is indeed a considerable reduction in anxiety in relation to the range of feared situations, there are then indications that exposure to the actual frightening situations should indeed yield an ability to confront the situation without great fear.

As Bandura (1969) has pointed out, in reviewing relevant outcome studies, the indications are, on the whole, quite convincing that, at least in the case of phobias, most forms of desensitization do lead to a reduction in anxiety during the sessions in connection with the various images that make up the hierarchy. Moreover, there is a much greater indication of approach responses to the feared situations themselves. A classic study by Lazarus (1961) carefully demonstrated with quite good controls that phobic behavior could be extinguished completely in a large number of patients on the basis of desensitization; the extinction of the fear persisted for a large number of the cases over a reasonably long period of time. Studies by Paul (1966, 1967) also yielded evidence of considerable improvement in the phobic response, as well as in related emotional behavior, for patients treated by systematic desensitization.

Bandura (1969) concluded that desensitization has a marked effect on increasing the likelihood of approach responses, but rarely leads to complete extinction, at least as evident in formal experimental studies. Based upon his follow-up of more than 100 (of his own) cases that Lazarus (1971) treated by a variety of behavior methods — but primarily desensitization — came evidence that there were some relapses. Relapses were particularly found in patients when emergencies occurred that could not have been anticipated in the therapy itself. There were, however, no indications of symptom substitution to speak of, and in a large percentage of cases, gains were maintained most noticeably when the life situations of patients were favorable, when, too, their spouses or other family members were encouraging or had obtained treatment which improved their own stituations in relation to the patient's.

On the whole, the results for the treatment of phobias and phobia-related symptoms by the method of systematic desensitization indeed appears effective. Certainly in terms of treatment time, often several months or fewer, and the possibility of the patient learning to practice some of the techniques himself, desensitization seems at this point superior to any other known method for the treatment of fairly circumscribed irrational fears, especially in individuals who are not grossly disturbed in a great variety of areas. The study by Paul (1966–1967) remains one of the most convincing and well-designed outcome studies in the vast psychotherapeutic literature. It clearly indicates the special advantage of systematic desensitization over a more dynamically oriented approach to psychotherapy.

A Closer Look
at the Components of Desensitization

Let us take a closer look at the key ingredients of the method. First, is relaxation. This procedure, which of course again involves a couch or comfortable chair, rather resembles the establishment of conditions in other therapies, such as psychoanalysis or the mental imagery techniques, that maximize the opportunities for the generation of imagery. Wolpe has proposed that the muscular relaxation is critical for producing a reciprocal inhibition effect and reducing the anxiety associated with the images. Evidence from a large body of physiological studies seems to contradict this interpretation of the effect of the relaxation. For example, Chapman and Feather (1972), Van Egeren (1970), and Van Egeren, Feather, and Hein (1971) all have provided evidence that "relaxation" tends to increase the intensity of affective reaction as measured physiologically and as rated by the subjects for phobic images.

In a rather sophisticated study, Chapman and Feather (1971) employed signal detection theory to examine the subject's ability to discriminate the degree of phobic threat of an item of neutral imagery from his anxiety hierarchy. Physiological responses associated with these phobic threat ratings were also obtained. The data from this study and other studies by this group make it clear that sensory decision theory analyses can be employed in procedures of this kind and suggest that relaxed subjects are actually more sensitive to the *phobic* properties of the controlled imagery than nonrelaxed subjects. That is to say, in the relaxed state, subjects experience the fearful emotion even more vividly. This would seem clearly contrary to the theoretical position of Wolpe and to the theory of reciprocal inhibition, but it does point up the fact that relaxation may have a genuine psychological effect in helping the individual generate vivid imagery and also to discriminate more clearly the associated autonomic characteristics of the experience. The possibility arises that treatment may depend not so much on a more peripheral learning experience, but rather on an enhanced central cognitive discrimination capacity generated by relaxed attention to these situations in the course of vivid imagining.

A very thorough review of the literature on psychophysiological measurements in desensitization treatment by Mathews (1971) led the author to conclude: "relaxation may augment both vividness and the autonomic effects of imagery, while at the same time maximizing responses decrement with repeated presentations [p. 88]." As research in my own laboratory has suggested (Antrobus, 1968; Antrobus et al., 1971; Singer, 1966, 1970), it seems likely that various fantasies or "task-irrelevant" or "stimulus-independent" thoughts spontaneously occur as the amount of external information and task demands are reduced. This would suggest that relaxation has as its probable effect the enhancement of the occurrence of imagery and, with this enhancement, the likelihood that the more intense response generated effectively can then be reduced more drastically by subsequent repetitions.

Data reviewed by Wilkins (1971, 1972) also have raised questions about Wolpe's original view of the function of the relaxation and indeed raises questions as to whether relaxation is even critical in the effectiveness of desensitization. Nevertheless, as Bandura (1969) and Mathews (1971) noted, the autonomic data suggest at least some support for relaxation as a useful feature in the desensitization technique. Rachman (1968) has called attention to the fact that the overall effect of desensitization may be to create a sense of calm and the likelihood of alternative images to the frightening ones. As Bandura (1969) pointed out, this view suggests that more centrally mediated or symbolic aspects of the process of desensitization are involved and that it may be worthwhile to consider the possibilities that positive imagery may have an effect in allaying anxiety. I consider this issue at least from a clinical standpoint later in this chapter.

If we turn our attention now to the component of the procedure which involves the use of a hierarchical presentation of both images, we again find relatively little support for the theoretical proposals of Wolpe. Wilkins (1971, 1972) has reviewed the literature on hierarchy construction. He concluded that hierarchy construction is a useful component of the treatment, but not an essential one. For example, Krapfl (1967) was able to show that subjects receiving hierarchy items in a randomized order, rather than in one of increasing intensity of fear, showed significant clinical improvement. As a matter of fact, even presenting the hierarchy in most frightening to least frightening order yielded significant behavioral improvement, but, as might be expected, it also led subjects to react rather negatively to the treatment process.

On the whole, it would appear that the construction of the hierarchy, although perhaps not crucial in desensitization, probably has many valuable clinical advantages. Initially, it provides the basis for a careful interview and for helping the client become aware of his own behavior patterns and begin to discriminate the relevant contingencies associated with their occurrence. In addition, it provides the therapist with a very precise picture of the symptom pattern. Finally, the graduated use of the hierarchy presents an easy entry for the patient into the process and avoids the likelihood that patients will feel such discomfort as to be unwilling to continue with the procedure.

What, then, is the critical component in the desensitization process? As Wilkins (1972) pointed out in his review and in his rejoinder to the criticisms of Davison and Wilson (1972): "[the] instructed imagination of fear relevant scenes is the only necessary element . . . [p. 34]." The importance of imagery, so long denied by behaviorists, can no longer be ignored: the most efficacious behavior therapy method depends essentially on the production of visual imagery.

Several theoretical explanations can be advanced as to why imagery is crucial to the procedure. Wilkins (1972) called attention to two possible models: the *respondent* and the *operant*. The former yields the interpretation that the phobia is extinguished because the imagined conditioned stimulus is not followed by the unconditioned stimulus. Indeed, one might add to Wilkin's view the possibility, based on two-factor learning theory (Rescorla & Solomon, 1967), that conditioned inhibition may play a role in the process. The operant model, on the other hand, with its more centrally mediated focus (Bandura, 1969) emphasizes the fact that in imagination one becomes aware of the absence of negative reinforcers and also perhaps experiences positive reinforcements for nonavoidant behavior through fantasy. In this sense, the operant method has qualities comparable to symbolic modeling or observational learning methods.

If we look a little more closely at the subject's situation in the typical desensitization experiment, however, none of the explanations provided is entirely satisfactory. The appeal of the desensitization technique, and at the same time its deceptiveness, lies in its apparent simplicity. The subject simply has to call to mind a set of images associated with the hierarchy. Despite all of the rigorousness of the behavior modification school, the critical independent variable—the continuity of the patient's self-generated image—is essentially controlled. Indeed, it is taken for granted in a way that seems contrary to the way human beings experience imagery and fantasy. Somewhere along the line, behavior therapists have not paid attention to William James' (1890) famous chapter on the stream of thought in *Principles of Psychology*. Weitzman (1967) has called attention to the fact that it is extremely difficult for a subject to stay focused upon a very specific image of the type employed in desensitization. Certainly, it would be difficult to stay attentive to such an image for a sufficiently long time to enable deconditioning to work as precisely as it is proposed to. Weitzman (1967) compared Gendlin's (1969) focusing method with Wolpe's in several studies and found indications that there was considerable movement in the imagery during desensitization and that perhaps the critical feature was again the vividness and emotional experience associated by the subject with the ongoing imagery. In my clinical work employing variants of the desensitization method, I frequently had patients report to me that from time to time their imagery drifted away from the assigned image. Indeed, sometimes patients rather forcefully interrupt when one is engaged in presenting the hierarchy and urge that they be given time for self-pacing so that they can generate the images as fully as possible. At other times they report a sequence of imagery associations that seem to call for at least some more dynamic interpretations.

Common sense suggests that a careful inquiry needs to be made at the end of any desensitization session about extraneous thoughts that may have occurred to the patient during particular sequences of visual imagery. In addition, there are advantages to the patient's becoming aware, as he proceeds, that he can generate imagery and to some extent learn to control it. The therapist has to be sure that the patient is simply not saying the words that are associated with the frightening event. If the patient merely thinks verbally, "little dog barking," and does not generate a fairly complete picture of the dog barking and perhaps even have an auditory image of the sounds of barking along with the picture of the dog, it is possible that the effect will be essentially "lip service."

Clearly further research is necessary to ascertain the degree to which the visual image is operating, as Paivio (1971) might argue, through a parallel-processing method. The visual image functions to provide a simultaneous extended scene, as compared to the more sequentially processed verbal phrase, to affect the patient's learning situation. Pending additional research, it can be conjectured that the patient not only has the advantage through the production of his imagery of perhaps a deconditioning or learning of new response patterns through symbolic modeling, but also of an experience of control over processes he may have been hesitant to develop in the past. This process is one of manipulation of imagery that is not often recognized as available to them by many people. To the extent that the patient gains some awareness of his capacity for self-control of imagery, he may experience an enhancement in self-esteem, as well as an improvement in his ability to confront a frightening situation.

An advantage of desensitization is that its requirements can be made extremely concrete and relatively explicit for the patient. Indeed, as

Darwin and McBrearty (1968) and Bergin (1969) have shown, the therapist can establish an atmosphere in which the patient experiences considerable control over his performance by compliance with a key set of agreements. Self-desensitization techniques have been presented by Reppucci and Baker (1969); their evidence, indicates that these techniques can be used privately by college students with good results, especially for more outgoing personality types. Clinical approaches to the use of desensitization and imagery for the purposes of helping the patient attain an experience of self-anxiety have been described by Goldfried (1971) and Singer (1971).

I shall discuss desensitization and its relationship to the whole process of imagery later. It seems clear, however, that the central role of the image-making capacity of man is at the moment demonstrated reasonably well by the effectiveness of the desensitization methods. What needs to be done now is much more careful research on the various manifestations of imagery in the ongoing therapy, the degree to which imagery "stays put" while the patient is carrying on a hierarchical sequence, the various functions of the imagery in relation to autonomic arousal and related effects, and the degree to which the imagery is indeed generalized for use in *in vivo* situations.

Positive Imagery
and Desensitization Approaches

In 1936, Chappel and Stevenson reported a remarkably well-designed study with a group of peptic ulcer patients. These patients had been ill for some time and were admitted to a hospital for medication and dietary treatment. During this period, 32 patients were given a special type of group psychological treatment that consisted of training them to become aware of their bodily processes and to use positive imagery by thinking about pleasant life experiences whenever they became aware of being anxious. The remaining patients were controls. By the end of a month, both groups were symptom free on the basis of medication and controlled diet. After a month of medication, control patients were encouraged to broaden their diet—with the result that within 2 weeks, 18 of the 20 reported a full recurrence of symptoms. The remaining two patients had significant symptom return within 2 months. In contrast, the experimental subjects, who were receiving approximately 6 weeks of daily training in the use of Positive imagery, were given freedom to eat anything. In a follow-up 3 years later, 28 of the experimental patients were located. Only two of the group had recurrences of symptoms comparable to their original lengthy history of severe peptic ulcers. Clearly, this method yielded a remarkable result in human benefit through the use of positive imagery. It is to be regretted that this brief report was not followed up by further research by these authors, nor was significant detail made available about the kind of positive imagery technique employed.

A quarter of a century later, Lazarus and Abramovitz (1962) explored the possibility of the use of a positive imagery with a group of young children for whom relaxation exercises had proven difficult to employ. They developed the usual hierarchy of frightening scenes, but also encouraged the children to develop scenes in which there were positive images that could be juxtaposed with the more frightening scenes in the hierarchy. Their results were reasonably good. A few years subsequently, working at the time without knowledge of the Lazarus and Abramovitz or Chappel and Stevenson studies, I began to explore the possibilities of positive imagery in psychotherapy. This interest initially grew out of my research on daydreaming and also the relationship of positive imagery and affect suggested by Tomkins (1962, 1963). In the procedure used the relaxation method, then developed for the patient very strong positive images that could be used to further enhance relaxation, and finally systematically juxtaposed the increasingly frightening hierarchy items with the positive imagery developed by the patient. Speaking generally of the positive images which the patients produced, they were linked to nature scenes with numerous references to lying on quiet beaches and watching the waves of the ocean or lakes, being in peaceful woods, or watching the snow fall on a pleasant hillside. These positive images generally were not self-involving, a significant finding in view of recent research by Greene and Reyher (1972), who reported that images of a positive nature, and not body oriented, can have a significant effect in reducing pain produced by intense electrical stimulation.

Lazarus (1971) has also described the use of *emotive imagery* for the treatment of a child with a dental phobia. In this case, the child was encouraged to imagine that Batman and Robin were accompanying him to the dental chair and to think about Batman and Robin in the situation. Again, the results were promising. Ahsen (1968), although somewhat closer in orientation to the European mental imagery techniques, also seems to make extensive use of positive imagery techniques, which he calls *eidetics*. In the case of a constipated adult who felt unloved by his mother, Ahsen encouraged the patient to develop a very vivid fantasy of physical closeness and warmth with his mother which he was to practice regularly. The result of this was a generally improved personality orientation and, most specifically, an increased regularity of bowel movements—a remarkable demonstration, indeed, of the power of positive thinking as an alternative to a laxative.

Pending further experimental research of the type reported by Greene and Reyher (1972), the significance of positive imagery and its long-range effectiveness in psychiatry remain to be explored. In discussing clinical possibilities and further research and theory, I shall return to this particular technique later in this volume.

A form of desensitization that combines some elements of the European guided imagery techniques with both positive imagery and desensitization has been described by Wolpin (1969). In the case of a snake phobia, for example, he encouraged the patient to imagine an extended trip, which ultimately involved walking up to a snake and then engaging in activity, holding the snake, and gradually bringing the snake closer to him.

Some Implications
of Systematic Desensitization for Imagery

If we take the cumulative body of research literature seriously, that systematic desensitization is the outstanding form of psychotherapy for the treatment of phobias, whether in fairly circumscribed minor problems of normals (snake phobias) or in the somewhat more serious problems presented by clinical patients (Marks, 1969). It is certainly true, as Marks pointed out, that for patients with massive phobic symptoms in a great number of areas and patients with very high general levels of anxiety, the treatment is less successful—but so are all treatments in such cases. The evidence suggests clearly that desensitization is an essential tool for any psychotherapist as part of his overall repertoire of skills.

Granting that systematic desensitization has limitations in its applicability, the fact remains that it points up even within these limitations the great power and importance of visual imagery in our behavioral repertoire. What seems perhaps obvious to the European practitioners of mental imagery techniques is now a significant lesson that must be learned by the behaviorists. The great upsurge of research on the role of visual imagery and other forms of imagery in the information processing and encoding processes of cognition reflects a similar recognition on the part of experimental psychologists.

The power of imagery for therapeutic proposes has been examined in association with relaxation and positive suggestion (Leitenberg, Agras, Barlow, & Oliveau, 1969). These authors found very clear evidence that continued suggestions of positive improvement by the therapist made a difference in ultimate outcome. Findings by Howlett and

Nawas (1971) indicated that single suggestions of improvement at the end of treatment could not affect significantly the benefits of systematic desensitization nor improve the minimal effects of mere exposure to the frightening imagery. These authors were careful to note that their suggestion procedure was not extensive as compared to procedures used by a number of other researchers; studies elsewhere suggest that placebo effects do indeed occur in treatment of phobias, although they are generally significantly less powerful than systematic desensitization. Howlett and Nawas (1971) as well as Mealia and Nawas (1970) have demonstrated that graded presentations of frightening imagery in association with relaxation indeed led to clear improvement in a specific phobic response: fear of spiders. The latter study also makes clear that simply thinking about the imagery that is frightening will not in itself lead to habituation, but that some process of graded increase in fearfulness from very low levels to higher ones is a necessary part of the procedure.

That imagery functions in special ways in relation to possible change in subsequent behavior opens important avenues for research on the function that private or covert rehearsal may have in a variety of human behaviors; that is, not simply in the removal of fears. The fairly positive results obtained in general suggestion [recall that Paul, (1966, 1968) obtained quite good results for his placebo group; indeed the results were close to those of the dynamic psychotherapy control group he used] raises an intriguing question about what we mean by suggestion. All too often, findings in control groups that show improvement upon receiving suggestions of improvement or harmless drugs to which some beneficial effects are attributed lead us simply to classify these effects on the basis of "suggestion."

Nonetheless, a more careful examination of the psychological process that underlies suggestibility effects is necessary. One possibility is that the positive benefits of suggestion are in terms of a set of anticipatory images that the subject generates which essentially play out in fantasy positive alternatives to the complaint for which treatment is sought. A hypothesis worth exploring in future research is that someone given positive suggestions begins, whether in the course of the treatment itself or in intervals between treatments, to fantasize positive outcomes. In these fantasies and images, the patient is in effect engaging in covert modeling of alternatives that may have some of the same qualities as Bandura's symbolic modeling or that are comparable to emotive imagery. In this connection, one can also raise the question of whether there may be a whole set of attitudes and private rehearsals or orientations around the desensitization treatment itself that plays a part in the patient's subsequent improvement. Certainly, it would seem appropriate for research in the future to pay attention to the fact that people do not produce imagery only on demand in specific therapeutic situations, but are thinking about these treatments at other times, playing out different possibilities mentally, and reacting to the new images that they produce as they reminisce or fantasize about the future.

Kamil (1970) carried out a study that raised some interesting questions about the more general personality implications of the desensitization treatment. Approaching the problem from a psychoanalytic point of view, Kamil proposed several alternatives to the recurrence of a symptom or occurrence of another symptom when desensitization effects relief of a phobic reaction. One possibility is that the symptom had become functionally autonomous before the treatment was instituted and that the original dynamics of the personality no longer require the symptom. A second possibility is that desensitization may actually adversely affect personality structure, but that methods employed have not penetrated deeper levels of personality through use of techniques such as projective tests and, therefore, have not elicited these changes. There is, of course, a significant exception to this notion in a study by Baker (1969) in which projective techniques indicated a general improvement for a group of patients suffering from enuresis following removal of the symptom by conditioning methods. The third possibility is that the removal of a symptom may indeed lead to a general change in the pattern of underlying conflict for the patient.

Kamil set about testing these possibilities in an ingenious fashion. He employed the usual snake phobia pattern with the following modifications. Subjects were chosen for systematic desensitization and as nontreated controls from a group of volunteers who clearly showed circumscribed snake-phobic reactions. A third group of persons who were generally fearful in a great many areas, but not specifically phobic about snakes were matched in other respects with the snake-phobic subjects. Finally, there was a group of normal subjects who showed minimal scores on the Fear Survey Schedule.

A critical feature of this study, from the psychodynamic standpoint, was to be able to demonstrate that snake phobics like general phobics shared a common underlying anxiety, obviously the castration fear that is fundamental in psychoanalytic thinking. Several cards of the Rorschach test and pictures from the Thematic Apperception Test (TAT) were employed and were scored for specific categories that would represent evidence of castration fears on these cards. For example, on Card VI of the Rorschach, evidence of physical damage to an organism (deformity, protruding part missing, squashed, splattered, cut) was one of a number of categories used to ascertain evidence of presumed castration fear. On the TAT, the scoring categories for the cards included such items in the subject stories as "genital injury or less; including total mutilative destruction of the body."

Kamil was able to show that there was reasonable interrater reliability for the scores of castration anxiety on both the TAT and the Rorschach. He was also able to show that the castration anxiety categories on the Rorschach and TAT differentiated the phobic subjects, both snake and general, from the normal subjects. The general phobics and snake phobics did not differ significantly on the castration anxiety measures, which, Kamil (1970) proposed, "lends support to the psychoanalytic position that the presence of castration anxiety is central to neurosis, or at least to phobias in general [p. 201]."

Following the systematic desensitization treatment, the snake-phobic subjects receiving treatment showed a greater reduction in manifest anxiety than did the untreated group of snake phobics, but still maintained a somewhat higher level of fear than did the normal subjects. On the question of snake avoidance, initially none of the 20 snake-phobic subjects had dared to touch the harmless live snake used in the study. The normals had all been able to touch the live snake in the experiment. On posttesting, nine of the ten desensitized phobics were able to touch the snake, while none of the untreated snake phobics dared do so. All normal subjects again were willing to touch the snake. Clearly, then, systematic desensitization not only reduced the manifest anxiety associated with the symptom, but it also removed this very clear-cut phobic reaction, at least at the time of posttesting.

The critical test of the more general notion in this study comes when one considers the results for the Rorschach and TAT measures of castration anxiety. On posttesting, the snake-phobic subjects in both groups did not significantly differ and continued to show a much higher level of castration anxiety than the normal subjects. At least on this measure, the removal of the symptom had not affected the indications of castration fear as an underlying conflict. For the TAT, however, the treated group of snake phobics did indeed show a significant reduction in castration anxiety, although (compared with the nontreated snake group) the results still fell to the same level as the normal subjects. Kamil interpreted this finding as indicative that the removal of the symptom has some more general positive benefits for subjects and increases their level of self-esteem, as manifested in the changed quality of stories told to the TAT; at a deeper level (on the assumption that this is what the Rorschach taps), however, the castration conflicts were not modified.

One need not accept the specific notion that the Rorschach and TAT measures used by Kamil tap a very specific conflict in an individual, namely castration anxiety. His very definition obviously includes more general scores of mutilation and fears of destruction or attitudes toward bodily impairment that might indeed have been learned early in childhood from overly sensitive parents and might not specifically be related to the genital area in these subjects. It is almost impossible to support the hypothesis of such specificity as a castration complex without some at present unfeasible follow-ups of carefully observed children. Nevertheless, Kamil's data, in addition to providing interesting further evidence of the power of imagery and relaxation in removing a potent symptom, suggests further interesting possibilities about the feedback effects of the patient's experience of success in the course of undergoing treatment. Presumably, the TAT results reflect some degree of self-awareness of mastery and increased competence; these are generalized to the stories which reflect more positive outcomes and more heroic types of figures.

One need not limit oneself to measures such as projective techniques to evaluate the effects on fantasy and thinking of an ongoing treatment. It would seem appropriate to sample widely from subjects' daytime fantasies, night dreams, and various other ongoing daydreams or expectations in order to get a view of what is going on inside a patient in the course of a treatment such as systematic desensitization. While such an ongoing sampling of mental activity cannot help but influence outcome to some extent (a kind of psychological version of the Heisenberg effect in physics), various controls could possibly avoid this and it might give us a much better understanding of the overall experience of the patient undergoing a treatment such as systematic desensitization. Naturally, this proposal applies to all kinds of ongoing psychotherapy. It seems especially appropriate for the behavior therapies, which tend to approach the patient in a relatively circumscribed manner and do not pay as much attention as other forms of treatment to the transferential characteristics of the patient–therapist relationship and to the pattern of expectations or the various hidden agendas that people bring to therapeutic situations.

COVERT AVERSIVE THERAPY AND RELATED PROCEDURES

Punishment Techniques

I have dealt thus far with phobias and various forms of social inhibitions for which systematic desensitization seems especially appropriate.

These behavioral difficulties, although unpleasant for the subjects themselves, are rarely seriously disturbing to others around them and certainly not to society. This may account for the fact that so gentle a treatment as desensitization is employed. If we look at behaviors that are strongly socially disapproved, however, such as various types of sexual perversion and fetishism or addictive behaviors, a different approach is used by behavior modifiers. The techniques usually involve some type of punishment, or aversive, therapy. Certainly if we look at some of the elaborate methods used to deal with sexual perversions, they somewhat resemble the methods of medieval torturers. All kinds of elaborate chemical and electrical shocking apparatuses and procedures have been employed, as well as, in some cases, methods for humiliating the patient in a fairly systematic way. Probably some of the gross misunderstanding of behavior therapy, represented, for example, in movies such as "A Clockwork Orange," reflects the reactions of many sensitive readers to descriptions of the aversive techniques in behavior therapy. Such techniques have a fairly extensive history in this century—perhaps the widest known use being that of the drug Antabuse in connection with alcoholism. In this section, however, I am concerned primarily with imagery techniques employed in various forms of aversion therapy, and I review some of the related applications of imagery growing initially out of the aversion therapies.

As might be expected, many psychologists and psychiatrists have serious questions about the employment of chemical or electric shock methods in the treatment of undesirable behaviors. Typical of some of the aversion methods, used particularly with sexual deviations, are those reported by Feldman (1966) and Feldman and McCullock (1965). These investigators projected slides of sexually attractive males for homosexually conflicted young men. A shock occurred at the appearance of the male picture, and both picture and shock were extinguished by the patient's flicking a switch. Subsequently, as a reward for anticipatory dismissal of the sexually deviant picture, the patient might be shown an image of an attractive woman so as to positively reinforce a heterosexual response. Some success was reported by this method, yet it seems quite complex. The method certainly is cumbersome for many kinds of patients and seems particularly ill suited for homosexuals who are a part of "gay society," where many of the features of homosexuality intertwine with social acceptance, vocational and social opportunities, and with many other positive attributes of urban life.

As Rachman and Teasdale (1969) pointed out, there are significant ethical questions, as well as social ones, that must be raised in connection with the use of chemical or electrical therapies. They have called attention, for example, to an experiment carried out by Sanderson, Campbell, and Leverty (1964) in which patients were injected with a drug that produced a cessation of breathing for up to 150 seconds. This extremely frightening experience certainly had some impact on the patients, but it is unlikely they would have undertaken the treatment if they had been fully informed in advance that it would involve such a terrible consequence. Rachman and Teasdale suggested that it is not very likely that patients can be motivated to cooperate for very long with such frightening treatments.

Noxious Imagery Methods

A much more tolerable alternative to mechanical or chemical therapy is one that rests fundamentally upon the patient's cooperation and his own personal self-control. The method pairs a noxious image with a behavior unacceptable to the patient and one he wishes to eliminate from his response repertory. An early example of this approach was reported by Gold and Neufeld (1965). In treating a homosexual boy, they made extensive use of his own imagery by having him imagine himself in different scenes in which he was close to men of varying degrees of attractiveness in public toilets (where he ordinarily carried on his homosexual solicitations) and then having him experience either repugnance or awareness of a policeman in the vicinity. After a series of pairings of the more frightening consequences or negative images with the previous attractive scenes, a shift was made to increasing scenes of a heterosexual kind, which were to be associated with positive imagery. A significant improvement was made in the young man's orientation in the sense that his homosexual behavior decreased markedly; however, he did not completely lose his interest in men. He was able, nevertheless, to enter into an appropriate relationship with a girl at that point.

A very vivid case study of the treatment of a boy troubled by a recurrent sadistic fantasy was reported by Davison (1968). In this study, Davison used an imaginative combination of techniques built around the patient's imagery capacities, as well as the use of actual pictures of provocative nude women. The patient was encouraged to masturbate with the pictures of the nude women and, at the same time that he was conjuring up images of the more sadistic kind, he was encouraged to generate a very disturbing image that evoked a nauseous reaction in him. He was very carefully brought to the point where the sadistic masturbation fantasies gradually faded because of the association with the noxious image, whereas the masturbation fantasies in the direction of heterosexuality increased to the point of becoming dominant. The persistence of this change in the face of 10 years of practice of the earlier pattern is a striking achievement and points again to some of the power of a careful manipulation of imagery.

Kolvin (1967), also working with adolescents, one a fetishist and the other a gasoline sniffer, had the subjects draw up a list of unpleasant images. Following arousal through imagery of the unwanted behavior, as soon as there was an indication of the patient becoming "turned on," he was encouraged at once to think of the unpleasant scene. Both patients made rapid recoveries within 20 sessions by the pairing of the unpleasant scene (one of a bad fall) with the unwanted attraction. It should be noted that some reassurance and psychotherapy was included in the treatment.

Probably the most extensive use of covert desensitization and of a variety of related imagery techniques for helping to extinguish unwanted behaviors or to increase the likelihood of desired behaviors has been by Joseph Cautela. In a series of papers in the mid-1960s (Cautela, 1966, 1967), Cautela described the use of aversive imagery techniques in the treatment of such maladaptive "approach" behaviors as obesity, compulsive stealing, smoking, homosexuality, and excessive drinking. Essentially, this method involves the development of a series of extremely noxious images, some constructed in advance and some developed along with the patient. These then are used in juxtaposition with the patient's presentation of an image of the very desired behavior. In addition to allowing the patient to generate the image and presenting the negative one in juxtaposition, Cautela developed a series of set scenes that can be used for particular problems. Here, for example, is the scene used in connection with attempting to help a patient overcome homosexual attraction:

> You are in a dungeon. It is dark, smelly and altogether loathsome. As your eyes get accustomed to the light you can just barely see an attractive nude male in the corner of the dungeon. He is gesturing for you to come nearer to him. As you begin to approach him, you think to yourself, boy, this is going to be good. As you think that you begin to get a queasy feeling in the pit of your stomach. Some chunks of food come into your mouth and taste bitter. You swallow them back down. Your throat feels raw. But you continue to approach the guy. The closer you go, the sicker you feel. Your eyes are watery. Snot and mucous from your nose are running down into your mouth. Your stomach is turning. Just as you're about to touch him, you start to vomit. You vomit all over him, all over yourself, all over the floor. You can see him all covered with yellow and brown bits of slimy vomit. His entire body is covered with it, especially his penis. You continue to retch your insides out. Your shirt and pants are full of vomit. You get sick over and over again and vomit all over everything again. You turn away from the guy and start to run out of the dungeon. He grabs for you and you

trip and fall down into a huge pile of vomit. The odor overcomes you and you
vomit again, but nothing comes up . . . you have the dry heaves. Somehow you
pick yourself up, push him away, and run from the dungeon. As you run out
the door you start to feel better and better. When you get into the clean fresh
air, you feel wonderful. You go home and clean yourself up [Cautela, unpublished manuscript].

Any reader who has read this paragraph and tried to imagine vividly
the material described may indeed experience some empathic nausea.
Clearly, there is a certain power to the imagery effect such scenes can
have and with repeated use of them, Cautela reports considerable success in the treatment of a variety of behaviors that people find they
want to carry out against their better judgment.

Cautela has developed a large number of scenes of this kind for use
particularly with alcoholics. One need not repeat in detail examples of
the scenes, but they involve such things as the patient imagining himself walking into a bar deciding he wants a drink, feeling queasy
and nauseous, vomiting all over the bar and over into his beer, and
trying to drink the beer amid floating mucous, and food particles.

After running through the 20 or so scenes in the office with the therapist, the patient is encouraged to carry out further practice. Indeed,
some behavior therapists have even prepared tape-recording methods
for use at home, joining shock and aversive imagery (Feingold, 1969).
Rather dramatic results are reported for the use of covert sensitization
in several studies that have at least to some extent more control than the
usual clinical reports. Anant (1967) used covert sensitization with 26
persons who were classified as alcoholics and had a long history of such
behavior. He found 100% improvement after only a relatively few sessions in the sense that all subjects were abstinent in follow-ups at 8–15
months — a remarkable record. A more controlled study by Asham and
Donner (1968) treated for 6 weeks 23 men classified as alcoholics. It
should be noted that these individuals did not show gross general
psychopathology and seemed in fairly stable family situations. They
were divided into a treatment group that imagined the noxious scene
after developing the drinking scene, a treatment group that imagined
the drinking scene after the development of the image that aroused
nausea, and an untreated control group. The second experimental condition presumably was employed to check on the possibility of this
being a pseudotreatment or placebo group. In actuality, however, it
became clear that whether the alcohol was thought of prior or subsequent to the nausea, the images fused, and both groups began to
react in comparable fashion so that results were combined for the two
of them. The treatment groups showed that, despite an average history

of 18 years of heavy drinking, approximately 40% of the subjects could abstain on a 6-month follow-up, whereas none of the control group showed any change.

Although it is hard to believe that covert sensitization is the answer to our alcoholism problems — consider all the external attractions and social structures built around drinking — the positive results reported so far are a tesimony to the effectiveness of some kinds of imagery techniques. A study by Weiner (1965) carried out in a more experimental vein has made it clear, within an operant conditioning framework, that imagining aversive consequences of a response and actually experiencing the direct aversive consequence of this same response both yielded a reduction in subsequent response rates compared with a control condition.

Cautela (1970) has turned also to control of smoking behavior and reported on some clinical cases. The technique essentially involves the same situation of using noxious imagery paired with the smoking behavior in fantasy and, in addition, use is made of self-instructions and "thought shifting." The patient is often urged to say "stop" when he is actually about to start smoking or feels tempted to smoke; at this point he is to imagine himself vomiting. Cautela reported an unpublished study by Muller where the average cigarette smoking in the covert sensitization group dropped from 15.3 to 3.6 cigarettes a day after six sessions, while a control group showed no special change from a comparably high level of smoking at the outset. Cautela reported other unpublished studies, such as one by Wagner (1969), which involved control groups and 90-day follow-up. They indicated that combined desensitization and covert sensitization may operate together effectively to reduce smoking.

Perhaps the best-controlled study that has appeared in this area is one by Berecz (1972). This study, however, focused not so much on the use of noxious images, but rather on a comparison of actual smoking with imagined smoking followed by an actual shock. Berecz' rather complex study involved an untreated group, a placebo group, and an imagined smoking and an actual smoking group. The last two administered painful shocks to themselves upon actually beginning to smoke or imagining that they were smoking. The groups were also divided into moderate and heavy smokers. The results, in general, indicated the following: For male subjects who were willing to administer sufficiently painful shocks to themselves, in the moderate smoking group, shocking oneself on the actual smoking behavior was somewhat more effective than shocking the imagined smoking, although both of these reduced levels of smoking compared with the control and placebo subjects. For the heavy smoking group, the shock proved completely ineffective when administered in relation to an actual smoking situation. It was, however, dramatically effective when administered for imagined smoking. This result was perhaps the most striking of all the findings in the study. Again, this study points up the significant power that imagery has as a human function. It would be worthwhile to repeat a study of this type with the use of noxious imagery, rather than electric shock, to see if one might get roughly comparable findings.

Cautela and Wisocki (1971) have reviewed the literature on the use of covert aversive imagery in the treatment of various sexual deviations. They reported reasonably good results in the treatment of homosexuality through this method in follow-ups of eight patients. They made the point that the advantages of using both an aversive stimulus and having the unwanted behavior appear in imagination are considerable. The most obvious advantage is that real stimuli are not required; moreover, there is much greater variability in the possibilities suggested, the patients are more willing to undergo the treatment and less likely to develop fear or a sense of being artificially manipulated, and it is a method highly susceptible to self-practice which can be incorporated into the patient's own behavioral repertory. The authors were careful to suggest that because of the complex social involvements that characterize much homosexual behavior and its relationship also to fear and inhibition in relation to women, it is necessary to set the treatment within a broader framework and to include training in self-assertion in relation to women and desensitization of certain fears about female sexuality.

An especially dramatic experimental demonstration of the control of deviant sexual tendencies through noxious imagery has been reported by Barlow, Leitenberg, and Agras (1969). These authors were treating a 25-year-old married man who had a long history of pedophilic behavior both in fantasy and in a number of direct molestations. The second patient involved in this study was also a mature married man with an extended history of homosexual activity. For both patients, a hierarchy of sexually arousing scenes was constructed based on their own fantasies and experiences. Similarly, noxious scenes were also prepared. The procedure essentially followed that described by Cautela, with the build-up to an especially revolting contact with either a child in a sexual situation for the first patient or another male for the second patient, followed then by the relief of an escape from this unpleasant situation. Careful physiological measurement was carried out to indicate the degree of arousal in the patients, as well as their own self-reports.

The results for both self-report and physiological measurement indicated a decline in the desire for the pedophiliac or homosexual experiences in both patients following several days of regular exposure to the noxious imagery. These investigators then tried a clever technique of suddenly discontinuing the pairing of the imagery with the noxious scene. What they did was to present only the sexually arousing scene for 10 seconds and then leave out the next 30-second period, which had been previously filled by the nauseating scene. During this period of no pairing of noxious imagery with the previously desired imagery, there was a dramatic increase in reports of positive arousal in connection with the pedophiliac or homosexual imagery. After 8 days of this procedure, pairing the sexually arousing scenes with the noxious imagery was reinstituted. At this point, there was a dramatic drop in the arousal affect of the previously very arousing sexual scenes. Both patients then showed considerable change with an increase in heterosexual behavior and in the arousal possibilities of heterosexual fantasies.

The study by Barlow *et al.* (1969) also pointed up the fact that covert sensitization was probably the significant factor in the study since the authors, in suddenly terminating the noxious imagery, indicated to the patients that this sudden termination was a regular part of the treatment. If suggestion alone were the cause of the positive results in the initial pairing of unwanted imagery with the noxious stimulus, then there should have been a continuous increase even when the pairing was not occurring, since the therapist had made it clear that this was a regular part of what they considered a valuable treatment program. Instead, when pairing did not occur, there was a dramatic change in desire and in actual overt behavior of the patients. When the pairings were resumed, the progress picked up at a somewhat higher level than before and overt behavioral changes were also manifest.

An important technical point is the fact that in all this work with covert sensitization, the patient is initiated through the use of the progressive relaxation method. This is intriguing since it suggests that primary focus of the relaxation is indeed to enhance the likelihood of generating vigorous imagery, rather than establishing an atmosphere contrary to anxiety. Certainly if it were a question of the relaxation operating to reduce anxiety, the occurrence of the noxious stimuli in connection with the relaxation state should merely reduce the power of the noxious images. Obviously, this is not the case, and instead it is likely that the relaxation essentially creates a situation that makes it possible for the patient to throw himself more deeply into the empathic mood and vivid imagery situation necessary for the noxious stimulation to operate effectively.

Theory of Covert Sensitization

The theoretical basis for the effectiveness of covert sensitization is by no means clear. There have been few studies carried out with sufficient care or attention to the technical facets and timing of juxtaposition to permit us to make the statement that a purely conditioning model is operative. The limitations of punishment in altering behavior, other than producing temporary suppression of certain responses, are well known. It seems much more likely that one is best advised to view the effects of the pairing of noxious stimuli with the attractive, but undesirable, behavior as a way of training the subject to delineate more clearly the situations which occur in fantasy and which lead almost inevitably to a sequence of overt acts that become increasingly attractive. Thus, one step would be to aid the patient in discriminating situations and then provide him with a series of devices for very quickly stopping the further development of the fantasy from leading to action. The patient can, if he is sufficiently motivated to change this behavior, now resort to the noxious stimulation and gradually make the fantasy less attractive and appealing than it has been over the past years. Clearly, there must also be some retraining and cognitive reorientation in other directions, as most of the workers with this technique point out. (Some case examples of my use of this method are presented in Chapter X.)

Covert sensitization lends itself fairly well to a rather structured and formal procedure that yields a possibility of experimentation and manipulation of variables. There are, however, a host of additional approaches to the use of imagery in behavior modification which have been somewhat less amenable to research evaluation, although they may in the future generate such possibilities. I consider these in Chapter VII. For the reader the contrast between the type of material described in the discussion of the European mental imagery approaches or those variants of the techniques now employed in this country and the behavior modification use of imagery must certainly be instructive. It is clear that built into some of the European imagery techniques are facets of both desensitization and covert sensitization, but in perhaps a random and haphazard fashion that precludes the possibility of systematic effects and also of evaluating their impact in any given case. At the same time, the complexity of the material that emerges in the more loosely controlled mental imagery method raises some serious questions about the perhaps oversimplified descriptions of imagery that occur in the behavior modification usage. It seems very likely that even during the fairly controlled presentations of images and paired noxious or positive stimuli that occur in the types of treatment described in this chapter, patients may also be drifting away in fantasies or carrying on some type of interior monologue and feeding back reactions to themselves about the very situation that is taking place.

The fact that covert sensitization and systematic desensitization seem to yield good results underlines the importance of helping patients work systematically at attending to their own processes. It is possible that suggestion effects may indicate that patients are generally being encouraged to value their own internal processes and to pay attention to them, thereby helping them discriminate between negative and positive feedback and providing them with a kind of broader cognitive skill that they can use in other situations outside the treatment hour. If this is so, then one might expect more general improvements in sense of competence and in self-awareness on the part of patients who have undergone training in relaxation and in some form of systematic use of imagery. Kamil's findings certainly support this possibility, but the area remains one requiring further study.

SYMBOLIC MODELING, COVERT CONDITIONING, AND IMPLOSIVE THERAPY

> *Given the existence of independent but partially correlated modes of response to significant stimuli, the psychotherapist can profitably concentrate his efforts on direct modification of the classes of response that the treatment is designed to alter, rather than embarking on a protracted search for unconscious causative agents that one predicts in advance will prove to be concordant with the therapist's particular theoretical predilections.*
>
> A. Bandura (1969, p. 593)

The methods of behavior modification, presented in Chapter VII may be said to have a somewhat circumscribed and almost static quality, at least in their conception. The imagery employed is more or less expected to "stay put." In contrast, when we turn to the various methods of symbolic or covert modeling, covert reinforcement, implosive therapy, covert extinction, or the various self-instructional techniques, the behavior modification approach moves closer to the more dynamic view of the stream of thought that characterizes the psychoanalytic and mental imagery approaches. I say closer, but with a very significant qualification. By employing fairly extended thought sequences that are necessary for covert extinction, modeling, or various forms of private rehearsal, the therapist is, in effect, recognizing the degree to which the patient's flow of imagery is more or less continuous and active. In this sense, there is some comparability to the much freer approaches of the psychodynamic or mental imagery therapist. Still, as suggested in the opening quotation to this chapter, for the behavior modifier, the focus of symbolic behavior, whether in the form of rehearsal, modeling, extinction, or reinforcement, is always very close to the specific behavior to be influenced. This is in marked contrast with the other approaches. Although Leuner occasionally deals with very specific symptoms by having the patient imagine rubbing on magic fluids or by suggesting that the image begin in the general motivational area of difficulty, most of the treatment is designed to modify broad, underlying complexes in conflict areas. The behavior modification uses of these more flexible types of imagery still seem on the whole to be aimed at relatively specific, consciously intended changes in overt behavior. No assumptions appear to be made about underlying conflicts or modification of an unconscious stratum of difficulties.

SYMBOLIC MODELING

With his long series of ingenious experimental studies, the thoughtful and comprehensive *Principles of Behavior Modification*, fine research on social learning and psychological modeling, and finally his strong public stand on such national issues as the effects of television on children, Albert Bandura has emerged as a major figure in psychology during the 1960s. Of special significance for the theory and practice of behavior modification has been Bandura's increasing concern with questions of the nature of imagery and self-representations or related internal processes. Too much of a behaviorist to be comfortable using terms like imagery or fantasy, but too astute an observer of man to deny the significance of central cognitive processes, Bandura has laid the basis for a more systematic understanding of the nature of private experiences, internal monologues, and private imagery as a critical part of the learning process.

A major feature of Bandura's influence in learning theory, as well as in applied psychology, has been his emphasis on observational learning or modeling (Bandura, 1969, 1971). He has been critical of many of the conditioning theories of learning on the basis that they remain atomistic and associationist and can scarcely account for the great rapidity of learning which the child shows. It seems obvious that children learn through imitating their parents, yet imitation thus far has not been the subject of sufficient research. A unique feature of Bandura's position on imitation is the emphasis on a more purely cognitive approach. He has moved beyond Sheffield's (1961) emphasis on the fact that matching of one's own behavior to that of another person or groups is a consequence of a perceptual image of the model events, generally a visual representation. Whereas Sheffield has stressed the association by contiguity to account for rapid learning, Bandura (1971) provided a more complex function for symbolic mediation:

> In the social learning view, modeling stimuli serve more as source of information than as automatic conditioners; observers often perform operations on modeling inputs so that transformational and organizational processes are involved, as well as associational ones: less structural correspondence is assumed between memory codes and the original model pattern; verbal representation is assigned a greater response guidance function; and reinforcement, . . . is treated in social learning as a factor that can facilitate observational learning [pp. 25–26].*

While cognitive theorists, psychoanalysts, and clinicians generally might react to the paragraph quoted above by saying, "What's new? Bandura has discovered thinking!," there are some rather striking differences and implications of the theory that need to be stressed. Bandura has attempted a more precise delineation of the specific processes involved in observational learning; these processes may form a basis for an operational test of specific components in a way not effectively carried out previously. It is certainly true that among dynamic theorists, Sullivan, influenced by the sociology of Mead, was in advance of his time in focusing on interactive processes in development and their role in personality growth. But Sullivan was not able to move more precisely beyond such terms as *empathy* in trying to describe how the child reacted to parental behavior. Bandura is guiding his theoretical system in a direction that permits an examination of the components of empathy and imitation.

Modeling may be viewed not simply as the direct imitation of overt responses, but as their imitation in symbolic form within the child. Modeling also has disinhibitory and response facilitative effects. Bandura, like Paivio (1971), emphasizes the separate coding systems available for verbal and imagery representations. He has called attention to the fact that most learning for greatest efficiency involves an effective interaction between symbolic representations in visual form and the highly condensed verbal coding of these representations. A series of studies by Bandura, Grusec, and Menlove (1966), van Hekken (1969), and Bandura and Jeffrey (1973) makes it clear that symbolic responses are extremely important in the learning and retention of model behaviors or observations.

Especially interesting for our purposes is the study by Gerst (1971) in which college students practiced rehearsal of a complex motor response (actually movements taken from deaf language) in one of several ways. One group simply imitated the original response through the members' own imagery. A second group translated the response by concrete verbal description. A third group tried to develop concise labels to incorporate the ingredients of the response; for example, describing a response involving much interweaving of arm movements as that of an orchestra conductor waving his baton at the end of a symphony. Control subjects performed extraneous tasks to prevent their using symbolic coding.

In the Gerst (1971) study, concise labeling and visual imagery proved equally effective in leading to immediate reproduction. The concise labeling method was especially advantageous when it came to later retention of matching responses and, particularly, when the representation of response elements in the exact sequence in which they had been modeled was desired. It is possible, however, that the concise labeling or verbal method here employed was somewhat contaminated with the kind of visual imagery representation emphasized by Paivio for its superiority in certain types of recall. The use of the image of the symphony conductor, for example, is a vivid visual image that is not unlike the techniques of expert mnemonists in recalling sequences of paired associates. While the purely informational aspects of modeling stimuli in symbolic form have generally been stressed and most studied by Bandura and various collaborators, it is clear that the private rehearsal of model responses is likely to have affective and decision-making implications that can also influence acquiring new forms of behavior or repeating established ones (Bandura, 1971). I discuss the implications of this position in relation to the cognitive–affective theory presented later.

Symbolic Modeling
in Behavior Modification and Attitude Change

A critical feature of the use of symbolic techniques for behavior modification is the indication that strong emotions can indeed be associated with imaginal representations. While this, of course, has appeared obvious to many clinical practitioners, it has rarely been effectively demonstrated in a laboratory situation. Studies by Barber and Hahn (1964) and by Grossberg and Wilson (1968) did, however, find fairly adequate support for indications that the imagined painful stimulation for the visualization of frightening scenes produced autonomic responses roughly comparable to those produced by direct exposure to the noxious stimulus. The importance of covert self-reinforcement has been supported in a study by Weiner (1965). He found that subjects exposed to an actual experience of negative events reduced, without reinforcement, their level of response to the situation; however, subjects also did so when imaging unpleasant scenes. The imagining effect was somewhat less powerful, but it does still point up that representations and feedback can be used in training people to modify behavior.

The large number of experimental studies that demonstrates the various parameters of modeling in children will not concern us here. The power of modeling for changing relatively simple behavior is demonstrated in a study by Luchins and Luchins (1966) in which they were able to show that college students performing a very complex sequence of behavior made tremendous numbers of errors and could not really learn the desired sequence when they were limited to simple verbal statements of right and wrong answers. By observing models who were reinforced for correct responses, these students were able to acquire the entire behavioral sequence rapidly, with a minimum of trial and error and attendant frustration.

The implications for work with children of vicarious modeling experiences in psychotherapeutic fashion, especially to modify disruptive or self-defeating behavior patterns, has been a major contribution of Bandura's group. Long before this development, however, a little-known study by Chittenden (1942) had already demonstrated that exposing preschool children to brief plays in which doll children demonstrated either physically aggressive or cooperative solutions to conflict led to decreases in aggressive conflict between children. Imitative reactions either increased aggression or increased cooperativeness compared with pretreatment behaviors; results were quite strong and persisted for a month. Modeling effects which indicate that extremely socially withdrawn preschoolers can be brought up to a reasonable level of social interaction on the basis of exposure to a film in which a child is initially withdrawn and then gradually interacts with considerable enjoyment have been reported by O'Connor (1969). Demonstrations that various forms of modeling and systematic training in make-believe play can increase the level of such play in preschool and kindergarten children, as well as in older children, have been carried out by Marshall and Hahn (1967), Smilansky (1968), Freyberg (in Singer, 1973), and Gottlieb (in Singer, 1973).

Small-scale studies have also indicated that modeling behavior can improve the effectiveness of pyschotherapy or interview behaviors. For example, Schwartz and Hawkins (1965) found that the availability in a psychotherapy group for adult schizophrenics of two patients who served as models by verbalizing their emotions generated a greater amount of affect than when the models added in the group simply produced neutral reactions. Meichenbaum (1971a, b) has made particular use of various exemplary procedures to improve the subject's ability to play the role of a patient in psychotherapy. Truax and Carkhuff (1967) also have provided some evidence that patients can benefit from examples of what it means to be a patient prior to entering a therapeutic interview.

Much of Bandura's work has involved what may be called vicarious conditioning or extinction through the use of motion pictures or slides. A rather striking study by Bandura and Menlove (1968) demonstrated that children who had a strong fear of dogs could be helped relatively quickly by exposure to brief movies in which model children played harmlessly and enjoyably with dogs. There was somewhat greater generality of the effect for children who observed a variety of models, rather than a single model, playing with dogs. This study had the especially interesting feature of picking up the control, untreated subjects at the conclusion of treatment and starting a course of therapy for them by the same method; in the control group there was subsequent dramatic improvement. Whereas Bandura pointed out that symbolic modeling may be slightly less effective than direct modeling, there are indications that it lends itself to a greater variety of modeling exposure for the child and, therefore, may have better generality in the long run, as well as being more practical for regular treatment sessions.

A well-known study by Bandura, Blanchard, and Ritter (1969) was successful in demonstrating the efficacy of symbolic modeling in comparison with desensitization in the relief of severe snake phobias in adolescents and young adults. The symbolic modeling did indeed involve exposure to an actual movie. Also employed was a method of graduated direct involvement with a snake and a model who encouraged each approach movement of the patient. Of special importance for our purposes is the fact that the symbolic modeling method was quite effective, indeed somewhat more so than desensitization, although all treatments were far superior to no treatment at all. Positive results lasted for at least a month on follow-up.

Bandura (1969) proposed the following formulation of the possibilities of modeling for producing significant behavior change and reduction of aversive reactions:

Repeated modeling of approach responses decreases the arousal potential of aversive stimuli below the threshold activating avoidance responses, thus enabling persons to engage, albeit somewhat anxiously, in approach behavior. Direct contact with threats that are no longer objectively justified provides a variety of new experiences that, if favorable, further extinguish residual anxiety and avoidance tendencies. Without the benefit of prior vicarious extinction, the reinstatement of severely inhibited behavior generally requires a tedious and protracted program. After approach behavior toward formerly avoided objects has been fully restored the resultant new experiences give rise to substantial reorganization of attitudes [p. 192].

My own experience as a patient in psychoanalytic treatment attests to the therapeutically useful effect of an incidental modeling experience and perhaps may make concrete for the reader some of Bandura's points. On one occasion in the course of my treatment, my analyst and I came down from the office to the lobby of the apartment building, where she proceeded to look at the mail. As I walked by the mail table, I noticed a magazine with an especially intriguing subject in its list of contents, and I commented on this to her. My analyst said, "Well, why don't you take this magazine along with you?" I was rather taken aback at such flagrant thievery since the magazine was clearly addressed to a resident in the building. "Oh, go ahead," she said, picking up the magazine and handing it to me. "These people are never here. They live in Texas and the mail just sits here for months and gets thrown out frequently."

I still found myself reluctant to commit a crime against the United States Postal Service, but seeing the freedom with which she handled this magazine I seized it and dashed from the building. Subsequently I was able to examine my inhibitions about this act in relation to a long history of being a "good boy" and found a certain liberating ability to be freer in a great variety of situations. I should point out (and this perhaps is not stressed sufficiently in the behavior modification literature) that my self-analysis and generalization of this incident went far beyond a relatively circumscribed set of behaviors as modeled from the analyst. I quickly was able to relate this inhibition to a larger number of seemingly proscribed behaviors in my past and, in thinking through the implications of the situation, was quickly able to see how many of them were largely unimportant instances of compliance with a frightening authority.

I worked most of this analysis out myself in a relatively brief period after the session and never particularly discussed it with my own analyst, who probably was unaware subsequently of the tremendous impact this particular example of modeling had on the analytic process. Needless to say, the modeling was clearly a combination of disinhibitory and, to some extent, facilitative effects. I certainly did not, however, become a mail thief, nor any other kind of gross criminal. One wonders, however, how much of what actually happens in many forms of psychotherapy is a consequence of modeling in situations where, as I indicated, the therapist may not at all be conscious of the extent to which imitative responses are taking place.

The effectiveness of modeling on reducing inhibitions is graphically presented also in an experiment by Lefkowitz, Blake, and Mouton (1955). These investigators found that a high-status well-dressed person who violated traffic signal regulations was more likely to generate a greater rate of subsequent pedestrian violations than the same violation produced by a sloppily dressed individual. Recently, we have experienced calls for reinstitution of the death penalty for a variety of crimes by the President of the United States and by various governors and local leaders. It seems tragic, indeed, that such leaders do not recognize that their calls for violence, however formally legalized, merely encourage positive attitudes toward violence as simple solutions on the part of the masses of the citizenry.

A potentially important consequence of the power of modeling through symbolism and vicarious experience has to do with the question of attitude change and development of self-regulatory, or internal control, factors. Carlin (1966), for example, was able to show that children could increase their preference for deferred gratification after observing an adult model who was able to wait for delayed reward, while at the same time showing a positive emotional reaction. Bandura (1969) has written effectively on some of the potential uses of modeling and internal reinforcement methods in the development of self-control and (to some extent) experiences of power and self-esteem. He called attention to what he has termed *intrinsic sensory consequences*, in which once certain skills are learned by the child, they may feedback self-generated visual or auditory stimuli that are positive. There are also anticipatory consequences that may be present in the form of fantasies or sometimes delusions. A third way in which behavior may become free of situational dependency relates to internalization of self-reward and self-punitive imagery in connection with specific events previously observed and perhaps moderated subsequently through private rehearsal.

Bandura has characterized some of the self-generated consequences we experience as fear controlled, whereas others are conscience controlled—the *shame* versus *guilt* distinction widely used in psychoanalytic formulations. He made the important further point, however, that such internalized standards are rarely completely free of external influence. In many cases, individuals seek an alliance in smaller reference groups that share similar orientations, and these groups not only may explicitly reinforce particular internalized values, but may serve as internalized models through imagery for subsequent self-reward or self-punishing behavior. These internalized reference groups undoubtedly contribute also to reactions of patients in therapy, not only to their therapists, but in a sense to the whole class of patients they know going to this or other therapists of the same school. Indeed, in places like New York City or Los Angeles, graduate students in clinical psychology or residents in psychiatry may bring pressure to bear on fellow students who have not entered psychoanalysis or some form of psychotherapy or do not report certain kinds of experiences as an outcome of their therapies.

COVERT MODELING, EXTINCTION, AND SELF-REGULATORY SYMBOLIC APPROACHES

Cautela and Covert Conditioning Methods

Whereas Bandura has been primarily concerned with the development of a theoretical system and the test of various components of the system of parameters of the observational learning experience, other investigators have moved more directly into a variety of psychotherapeutic approaches using symbolic modeling within a behavior modification framework. Some of the methods of symbolic modeling that have long been a part of psychotherapy need not be outlined here at any length. Certainly many aspects of Moreno's role-playing and sociodramatic methods, as well as the role-reversal technique, represent manifestations of modeling with the likelihood that some of their effectiveness comes about through subsequent symbolic or imaginal replaying of the experience by the patient in moments of privacy. Some of the role-taking techniques used by Kelly (1955) in his personal construct therapy similarly represent such covert modeling exercises. Within Gestalt therapy there are many "off the top of the head" introductions of modelinglike procedures in which an individual may talk to two sides of himself and empathize with one or the other in playing out a significant conflict of attitudes that he has uncovered. In effect, a procedure like this is usually demonstrated to some extent initially by the therapist or by other patients in a group or workshop, and then can be incorporated into private rehearsal periods. Quite recently Bandura and Barab (1973), on the basis of an experiment on effects of adult and peer-modeling upon snake phobia, have suggested that some forms of systematic desensitization may be special cases of vicarious modeling experiences.

A more explicit use of modeling has been proposed by Cautela (1972). As Cautela noted, modeling was used long ago by Mary Cover Jones (1924) in her classic study of fear reduction in children. His proposal is to approach the patient in a very straightforward fashion, describing the advantages of modeling, based on Bandura's research, and encouraging the patient to develop extensive imagery that can be used to change certain kinds of behavior. Through interviews with the patient, a set of scenes is then constructed specifically to present the patient with an alternative to the pattern of behavior that is causing him difficulty and he would like to change. These scenes are practiced in the session itself and are assigned to be practiced very extensively by the patient in private.

In the case of a homosexual who reported that he was troubled by the urge to have sex with both male and female at the same time, Cautela (1972) proposed the following image:

> I want you to imagine you are watching a movie, and the male has a woman by one arm and the male on the other. He is walking with both of them towards the bedroom. Just as he reaches the bedroom, he pushes the male aside and says 'Get away from me; I don't want you!' He then takes the girl into the bedroom, puts his arm around her, and kisses her tenderly, and looks very happy [p. 7].

For a woman who found that she got into rapid escalating arguments with her husband once he shouted or swore, Cautela proposed that she imagine herself at a movie in which a husband is shouting and raving at his wife. The wife in the movie, however, remains perfectly calm and does not seem at all troubled. The patient is instructed to repeat this kind of image consistently during the session and then again at home during regular practice sessions. It should be noted that the imaginary husband and wife are different people from the patient and her spouse.

As Cautela indicated, covert modeling primarily places the emphasis upon the imagining of someone other than the patient carrying out the act in a fashion that the patient then can emulate. It is possible that this approach gives the patient just a bit more distance from the scene and may make it easier to practice this type of imagery than if he himself is the subject under circumstances that might arouse considerably greater fear. A small study has been carried out by Cautela and his colleagues (Cautela, 1974) comparing overt modeling in the case of snake and rat phobias with covert modeling; the control group simply discussed fear of rats. After three treatment sessions, both modeling groups improved significantly on six different posttests of reduction in fear of the rat. The control group showed improvement only in willingness to take a few steps closer to the rat. The overt modeling group, which observed an experimenter actually fondling the rat, did not differ significantly from the covert modeling group, which merely imagined the experimenter fondling the rat. On five of the six measures employed, the overt group was superior only in scores on a self-report measure of fear.

While this study was on a relatively small scale and lacked some important controls, it did suggest that covert modeling is indeed potentially useful. It is taught relatively easily and less likely to arouse anxiety. Since many people find it difficult to picture themselves in an image, it provides an easier basis for them to develop scenes that will work in the session and in private rehearsal. The covert modeling technique also lends itself to combination with methods such as the technique of covert reinforcement. In some of the examples cited, a subject not only sees the model in his image resist the tempting, but socially undesirable act, but also is often rewarded subsequently or feels a considerable relief afterward.

Cautela (1974) pointed out the possibilities of other types of combinations, for example, covert modeling with covert sensitization, and the likelihood that increased generalization of the effect can be obtained by alternating covert modeling with scenes in which the subject himself is the significant model. Many patients in psychotherapy often report that they deal with certain unpleasant situations or help themselves get through unexpected dilemmas by imagining that their therapist is alongside them or is actually dealing with the situation. I myself have used this technique. This involves encouraging patients to imagine that I am with them in some difficult moment or that some other respected person is available with whom they can carry out an internal conversation as a way of diverting themselves from a great immediate fear or tendency toward an impulsive act. Such a method may also serve as a way of bringing to mind alternative modes of response.

Somewhat different from the specific method of modeling, but related to it, is the extensive use that Cautela makes of *covert reinforcement*. The first step in a procedure like this is to develop for the subject a set of images that can be shown to be effective for him. Cautela and Kastenbaum (1967) have developed what they call a *reinforcement survey schedule*, which is used to help identify these reinforcers for a given person. This schedule includes (1) a group of reinforcers that either can be presented directly to the subject, or in modified form, or are available for imaginary representation; (2) situations reinforcing to the subject; and (3) frequently occurring behaviors of the kind that lend themselves to the operation of Premack's principle. The schedule is in keeping with the notion that any behavior that is highly prepotent for a given individual can serve as a reinforcer for some other form of behavior. If the subject reports a particular kind of music or aesthetic experience as high on his list of reinforcements—something he enjoys very much on frequent occasions—the subject then can be encouraged to regularly imagine these types of scenes so that he is used to producing them relatively at will in the session. The relative speed with which the patient can produce the image is important. Its production should come close enough in time to the situation to be reinforced to insure some associative link. Cautela, of course, has explored other types of images besides the ones on his schedule to make sure that he is getting a sufficiently diverse and powerful group of potential stimuli from a given subject. It is important, to vary reinforcers lest they lose some of their effectiveness through repetition.

In many ways, the covert reinforcement procedure is close to the emotive imagery or positive imagery technique described in Chapter VI. The patient may report difficulty in carrying out a particular sequence of actions about which he is rather shy. He is first trained to have available a series of reinforcing images that will come to mind as soon as the therapist says, "Reinforcement!" Next the patient is encouraged to go through each step of this difficult action sequence, for example, asking a girl for a date, walking up to a girl at a dance and asking her to dance, etc. At each phase of the overall behavior sequence, as soon as the image is clear, the subject is to signal with his finger; at this point, the experimenter calls for reinforcement, and the subject immediately produces the appropriate image. Thus, practice at home is strongly recommended in covert reinforcement.

In the case of attempts to control socially undesirable behaviors, covert reinforcement is often combined with thought-stopping, covert sensitization, and covert modeling. For example, in a covert sensitization approach to homosexuality, the patient may be encouraged to imagine himself becoming violently ill as he approaches a male nude; as he moves away from this contact and starts to give up the contact, he is encouraged to imagine he feels better and then to think of the reinforcement image. The farther he gets away from the situation, he is encouraged to imagine himself saying, "What the hell, am I crazy to do something so disgusting?," which is followed immediately by the reinforcing image. The same technique is used to encourage positive attitudes toward girls in the case, say, of homosexuals. Cautela (1970) gave an example: "I want you to imagine you see a luscious-looking girl on the street, and you say to yourself, 'Oh, boy, I'd love to feel her soft skin against my body [p. 11].' " This then is followed by the instruction for reinforcement, and the patient immediately produces a vivid reinforcing image. Next the patient is encouraged to think to himself that actually girls are more fun sexually than men; at this point, he again is given the signal for reinforcement and thinks of the positive image.

This technique has also been tried by Cautela in keeping with Premack's (1959) conditioning principle to change a thought sequence from one predominantly negative in tone and self-denigrating to a more positive one. This has been applied in the case of somewhat obsessive types of rumination, wherein, for example, a young man who is concerned about sexual adequacy with girls may be encouraged to think a whole series of thoughts contrary to his usual trend—"I can satisfy girls as much as any other fellow"—followed immediately by a reinforcing stimulus. Extensive practice on thinking new positive thought, followed immediately by reinforcing images, seems to have been effective in changing some of the belief systems of clients. This result is indeed remarkable if it can be verified in subsequent research, for it has the promise of getting at some of the most disturbing and difficult symptomotology of neurotic patients—their endless rumination about potential failure and their self-recriminations.

The use of covert reinforcements clearly relates to the development of a repertoire of techniques that a patient can begin to rely on for himself to overcome the frequent experience of helplessness or powerlessness in the face of well-established neurotic trends. Cautela has tried to draw the parallel between the so-called "learned helplessness" found in animal research studies and reported more recently in observations of children (Reppucci & Baker, 1969; Dweck, 1972). This is an important contribution of much of the work on covert modeling and covert reinforcement. Essentially, these are techniques that the patient can begin to master for himself and can help to raise his own self-esteem as he is aware that he has skills that can be used in his own best interest.

Again we see that some of the criticisms launched at behavior modification therapists by psychoanalysts or other groups such as the client-centered therapists are unwarranted in cases where, in effect, the effort of the therapist is to provide the patient with methods by which he can ultimately feel a sense of greater self-control and independence because he has alternatives to "running to the therapist" when he experiences fears or obsessive doubts. In keeping with his learning theory orientation, Cautela (1969) called attention to the fact that reinforcement, while initially at the 100% level in training sessions, gradually should be reduced to a ratio schedule of partial reinforcement so that the final schedule, once a response has been well established, is probably a one-to-five ratio of reinforcement images to actual production of the image to be reinforced.

Cautela has carried out some experimental studies designed to demonstrate that imagery reinforcements can indeed change attitudes or beliefs. For example, Ascher and Cautela (1972) tested the notion that, by pairing a noxious image and the reduction of that noxious image with a neutral stimulus, they could use the neutral stimulus to modify estimations of size in simple geometric figures. The results generally supported the findings and, thus, presumably strengthened the general use that Cautela has made of covert reinforcement techniques. Studies by Cautela, Walsh, and Wish (1971) have also provided some support of the possible effects of covert reinforcement on changing beliefs and attitudes. In this study, attitudes of the subjects toward mentally retarded persons were increased in a positive direction by pairing of thoughts about retardates with reinforcing scenes. A study by Cautela and Wisocki (1971) was able to show that attitudes toward the elderly could also change in a positive direction by pairing images of old people with reinforcing scenes. Another study by Cautela, Steffen, and Wish (1974) also indicated that covert reinforcement could be effective in modifying size judgments.

A brief note of skepticism must be introduced at this point in connection with Cautela's work. Although there seems little doubt of its findings, the experimental studies of Cautela's group are on a relatively small scale, modest, and lack some major controls. They need also to test alternative models to be thoroughly convincing. Cautela has proposed a great proliferation of covert techniques. One is something like covert negative reinforcement: the person pictures a more frightening scene than the one he is trying to overcome and then the less frightening one. In getting rid of the more frightening scene, he experiences a sense of relief when he thinks of the less frightening one. An example of this would be a man who doubts his sexual adequacy and is encouraged to think of a much more frightening scene, perhaps being shouted at and fired by his boss. He begins the image of this more frightening scene and then is told to substitute for it the less frightening scene of being in bed with his wife; subsequently he experiences relief. Many of these methods sound "gimmicky" and are not yet supported by any extensive research of the kind carried out in connection with other methods cited earlier. One need not doubt the word of any given clinician about the effectiveness of a specific technique. However, it remains to be seen whether the techniques will work effectively in other hands and are indeed working for the reasons that Cautela suggests. This makes it essential that we mount further research, testing specific facets of the covert techniques.

Nevertheless, Cautela is to be congratulated for his own imaginativeness in examining the potential of imagery for effective use in a great variety of conditions. His work also points out that many patients such as alcoholics or sexually confused persons are capable, with help, of generating a great range of imagery that can be put to use for their own benefit. These findings open new vistas for the therapist who in the past has relied too often on simple verbal interchange. Cautela's work also frees the behavior modifier of an excessive concern about developing mechanical apparatuses suitable for shocking or projecting pictures or providing a kind of laboratory atmosphere which, while impressive initially, is not terribly practical for the many patients who must ultimately rely on their own resources in a great variety of social situations.

Meichenbaum's Self-Regulatory Techniques

Quite recently, a very interesting series of covert modeling and self-reinforcing techniques, as well as methods for developing internal controls that stem in part from desensitization, has been generated by Meichenbaum (1972). Beginning with an intriguing study of the modification of operant levels of schizophrenic speech, in which he was able to show that schizophrenics could increase the level of "healthy talk" they emitted (Meichenbaum, 1969), this investigator applied some of these self-talk and related internal imagery methods to a great variety of clinical and quasi-educational situations. For example, Meichenbaum (1971), using the cognitive style measures of Kagen (1966), was able to show that when impulsive and reflective children were studied directly, the impulsive children's verbalization tended to be of a less mature, less directed quality compared with those of the more reflective children. They tended to imitate sounds or animal noises or repeated words, but did not organize their speech in self-guiding fashion compared with the speech patterns of the more reflective children.

In a second study, Meichenbaum and Goodman (1969) were able to show differences in the way in which kindergarten children actually made use of suggested verbal descriptions in the course of various tasks requiring motor control. The impulsive children seemed less able to organize their speech around self-instruction and tended merely to say the words without any clear understanding of meaning, whereas the reflective children used the words actively to modulate behavior.

In a subsequent study, Meichenbaum and Goodman (1971) developed special training procedures for children in which the experimenter performed a task to serve as a model for the subject and then had the subject perform the same task, while the experimenter carefully instructed the subject aloud about the task. The subject then was trained systematically to perform the task *instructing himself* aloud while carrying on the task, then gradually internalizing these instructions by whispering, until finally the instructions took place covertly. The self-instructions involved questions about the nature of the task, answers to the questions (including a certain amount of anticipatory rehearsal), the use of these self-instructions for self-guidance, and finally a certain amount of reinforcement in the sense of saying something like, "That's good!" The study was carried out in fairly careful experimental format with placebo and assessment control groups and resulted in the improved performance on a variety of cognitive tasks. The improvement lasted for a month at follow-up.

A study by Meichenbaum and Goodman (1971) was also able to demonstrate that the modeling of the experimenter was not crucial in the study, but that the behavioral rehearsal was especially important. The authors pointed out that more recent clinical work is aided by the use of imagery methods such as, "I will not go faster than a slow turtle, slow turtle [Meichenbaum, 1972, p. 101]." The importance of such training taking place within a make-believe setting also is stressed and fits in well with the body of research on the importance of self-control in children (Singer, 1973). Thus, Meichenbaum (1972) described the impulsive child playing with the therapist and being told, "I have to land my airplane, slowly, carefully into the hangar." The child is then encouraged to follow the same pattern, but to talk for the control tower and instruct the pilot to come in slowly. In this way, the child gradually learns to slow down his own movements through a combination of imagery and self-instruction.

A basically similar method was employed by Meichenbaum and Cameron (Meichenbaum, 1972) in training hospitalized schizophrenics to improve their performance on a variety of cognitive tasks and to focus their attention more effectively by self-communication. It is felt the effectiveness of self-communication in connection with motor tasks is an important first step, as the authors realized, but they also called attention to the fact that since most schizophrenic symptoms are a consequence of feared social interaction, this type of procedure would have to be gradually expanded to a variety of social settings to be fully effective. Meichenbaum pointed to the uses of imagery and fantasy play as a means of helping some patients carry out certain types of cognitive tasks, for example, imagining that a light they are monitoring is actually a radar signal for a plane approaching. It is suggested that such methods might encourage patients to begin modeling more "task-relevant series of images."

A second general approach by Meichenbaum and his co-workers has been applied to phobic and speech- and test-anxious subjects, as well as patients wishing to control smoking behavior. Again, self-instructed methods were used with the attempt to control more negative self-statements and substitute for them a series of positive self-statements, as well as fairly clear-cut instrumental alternatives that could be carried on covertly through imagery and interior monologue. Meichenbaum (1972) also carried out a small study in which a cognitive modification technique which involved "coping" imagery on how to handle anxiety and self-instructional training proved to be, if anything, somewhat more effective than desensitization in helping students reduce test anxiety. Follow-ups and grade point averages also supported this finding. There seemed to be a general reduction in broader aspects of anxiety. The desensitization groups in a similar study of speech anxiety showed reduced speech anxiety; yet, desensitization was limited largely to a very specific situation, whereas self-instructional techniques used by Meichenbaum usually were more successful for general anxiety.

Meichenbaum and his co-workers use of coping imagery is a method that combines some of the elements of covert modeling, emotive imagery, and covert reinforcement. A critical part of this method is that it does indeed provide a series of steps that the patient can "take home" in the way of dealing with difficult situations. A particularly intriguing study by Meichenbaum was one in which a group of students considered relatively low in creativity was offered a series of self-instructional techniques. One group received self-instruction training involving both imagery and some of the focusing techniques of Gendlin (1969). There were also control groups. The subjects were trained first to identify the many negative self-statements they made in interior monologue about their capacity to perform. They then were encouraged to produce incompatible positive attitudinal self-statements and also to carry out a variety of task-relevant problem analyses and descriptions of their ongoing performances. Finally, they were encouraged to engage in a variety of fantasy and reverie activities involving imagery. A group simply concentrating on the production of its own feelings and allowing the feelings to come to the surface without the additional self-instructional methods was used as the control. The experimental subjects demonstrated significant improvement both in originality and flexibility on tests of divergent thinking. They also showed an increase in their preference for complex materials which clearly related to creative tendencies and also showed significant improvements in their production of human movement responses to inkblots, which are associated frequently with imaginativeness. Last, they showed positive changes in self-concept. The subjects receiving only the focusing training, although becoming more aware of bodily feelings and feeling themselves to be more creative on the basis of the experience, did not actually improve in performance on a variety of tests. The importance of the more specific pattern of imagery training and self-instructional techniques for improving the level of creativity of subjects seems to be strongly suggested by this ingenious experiment.

Meichenbaum has also developed from these methods a series of *stress inoculation techniques,* which make use of training people to modify what they say to themselves, to replace negative with more instrumental and positive imagery. In a series of reasonably well-controlled experiments he has been able to show the advantages of such procedures. In general, this relatively recent body of research and technique development seems impressive and encouraging because it combines therapeutic effectiveness and a series of well-formulated procedures that seem eminently researchable.

Implosive Therapy and Flooding Techniques

A treatment method that has attracted considerable attention and a flurry of research activity in the past 6–7 years was introduced by Stampfl (Stampfl & Levis, 1967). *Implosive therapy* is a mix of a psychoanalytic catharsis orientation with an approach derived from the theory of extinction through massive adversive stimulation, or "flooding" (Malleson, 1959; Rachman, 1968; Wolpe, 1958). This procedure is based on the following principle: if a subject is exposed in imagery to a series of extremely frightening consequences of a feared situation, without actually experiencing directly these consequences, the original fear will be extinguished for lack of reinforcement.

Suppose that someone is suffering from an exaggerated fear of dirt to the point where he will not touch the seat of a bus or the hanging strap in a subway for fear of contamination, or he is afraid to empty the garbage for fear of getting dirt on his hands. A massive imagery attack on this phobia is launched. The subject may be expected to imagine that, when he picks up the garbage pail, a huge host of revolting insects crawls out from it. He next imagines that someone has urinated or defecated all over the can, that fecal matter of animals is there and drains onto his hands, etc. In the course of vividly picturing all of these frightening consequences with considerable associated affective expression, the subject in actuality is not experiencing the direct consequences of this fear. As a matter of fact, no act of emptying garbage or of touching objects is likely to be anywhere nearly as stressful as what he has gone through in his imagination in the course of the sessions. Bandura (1969) quoted Stampfl's comment: "He who has lived in a septic tank need not fear the dirt found in a waste basket [p. 402]."

Hogan and Kirshner (1967) have proposed that symbolic or imaginary expression of the cues to which the original anxiety response has become conditioned leads to the likelihood of extinction of the learned phobic reaction because (1) the unconditioned stimulus, which may actually be significantly harmful to the subject (the terrible smells and crawling things on the body), do not occur when actually paired with the conditioned stimulus; and (2) the effect of anxiety as a secondary source of reinforcement has become weakened by repeated use without the occurrence of the initial unconditioned stimulus.

In general, implosive therapy begins with an exploration in some detail of the nature of the phobia to be treated and then calls for the institution of very vivid imagery practice of the most noxious consequences of the fear. Most of this material is played out privately in the presence of the therapist, who encourages the patient to act out the material as dramatically as possible, with as full an expression of affect possible in the clinical setting. Individual case reports are rather dramatic, indeed, in a description of the patient's reactions (Boulougouris & Marks, 1969; Boulougouris, Marks, & Marset, 1971; Hogan & Kirshner, 1967, 1968; Levis & Carrera, 1967).

A review of the literature by Ayer (1972) makes it clear that the more experimental attempts to examine the process of implosive therapy are far from conclusive and often seem to contradict the theoretical position, despite some individual case reports of good success. In practice, implosive methods have involved a number of variations, each of which has somewhat different relationships to learning theory and also different possible consequences. One of these grows naturally out of Wolpe's approach, namely, the notion that an intense grouping of imagined scenes from a hierarchy under conditions of relaxation should lead to extinction of the fear in this area because of reciprocal inhibition. A second approach, closer to Rachman's (1969) concept of *flooding*, calls for the imaginary reconstruction of a very large number of frightening or dangerous scenes without, however, imagining specific involvement of the patient himself. No relaxation training is required for this particular treatment. Closer to the original implosive theory approach is the third variation in which the imaginary situation involves the patient himself as the victim of often wildly improbable consequences of the frightening situation.

A major problem with the third type of implosive therapy has to do with eliminating sources of expectation and therapist variables from the treatment. Kirchner and Hogan (1966) tried to get around this problem by actually tape-recording instructions and attempting to help patients thus overcome rat phobias, but their results were far from conclusive. The control condition, which consisted of listening to music while thinking of pleasant scenes, could scarcely be expected to create the anticipation of improvement on the part of the subjects that was expected from the much more dramatic implosive method. As a matter of fact, it would be a rare subject who would *expect* to do better after an instruction merely to listen to music. The fact remains that more than one-fourth of the subjects did improve after the control condition. Although this percentage was significantly lower than the percentage of subjects who improved after the implosive therapy, it makes one wonder whether the clinical situation was sufficiently realistic for us to take this experiment seriously as a test of implosive therapy. Studies by Borkavec (1972), Fazio (1970), Hodgson and Rachman (1970), and Watson and Marks (1971) have raised serious questions about the theory and process of implosive therapy. Indeed, on the basis of reviews of the theory and relevant research, Morgenstern (1973) and Zachary (1974) have proposed that implosive techniques may be better understood in relation to a cognitive expectancy situation.

Zachary (1974), for example, suggested a model of the implosive therapy method that attempts to incorporate the following results, which have actually been reported in the literature:

1. Implosive procedures have had mixed results, with at least some degree of positive outcome, but with many instances of negative outcome, too.
2. Under some situations, there may actually be a worsening of the condition of the patient following a flood of negative imagery (Bandura, 1969; Rachman, 1969).
3. In many cases, reduction of avoidance behavior may be produced by the subject imagining irrelevant scenes, as well as those directly relevant to the initial complaint (Watson & Marks, 1971).
4. Watson and Marks also found that if one used as a criterion actual reduction in the level of autonomic arousal and in the reports of anxiety, then irrelevant imagery was more effective than imagery directly related to the frightening event.

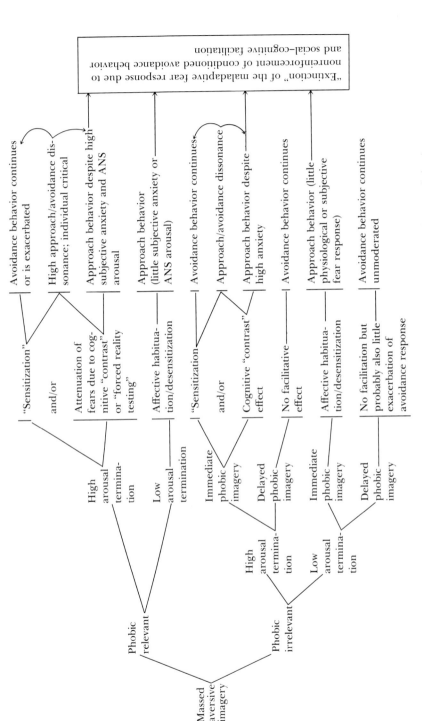

Figure 1. A cognitive-affective model. (From Zachary, 1974, reproduced by permission.)

169

5. In at least one study (Fazio, 1970), a rational examination of the phobic situation turned out to yield better results in overt behavior for subjects than imagination of frightening events relevant or irrelevant to the actual feared situation.
6. The timing of the relationship between the period of arousal and the occurrence of the imagery specifically related to the feared object is also a critical condition with evidence (Hodgson & Rachman, 1970), indicating that subjects who experience the emotional arousal and the phobic imagery in close proximity are more likely to show subsequent improvement in behavior.

In Figure 1, Zachary (1974) has analyzed, on the basis of these empirical results, a series of potentially different outcomes for an implosivelike treatment situation and this figure is reproduced here as an example of the kind of analysis of the cognitive–affective situation which may prevail in a variety of psychotherapeutic approaches.

Examination of Figure 1 suggests that under conditions in which the subject experiences a high degree of flooding of negative imagery associated with a specific fear and terminates the treatment session in a state of high arousal, one might expect the real danger of an increase in the frightening behavior or in an increased conflict situation. Because of a "contrast" effect, the possibility exists that the subject may come to tolerate his high level of fear more and approach the frightened object, but remain quite as fearful as before. This is not a bad outcome, but clearly not as desirable as a treatment capable of relieving the subject of the anxiety itself. If one follows Figure 1 under outcomes down or across, one sees a variety of possibilities, some of which are clearly susceptible to more extended experimental tests.

It is undeniable that there is a great attraction about implosive techniques. I have had some positive results using implosive therapy in the instance of an individual unrealistically frightened about possible attacks by street-corner boys. The method also has some of the appeal that the primal scream and related cathartic approaches seem to have. That it also has dangers of worsening the condition of the patient, as Bandura (1969) has noted, cannot be doubted. My view is that extensive application of the original Stampfl approach is not warranted at this point, and better methods are now available for dealing with phobias without the risk involved in the implosive approach.

CHAPTER VIII

THE SCIENTIFIC STUDY OF IMAGERY AND DAYDREAMING PROCESSES

> . . . *afferent sensory information is not directly transformed into a conscious report. What is consciously perceived is* imagery *which is created by the organism itself . . . the world we perceive is a dream we learn to have from a script we have not written. It is neither our capricious construction nor a gift we inherit without work. Before any sensory message becomes conscious it must be matched by a centrally innervated feedback mechanism. This is a central efferent process which attempts to duplicate the set of afferent messages at the central receiving station . . . matching the constantly changing sensory input is a skill that one learns as any skill. It is this skill which eventually supports the dream and the hallucination, and which central sending produces as the conscious image in the absence of afferent support.*
>
> SILVAN TOMKINS (1962, p. 13)*

We have traveled a long distance through a complex series of approaches to psychotherapy and claims for the nature and function of imagery or fantasy approaches in the attempt to ameliorate emotional distress or modify personality. The reader by now should be aware of the Tower of Babel effect in the mental health field to which attention

---

was called in the beginning of this volume. Can we now, at least in a beginning way, move toward relating the vast range of imagery usages in psychotherapy to some basic notions about the nature and function of imagery and stream of consciousness, and also to material that is to some degree susceptible of scientific evaluation?

I use the word *beginnings* quite seriously. We are at a time of a sudden and exciting upsurge in awareness on the part of behavioral scientists and, more specifically, experimental psychologists working in fields such as learning, memory, and, more broadly, cognition. The experimentalists at last are turning their ingenious flair for methodology to the study of the covert processes that clinicians take for granted. The position I take in this volume is that imagery and fantasy processes are not mystical effluvia of some spiritial essence or processes grossly different from ordinary motor or cognitive behaviors. I believe it sad indeed that experimental psychologists for most of this century have failed to attend to the systematic study of a variety of covert behaviors which most human beings easily report are going on "within" them and which no truly alert adult can now deny are critical features of the experience of being human. But the delayed incorporation of imagery and daydream or fantasy processes into the mainstream of scientific psychology is water under the bridge. It would be best for us to turn our attention to the findings of the most recent research and also to newer theoretical conceptions which might make possible the ultimate understanding of what goes on in the variety of therapeutic usages of imagery.

THE TREND TOWARD SCIENTIFIC STUDY OF IMAGERY

As suggested earlier, the revival of interest in imagery stems from the confluence of several streams of research. One of these has to do with the important advances in our understanding of the psychophysiology of sleep and dreaming (Kleitman, 1963; Oswald, 1962) and the emergence of the truly impressive interdisciplinary effort that has characterized the membership of the Association for the Psychophysiological Study of Sleep (Chase, Stern, & Walter, 1972).

Of particular importance in the information being generated by the sleep research movement is the very clear evidence that throughout much of the night, sleeping subjects appear to be processing very complex information. Although the exact nature of the association between vividness of dreaming reports and the emergent Stage 1–rapid eye movement (REM) phase of the sleep cycle has yet to be well understood, the fact is that considerable content can be elicited from the other sleep stages as well. It would, therefore, appear that even in the most profound state of withdrawal from external stimulation, some degree of covert self-stimulation in forms of images or interior monologues seems present.

The relationship of our important discoveries about the sleep cycle to waking daytime behavior has not been extensively studied as yet (Johnson, 1973). An important implication of the evidence of such a considerable degree of interior activity during sleep suggests that many kinds of private rehearsal in imagery or verbal modes are under way much of the time in adults and children. It is entirely possible that even waking behavior is characterized by a comparable complexity of covert information processing along with the kinds of directed thought or cognitive activities that we normally view as a part of consciousness. There may even be fluctuations in the degree of awareness of such processes or perhaps in their intensity or frequency as a function of a daily cycle (Krippke & Sonnenschein, 1973).

If it is indeed the case that so much is going on, then experimental psychologists studying how we learn about the world or what role memory plays in sorting out new experiences in the environment, or attempting to study the role that imagery plays in a specific learning situation, will have to take into account the fact that a tremendous amount of ongoing rehearsal is already in progress and that the experimental manipulations introduced in the usual cognitive experiment must be viewed against a background of this complex processing. Studies I have carried out with various collaborators on the ongoing stream of thought (Antrobus *et al.*, 1971; Singer, 1966, 1970) make it all the more evident that even in tasks demanding considerable attention in order to produece accurate responses, subjects once cued to be aware of task-irrelevant mentation will report a surprising degree of such thought even though accurately performing their tasks.

A second major stream of research that has contributed importantly to the necessity for cognitive experimental psychologists to take note of imagery and fantasy processes has come from research on sensory deprivation. These studies originally were set up presumably to tap significant aspects of the nature of brain function in the absence of sensory input (Hebb, 1960). However, they soon began to produce very striking evidence of the degree to which ongoing imagery processes are a central feature of human experiences, particularly when reduced demands are made on the perceptual apparatus to process the complex stimulation ordinarily available in the physical environment of the individual. (Holt, 1972). Quite possibly, the rather dramatic results obtained by the ingenious experiments on drastic reduction of sensory inputs in these experiments have been especially influential in forcing upon the more behaviorally oriented psychologist the necessity for including some research on imagery in their attempt to describe human cognitive processes.

Holt (1972), who has been especially active in documenting the revival of interest in imagery, also has called attention to the effects of "psychedelic" involvement in hallucinogenic drugs, which has in the past decade created much greater awareness on the part not only of the young people but of the scientific investigators (some of whom have emerged from this younger generation) of the potent effects of private imagery. Certainly, the similarities of language from the LSD trip to the imagery travels under the direction of a guide as used in the mental imagery therapies is far from accidental. For a variety of reasons that themselves call for very thorough sociological analysis, there has been among young people, in particular, and intellectual groups, more generally, in Western civilization a revival of interest in consciousness as a specific experience and in attempts at self-understanding and self-analysis. This development has sent thousands of students flocking into psychology classrooms (only to be turned off frequently by demonstrations of operant conditioning in rats and pigeons). The trend also has made fortunes for practitioners of the various forms of mind expansion and self-awareness that have been developed in prepackaged form and sold as franchises like frozen custard stands.

In the 1960s, many young people, as well as radical or liberal leaders, became scornful of psychoanalysis for its "mind fucking" tendencies, viewing self-analysis generally as an evasion of responsibilities for social action. The new, accelerated interest in private processes may be a reaction against the manifest failure of direct-action methods to modify in any substantial way the structure of our social system or to relieve in any major fashion the gross social injustices in racial and economic areas that characterize our society. The reaction against social radicalism does not seem a sufficient reason for the increased fascination with images, fantasies, and also with the more fantastic possibilities of the human condition that have in the past been viewed as unscientific or associated primarily with religion and superstition. The revival of interest in fantasy in literature (such as the response to the books of J. R. R. Tolkien), the interest in science fiction, novels of witchcraft and possession, and the increasing attention paid by relatively educated young people to various forms of Satanism, astrology, and psychic phenomena such as ESP, thought transfer, or reincarnation are surprising indeed. To what extent some of this interest will pass as another fad in an era in which the extensive communication process quickly satiates interest in specific areas (much as popular songs zoom to the top of record lists and fade almost as quickly) remains to be seen. Nevertheless, this movement, as is often the case with such movements, has forced greater interest on the part of serious investigators toward processes such as imagery and daydreaming that can only gain from systematic scrutiny and can, if treated intelligently, increase the scope of our understanding of the total human experience.

Given, then, the varied forces at work to produce an interest in research on imagery and related processes on the part of the experimental psychologists, can we briefly document some of the general directions that this new interest has taken in the areas of systematic research in psychology? McKellar (1957) beautifully summarized the literature to that date, particularly in the areas of imagery and undirected thought. A major conclusion he drew was the distinction between what he termed *A* and *R* thinking, that is, highly personal thinking, oriented around private needs (*A*) as against thinking oriented toward realistic interaction with the environment. Such a dichotomy was in itself not a major advance over Freud's (1962) early distinction between *primary* and *secondary process* thoughts or over the even earlier delineation by Jackson (1958) of *propositional* and *referential* thought. McKellar was able, however, to bring together systematically a great class of human experience described in the diverse literature, but rarely integrated for clear presentation. This classification of the great variety of hypnagogic or of various kinds of hallucinatory experiences set the groundwork for subsequent efforts such as those by Richardson (1969) and Horowitz (1970). If we move to even more recent works in this field, such as Paivio's (1971) impressive review or Segal's (1972) or Sheehan's (1972) collection of papers, we suddenly find ourselves in the midst of a vibrantly active field in which a whole host of information is being generated and, in addition and quite important indeed, more systematic organization of the phenomena and parameters of imagery in relation to a variety of adaptive functions such as learning and memory can now be represented.

Imagery

An example of this kind of advance is the by now reasonably well-established finding that imagery and perception seem in effect to be manifestations of a common brain process (Segal, 1971) and probably use the same common pathways in the brain. Such a proposition greatly increases our willingness to regard imaginal activities without the kind of suspicion and skepticism previously characteristic of the scientific psychologist. This susceptibility of imagery to rigorous experimental study in a variety of situations, as Segal demonstrated in her group of experiments, for example, has carried us a long way toward losing our sense of mystique about this covert process. The fact that results from very different experimental methods may lead to a common conclusion about the functional role of imagery in relation to perception also is an indication of the potential power of the experimental method in this area.

Segal (1971) carried out her research on what has been called the Perky phenomenon. As we have discussed, if one imagines a particular object as if appearing on a blank screen and if a picture of the object or almost any visual signal is flashed faintly, but ordinarily discriminably, on the screen while a subject is imagining, the imager may not be aware of the "real" stimulus in his visual field. Segal explored a great variety of the parameters of the Perky phenomenon and was able to demonstrate in many experiments that it was a genuine human experience in which, if one studied the relative role of detecting the external signal in the auditory, as well as in the visual, realm as a function of the concurrence of a same or different modality signal, it could be shown that blocking of the external signal was modality specific. This finding would suggest that imagery and perception share common brain pathways. A similar result was obtained by Antrobus *et al.* (1970), who used a very different format. They found that subjects processing visual signals were less likely to report visual daydreaming concurrently while their reports of auditory fantasies were unchanged. When processing auditory signals, subjects reported few auditory daydreams, but a constant level of visual fantasies.

Extremely important studies of the role of imagery in learning and memory and in relation to the nature of the language process itself have been extensively documented by Paivio (1971). For example, it is increasingly clear from a variety of experiments that one function that imagery serves is to assist in certain types of recall where the specific vividness of an image arousable by a certain word may give it greater probability of recall or recognition compared with the kind of word that, by its abstract nature, is less likely to provoke an image. Paivio cited dozens of studies that bear on the question of interrelation of a concrete image to recall processes and has also called attention to the interrelations of meaningfulness and imagery in a variety of verbal processes. Paivio emphasized what is now an increasingly accepted notion in psychology: different coding strategies and, perhaps, even learning principles obtain for concrete or abstract materials or for materials that involve visual, as against verbal, imagery components. In an elaborate effort to tease out the different implications of visual imagery and verbal mediation in a variety of learning situations, Paivio (1970) proposed that superior memory depends on increased availability of a number of different coding systems for the effective storage and retrieval of perceived materials. Paivio (1971) stated:

> The superiority of imaginal and verbal mediators over rote repetition presumably can be attributed generally to the discovery, under the mediation instructions, of higher-order visual–spatial or verbal–sequential units that incorporate to-be-associated items as components and from which the response can be decoded by a process of implicit labeling or associative responding. The decoding may involve a search process in which appropriate responding is dependent upon recognition memory once the mediator has permitted the generation of possible alternatives. Visual imagery, when readily generated may be more effective than verbal mediation because the information in the image is spatially organized permitting a rapid read-out of the relevant components, whereas the information in verbal storage is sequentially organized as a string of 'mental words' that may take up more space in memory, or require longer search time with less efficient retrieval of the relevant response during recall, or both. In addition, a symbolic motor component may contribute to the transformational efficiency of mediating imagery. Where both systems are relevant to the task, however, they preesumably interact continually in their mediational functioning, and imagery mnemonics may be especially effective because they enhance the probability that both symbolic systems will be brought into play in the learning task [p. 391].

I quote Paivio at length to convey to the reader the degree to which increased sophistication about the overall cognitive process is now capable of incorporating imagery into its structure. The role of imagery can be seen to be one of substantial significance in the overall method by which we come to learn about our environment and to store information for effective retrieval when external situations demand such careful searches of the stored material.

Recent experiments have gone even further in attempting to understand how imagery operates to increase the effectiveness of certain types of learning activities (Bower, 1970, 1973). Viewing verbal and visual processes as separate representational systems for the brain has yielded extremely interesting new information on learning processes and also poses intriguing challenges for theorists about the nature of the underlying neurophysiological structures. Bower (1970), for example, showed that if a subject is to learn sets of word pairs, then free recall of such pairs is more effective if he generates images about the pairs, such as dog and locomotive, and then puts the two words to be learned in an interactive representation. Thus, the image of a dog driving a locomotive is likely to lead to better subsequent recall of both the words *dog* and *locomotive* than simply trying to remember the words without generating images, or when images of a dog and a locomotive are generated independently. This type of research, which has been elaborated further in other experiments (Seamon, 1972; Sternberg, 1969), seems in general to indicate support for a notion that language processes are sequential and, therefore, time consuming in their storage and retrieval characteristics, while images are parallel in processing form, that is, one can scan all the details of an image at a "glance," rather than have to produce each in turn to the same degree, as is necessary in recall of a sentence. The interactive image takes advantage of the superior parallel scanning possibilities inherent in the visual imagery system.

Without going into more detail on many of the technical implications of research on imagery for learning, I wish to note again that once serious scientific investigation is addressed to the problem of imagery, important new findings on the structure of imagery in relation to the cognitive capacities of human beings become possible. Indeed, extremely important new findings scarcely anticipated have emerged from studies of ocular activity during processing of imagery and fantasy (Singer, 1966; Singer, Greenberg, & Antrobus, 1971; Meskin & Singer, 1974), studies of interactive imagery representation (Seamon, 1972; Bower, 1970), and studies of eye shift during cognitive activities (Day, 1967; Bakan, 1969, 1971; Kinsbourne, 1971; Kocel, Galin, Ornstein, & Merrin 1972). These researchers have suggested, first, that the brain is differentially specialized for representation of verbal and visual kinds of material or storage of verbally coded materials or imaginal representations. They also have suggested that there are intriguing individual differences in the tendency of people to rely heavily on verbal or imaginal processes in ordinary responses to questions and perhaps also as a reflection of differential development of the different halves of their brains. This new area itself has just begun to generate research, but it may open new directions for exploring how imagery processes operate, what relation they bear to the structure of the nervous system, and how significant individual differences may be in their effective employment.

The question of individual difference in imagery and fantasy processes is being revived vigorously on the basis of these new approaches to the cognitive process. Thus, Bakan (1971) has accumulated considerable evidence that subjects who tended to shift their eyes to the left when engaging in reflective thought were more likely to be persons much given to imaginative thought, aesthetic sensitivity, and emotional, religious, or spiritual orientation, whereas subjects who relatively frequently shifted their eyes to the right during reflective thought tended to be more verbal or quantitative in orientation, more objective and dispassionate, and more "logical" in their organization of thought. Meskin and Singer (1974) also found that subjects who might be described as inner attentive were more likely to be those who shifted their eyes to the left while thinking of answers to complex questions or trying to remember early childhood material; on the other hand, persons low on measures of daydreaming and inner sensitivity were more likely to be those who shifted their eyes to the right in such a situation. Seamon (1973) reported that subjects engaged in interactive imagery in learning paired words were more likely to respond more rapidly to material depending on the arousal of the right hemisphere of the brain, thus suggesting that the right hemisphere was indeed more involved in imaginal processes and the left, in verbal processes.

Aside from the specific question of brain asymmetry, there is, from these new approaches, increasing evidence of important differences in the orientation to the use of imagery or related mediating processes. Dunn, Bliss, and Silpola (1958) found that persons who showed what might be called *extraceptive* values — that is, greater interest in objectivity, impersonal, and practical issues — tended to differ considerably from those high in *intraceptive* values — that is, persons who were subjective, "tender minded," and oriented toward aesthetic, religious, and social values. The former group responded more rapidly in a variety of situations and gave more associations involving contrast and also seeming to involve much less use of mediating processes. The intraceptive subjects took longer to respond, were more likely to give descriptive associations, and also were to provide responses indicating complex mediating activities, particularly visual images. This finding is similar to the report by Meskin and Singer (1974) that the inner-attentive subjects, who were also more likely to be the persons who shifted their eyes to the left during reflective thought, were also likely to give more extensive responses to questions involving visual recall of complex material from the past or fantasy material of some kind. Results such as these would clearly have ultimate implications for the techniques of psychotherapy, which have until now ignored almost completely the predisposing set of the patient to produce or attend to his own ongoing imagery.

The power of imagery to evoke physiological change has been supported fairly recently in a series of studies. Simpson and Paivio (1966) have reported on the changes in pupillary size during images produced to both abstract and concrete words. Schwartz (1971) developed a clever technique for presenting subjects with word cues that generated private images and measured physiological changes pegged directly to these time-locked cues. May and Johnson (1973) measured the heart rate and galvanic skin response of subjects who were thinking images of an arousing, neutral, or inhibiting nature in a time-locked cue sequence. Thus, for arousal the subject was given words such as "murdered," "massacred," "mutilated," for inhibition, "peaceful," "tranquil," and "restful," and neutral words included "particle," "triangle," and "rainfall." The results for heart rate in particular showed rather striking changes. Heart rate was elevated relative to the neutral word base for the arousing words and depressed (although not significantly so during the inhibiting word presentations.

This very sketchy review of some developments in the field of imagery has been presented hopefully to whet the appetite of the serious reader for much more extensive investigation in references dealing specifically with the topic. My concern is not so much with presenting an extensive review, but rather with pointing to the fact that a significant and sophisticated body of literature on the nature of imagery is now developing that has relevance for understanding the various effects occurring in psychotherapy. The reader may also note that the language used by investigators such as Paivio becomes, if perhaps a bit drier, at the same time somewhat more precise and related to the information-processing tasks of the organism. The importance of terms such as *coding strategy, retrieval processes,* and *rehearsal* stems from the fact that they can, in general, be defined fairly precisely in experimental settings and quite possibly even in therapeutic situations. The important point in this connection is that imagery has its place in the general array of cognitive processes.

It is now reasonably possible to demonstrate the role of imagery without relying solely upon the verbal report that an image was or was not present. Some learning experiments make it clear that no other method of representation could have produced the particular learning outcome. The experiments and application of signal detection theory by Segal (1971) and Fusella (1972) to the study of imagery in the Perky experiments also make it clear that the impact of imagery is demonstrable without specific verbal report. Indeed, although we are still far from knowing clearly how to ascertain, by the use of objective methods, if a person is engaging in an image or fantasy in an ordinary social situation, there is increasing evidence that a shift of gaze and a fixation of the eyes may both be reasonably adequate indications that some type of "extended search" of the long-term memory system is under way or that the subject is processing a fantasy (See, for example, Antrobus *et al.*, 1964; Day, 1967; Marks, 1972; Meskin & Singer, 1974; and Singer & Antrobus, 1965). It appears as if important battles in the struggle for recognition of imagery as a fundamental part of man's behavioral repertory have been won; we must now progress, as the work of Paivio suggests, to detailed examination of the various parameters of imagery in a range of cognitive processes.

Dynamic Imagery and the Stream of Thought: Structural Factors and Individual Differences

Thus far, the focus has been primarily upon the single image or the relatively delimited or circumscribed scene that is, of course, most likely to be studied in systematic research. As William James noted, however, our own ongoing consciousness is characterized much more by the metaphor of a stream which like Heraclitus' river is never the same at each point that we dip into it. Indeed, it can be argued that much of the reliance upon the single image, which characterizes work such as that of Paivio or Bowers or even the assumed relatively fixed imagery characteristic of behavior modification methods (Weitzman, 1967), would fail to address the issue of the ever-changing nature of spontaneous conscious awareness. Most experimentalists who have studied imagery are in the position of portrait or landscape painters or still photographers when perhaps the phenomenon they seek to understand is best captured by the flowing style of a James Joyce in literature or by the art of the cinematographer in movies like "The Pawnbroker" or "Midnight Cowboy."

In a series of studies I conducted with John Antrobus and others we attempted to study the daydream or various manifestations of the ongoing stream of thought, to date with modest success. And only brief beginnings of efforts by other investigators in this field can be cited (Klinger, 1970; Krippke & Sonnenschein, 1973; Singer, 1971). In one series of studies, for example, Antrobus and I set up situations in which an individual had the primary task of detecting some signals or of maintaining a watch requiring vigilant attention to a light or a tone over long periods of time under conditions precluding much external attraction other than attention to the task at hand. In these circumstances, by having the subject free associating aloud continuously so that we could monitor his ongoing speech or by interrupting regularly (every 15 seconds), we could obtain reports either of the presence or absence of stimulus-independent mentation or task-irrelevant imagery over long periods of time. Results from quite a number of studies seem to make it clear that under these conditions, the investigator obtains considerable evidence of much ongoing thought that is unrelated to the actual attentiveness of the signal or the self-feedback about the subject's own performance during the task. It should be kept in mind that subjects were generally paid for correct responses, and in most of the experiments 90% accuracy in literally hundreds of detections of signals was maintained by the subjects. Thus, there is evidence of a very impressive rate of processing of private ideation that is generally far removed from the particular task. One may grant that other perceptual attractions are limited by the circumstances of the experiment and that the experiment itself is what may be called an "understimulated task" in the sense that there is nothing terribly interesting about paying attention to lights. The fact of subject accuracy, however, makes it clear that the amount of fantasy produced under these circumstances is not simply a consequence of gross sensory deprivation. Indeed, many of the environments in which we find ourselves in daily life—riding on buses or subway trains, driving long stretches of well-known highway, sitting in our homes or business places amid objects we have seen thousands of times—all these constitute relatively understimulating environments, as well, and it is likely that the laboratory situation is not as different as it at first appears to be.

Our data and data obtained by Klinger (1970) and Krippke and Sonnenschein (1973), in addition to recent studies by Filler and Giambra (1974) and Horowitz (1970), all point to the fact that a good deal of the time we are indeed carrying on complex processing of imagery sequences and fairly elaborate chains of thought that are often unrelated to some specific task or social situation in which we find ourselves. Our data has suggested it is not easy to suppress such ongoing thought (Antrobus, Singer, & Greenberg, 1966; Antrobus et al., 1970; Drucker, 1969).

The indications from quite a number of these studies of signal detection behavior and of concurrent task-irrelevant thoughts suggest that some kind of active processing is under way much of the time in the waking behavior of the individual, as well as during the night. These thoughts are of great variety and scope. Although many of these experiments seem somewhat artificial in the sense that they isolate subjects in a booth, the content of the material reported has also been shown to be comparable *thematically* to the content of reports of night dreams by the same subjects (Starker, 1974).

Growing out of attempts to tap into the ongoing stream of thought are studies of some of the individual differences in predisposition to be aware of, or to report, the type of material. Antrobus, Coleman, and Singer (1967) found that subjects who reported on questionnaires that they were given to a great deal of inner fantasy and daydreaming were more likely to report a considerable amount of stimulus-independent thought during an ongoing signal detection task. They also differed in the pattern of their responsiveness to this situation.

Daydreaming may be carried out both concomitantly with the processing of external information (*parallel processing*), but there are also indications that sequential processing occurs, that is, shifting between attention to private material and processing external information. Such shifting can lead to some decrements in signal detection. Since much of the information in our environment is redundant, it is possible to get away with a good deal of daydreaming without necessarily missing too many of the external signals of our environment. True, there may be some cost in engaging in, or in being aware of, ongoing daydreaming for various tasks (Antrobus & Singer, 1964; Antrobus *et al.*, 1966; Antrobus *et al.*, 1970). Such losses in alertness may be made up for by advantages in maintaining interest, generally positive emotional responsiveness, and reduced irritability in the face of long waits or boring tasks. There are also indications that many people make use of fantasy opportunities for planning. Some of this planning may be explicit and involve anticipations of immediately forthcoming events, such as how to deal with an interview or preparation for an examination. In many instances, however, it seems likely that the planning is more subtle and complex and has many of the characteristics also now shown for dreaming that involve examinations of major unfinished business in the individual's life and anticipation of a far-reaching nature about a variety of modes of dealing with these "current concerns" (Breger, Hunter, & Lane, 1971; Klinger, 1971; Singer, 1966).

A fairly extensive series of studies has attempted to determine more precisely the individual patterns or styles of attentiveness to inner experience or awareness of ongoing daydreaming (Fusella, 1972; Singer & Antrobus, 1963, 1972; Starker, 1974). Essentially, many data seem to suggest that individuals differ in the styles of daydreaming they show along about three dimensions. One of these dimensions involves a tendency to produce vivid and elaborate content with a generally positive cast to it and with an acceptance of daydreaming and related inner experiences. A second dimension that has been identified in a series of factor analyses has been a tendency for persons scoring high on this factor to report much negatively toned inner activity often strongly linked with guilt fantasies and with experiences of "tortured self-concern." A third pattern is characterized by fearfulness and anxiety, distractibility, boredom, and fleeting, rather than elaborated, daydreams with content minimally developed.

There is increasing evidence that self-reports of ongoing day-dreaming, as measured by questionaires of this type, represent more than test-taking attitudes. Fusella (1972), for example, found that subjects scoring high on measures of positive–vivid daydreaming, as well as other measures of "inner acceptance," proved more likely to report their imagery in an experimental situation as more vivid. In fact, they tended to miss the occurrence of an external signal while they were producing such vivid imagery in experiments dealing with the Perky phenomenon. Antrobus *et al.* (1967) also found evidence that both reports and accuracy of detections during a signal detection experiment reflected differences comparable to those in the questionnaire studies of daydreaming. Meskin and Singer (1974) found intriguing differences in patterns of eye shift, as well as in the type of memory material produced by subjects who differed in their predilection for different patterns of fantasy as measured by questionnaires. Feldstein (1972) also found that persons differing in daydreaming style responded differentially to deprivation of the REM sleep stage.

The studies of individual differences do not yet permit us to ascertain whether different reports of daydreaming frequency or styles reflect in general different degrees of *attentiveness* to ongoing experience, or completely different patterns of *content* in these experiences, or possibly differential patterns of *willingness to describe* certain types of experiences. It seems likely, however, that even in the case of subjects who report relatively less frequent daydreaming or more vague content, some degree of ongoing inner processing is taking place much of the time. I would hazard a guess that if most people were put into situations in which they were periodically questioned about "stimulus-independent thoughts" during the performance of ordinary day-to-day tasks or routines, we would indeed find a tremendous amount of such activity. Probably the results would be comparable to those of night-dream studies in the laboratory, where practically every subject ever studied has produced considerable amounts of material upon being awakened—despite the fact that many people profess they do not dream at all, or certainly do not remember any dreams.

I have again gone at some length into this area, not because we have clearly definitive results as yet and a full knowledge of the phenomenon, but rather to point out that the technology is now available for a considerably more sophisticated gathering of data on various parameters of ongoing imagery sequences and the continuous nature of the stream of thought. Detailed accounts of much of this research are available elsewhere (Klinger, 1970; Singer, 1966, 1970; there also are many studies in progress). The important thing for the clinically oriented reader is to recognize that the tools are becoming increasingly available for establishing a scientific base line against which to evaluate ongoing imagery as it is used in psychotherapy, as well as to evaluate it against broader principles of the nature of imagery sequences and the normal process of daydreaming.

THE INTERACTION OF AFFECTIVE PROCESSES AND INFORMATION PROCESSING

Emphasis thus far in this chapter has been primarily upon the information-processing activities of the organism. This would be, however, insufficient to account for the obviously dramatic and personally significant results that emerge in psychotherapeutic uses of imagery. Where does the dimension of human emotionality come into play? Here I propose that the psychology of emotion or affect has also achieved only recently a new measure of significance. Psychologists and psychoanalysts have always talked extensively about emotion and paid lip service to the notion that "feelings" are what really count in psychotherapy, yet there was no real, systematic theory of affect developed in the field until the beginning of the 1960s. In 1959, Schachtel published his seminal work on the close relationship between memory and a differentiated affect system. McClelland, Atkinson, Clark, and Lowell (1953) had already called attention to the significant role of emotion as the basic motivating pattern rather than drive. There is now increasing support for attention to the affect system in human beings as a critical feature in understanding incentives both to continue and to terminate patterns of behavior, to be curious, to become violent, or to demonstrate nurturing or peaceful responses.

Perhaps the most developed and sophisticated theory of the interrelationships of affect or emotion and information processing has been presented by Tomkins (1962–1963). Tomkins' position essentially represents a Darwinian view that man has evolved a fairly large, but circumscribed, number of emotions which provide him with information about his own motivational structure and which also, through manifestations primarily from facial expression and more general body response, communicate to others emotional experience and potentially motivating information.

Tomkins' theory proposes that affects or emotions are one of five basic systems which combine to determine man's behavior: *homeostatic, the autonomic regulatory system, the drive system, the affect system, cognition,* and *the motor system.* Although drives may in most instances be essential for survival, their primary role in human motivation is to signal the presence of deprivation states. It is the affect system that is viewed in Tomkins's theory as the major motivating system. Affects may amplify drive signals or may in their own right provide the organism with rewarding or punishing experiences. Affects themselves, however, are subject to the information-processing activities of the brain and particularly the rate and complexity with which new material has to be processed.

In Tomkins' position there is a limited number of differentiated affects that may be triggered by fairly specific differences in the information-processing tasks that man faces. For example, massive inputs of new or unassimilable information produce startle or fear responses; moderate rates of new information generate interest or excitement, which are positive affects; and the sudden reduction of high levels of seemingly unassimilated information (as in delayed recognition of an old friend, seeing the point of a joke, or finding good news upon opening a letter) leads to the positive experiences of joy or laughter. High rates of unassimilable or complex information persisting over long periods of time lead to the negative affects of anger, despair, and sadness. Thus, the flow of information, the readiness of the individual based upon his past experience, cognitive style, his anticipation of a situation, or his planning for the situation—all these play an important role in whether negative, punishing affects emerge or whether the positive rewarding affects of interest (a moderately rising gradient of new information) or joy (a moderately declining gradient from a high level of novelty) are experienced.

Inspection of Figure 2, which is drawn from Tomkins' (1962) *Affect, Imagery, and Consciousness,* will help the reader grasp what has been presented in very condensed form here. Tomkins employs the term *density of neutral firing,* which implies the degree to which there is a massive involvement of neural activity from various brain areas. Since this is not an easily measured variable, I have preferred to translate it into assimilability of information. If the doorbell rings and one goes to the door and it is a child returning from school at the usual time when he is expected, then that information is easily assimilated since it was largely anticipated in advance. If, on the other hand, the doorbell rings and a long-lost relative, a gorilla, or two FBI men are there, one is most likely to respond with a startle reaction. In the first case, after the initial startle response, recognition of the relative should lead to the experience of joy and much smiling. In the cases of the gorilla and the FBI men, a great deal depends on what follows from the situation; but the chances of a persisting high level of density of neural firing and, hence, negative affect are much greater.

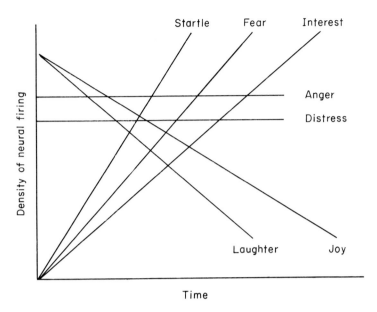

Figure 2. Graphical representation of a theory of innate activators of affect. (From Silvan Tomkins, *Affect, Image, and Consciousness,* p. 251. Copyright © 1962 Springer Publishing Company, 200 Park Avenue South, New York, N.Y. 10003)

The combining of affects and the learned patterns of manifesting affects are, of course, of great significance and depend heavily on particular cultural and family experiences. Nevertheless, as Figure 2 suggests, the innate triggering of affects is closely related to the information-processing load and patterning of environmental stimulation. One can add to this notion the possibility that one's ongoing stream of thought presents an alternative stimulus field to the material available from the external environment (Singer, 1966). Sometimes in the course of an activity that demands considerable attention to the external environment, we may suddenly be reminded of some significant bit of unfinished business in our lives.

Consider the example of a man at work who is asked by a co-worker to help him find the key to the storeroom. Suddenly, the man realizes that he has his own car keys in his pocket and that he left home with them and failed to give them to his wife, thus preventing her from using the family car for shopping and taking the children to the doctor. The full impact hits him and he pictures the scene of the car parked in front of his house and his frantic wife looking desperately for the key. He may startle and then become quite distressed since there is little he can do for the moment about reducing or assimilating this new information. His co-worker may perhaps notice his distress and be puzzled since all he did was ask about the keys to the office storeroom. In effect, then, a private event and unrolling of a memory sequence triggered perhaps by some external cue (although not necessarily so) may have much the same psychological impact and capacity to trigger affect as the complex externally derived information may.

A similar example may be used to point out how positive affect can be aroused on the basis of a sequence of private events. Suppose that the same man has now been showing this distress for a few minutes to his puzzled co-worker and is frowning and perhaps pounding one fist into another in annoyance, self-recrimination, and frustration. Suddenly, he recalls that for emergency purposes he once hid a set of keys under a flower pot on the back patio. As the image of the flower pot comes to his mind, but without the knowledge of his puzzled companion, he may suddenly feel a dramatic drop in the persisting level of unassimilable material and break out into a grin or chuckle and maybe snap his fingers. He now is showing strong positive affect, and yet all of this may seem utterly confusing to the co-worker.

I believe the reader can amplify extensively on many instances of the unrolling of private sequences that have both positive and negative affective consequences, sometimes more or less openly revealed depending on the subject's own emphasis on control of affect, the nature of the social situation, and so on. Needless to say, the social context is a critical factor in the consequences of any arousal of affect privately. Consider the possibility that in the course of sexual passion a young woman may make a remark in a tone of voice that almost exactly duplicates a scene in a comic movie. Her lover may recognize the remark and suddenly break into laughter only then to be accused of not really feeling passionately about the wonderful experience they are sharing.

A FORMULATION OF ONGOING THOUGHT

Storage and Retrieval Patterns

Tomkins' (1962–1963) integration of the information-processing tasks of the organism with the affective system and the elaboration I have suggested based upon the novelty and differential assimilability of sequences of *private* events, as well as externally derived information, lead to a more complex feedback notion of ongoing experience than is ordinarily available in the usual stimulus–response formulations. In view of the tremendous complexity and changing quality of available external stimulation and the fact that the eyes or body are fairly actively moving in both situations, some combination of anticipatory models with a filtering system organized by some "central executive" in the brain must be postulated. This formulation, put forward very effectively by Miller *et al.* (1960), has also been elaborated upon by many other cognitive theorists. Neisser (1967) has argued that the notion of such an executive is strongly defensible by analogy with the computer usage of routines and subroutines, which permits hierarchial structures and the unrolling of certain sequences that can be stored for use in dealing with each set of new inputs available to the sensory systems. Human development calls for learning various anticipatory routines and subroutines so that, as new information becomes available to us, we can process it rapidly, assign it to appropriate categories, screen out superfluous material, and still perhaps have time for appropriate physical activities or have "channel space" for private elaborations of the ongoing activity (Singer, 1966).

But this cognitive view of routines and subroutines would be misleading if we limited it to the notion of highly organized sequences of thought. Indeed, this unfortunately is a limitation of many computer models and of many of the earlier views of perception. Freud's (1962) insight into the nature of primary and secondary processes in thinking or McKellar's (1957) *A* and *R* thinking need to be incorporated into this kind of system. Neisser (1967) proposed that much information that we take in is stored or processed continuously in more or less the modality in which it occurred, most especially, the visual modality. It thus lends itself to parallel processing more readily [as Paivio (1971) has noted] and is evident in the many diffuse visual images or phrases of conversations that make up our conscious experience. At the same time, we make efforts usually more organized around verbal coding systems to classify abstractly or to schematize these sequences for more efficient coding and retrieval. These processes involve more of a sequential system in which one verbal code must follow another by contrast with the more "chaotic" parallel structures of images that occur to us as we carry on a conversation or try to make a point.

As an example of this combination of parallel-processed imagery material set against the more sequentially processed highly organized material which we use for communication or in order to engage in the most formal operation of thought, I can cite my own response as I write this particular section. As I attempt to present some of Neisser's position and also refresh my memory by looking up material in his book, pictures come to my mind of Neisser himself—when I have met him. I have an image of him presenting a talk at a research conference in which we both participated. Images also of other persons who are mutual friends and an image of a colleague who has tragically died since then come to mind. Much of this information is not formally usable in expounding Neisser's view.

The concurrence of images and sequences of phrases or other events that parallel the ongoing expository process of directed thought or communication of thought has also been adduced by Neisser to provide a broader basis for incorporating Freud's view of the slip of the tongue into the general cognitive system. Since a speaker not only has the organized routine that is unfolding to present to his audience, but also is fleetingly aware of an array of seemingly more or less relevant images, chances of incorporating some of this other material into the communication process do exist. The slip of the tongue that seems particularly meaningful may be just one example of many possible slips that occur because of the special potency of the material and the urgency with which the speaker experiences conflict about the communication he would like to make.

A rather striking instance occurred at a recent open meeting of a regional psychological association. A motion had been put forward by some more radical members and was being discussed heatedly on the floor. The chairman of the session, while attempting to be impartial, could not from time to time conceal his irritation with the apparent impulsivity of some of the self-identified radical speakers. Finally, when the time came for a vote, he said, "All in favor of the revolution say 'Aye!'." Clearly, what happened was that he had been carrying on a parallel process of images, probably particularly related to one young woman who had spoken not long before and had especially identified herself as a revolutionary and had presented her position on the resolution in very intemperate terms. Undoubtedly, the chairman had been reflecting on all of these recently occurring events as he prepared his own formal statement and while obviously not wanting to take an open stand, his annoyance and the vividness of the imagery of the recent scenes combined to permit him to reveal his true picture of what was behind the resolution.

Neisser's (1967) important point about the primary and secondary processes is that both are essential for effective thought. The primary process material, perhaps stored without complex labeling initially and being somewhat vague, can be acted upon again through rehearsal and reexamination until it becomes stored in a more sequential fashion that can be ultimately quite useful. Rather than limit this notion to the special case of creative thought, Neisser emphasized that all visual and auditory perception, as well as directed thinking, are dependent upon earlier forms of a more holistic grouping of inputs.

By emphasizing similarities between visual perception and memory processes, Neisser is laying the groundwork for the position taken in this volume and in earlier research on daydreaming (Singer, 1966) that one's own ongoing stream of thought represents a competing stimulus field with the material to be processed from the external environment; and, furthermore, our routines and subroutines must filter and process new environmental information and must also be filtering out the ongoing imagery of the parallel stream of stimulation from long-term memory. Survival depends usually upon our being more attentive to external sources of information and giving this direction of information a greater priority. As Rapaport (1960) put it—there is a permanent gradient toward external cathexis. Nevertheless, there are also important routines and predisposing sets in given individuals which more heavily weigh ongoing material from long-term storage. These may also be adaptive under particular sets of circumstances.

At a boring formal reception, tea, or cocktail party, a professor or a businessman may find himself going through the motions of conversation while actively processing some important material relating to his own work. Indeed, he may even realize something important and may break into a smile or laugh of pleasure at this private discovery and then have to cover up his response by some social rationalization. The practiced writer or playwright may similarly be more involved mentally replaying scenes and possibilities that occur while he is actually participating in a social situation. He may hear a phrase in a conversation or notice a gestural nuance which intrigues him, and he may mentally code these incidents for later retrieval and possible use in some dramatic or fictional form.

Many writers habitually carry notebooks and often interrupt ordinary conversations in order to scribble notes. In effect, however, the notebook is simply a more efficient way of insuring storage of the material; psychologically, the act carried out completely privately of "ticketing" certain images or events for assignment to particular categories or for subsequent replaying of them in privacy may reflect the selfsame attitude. We all do something of the same kind with much of our day-to-day perceptual activity—we code it and assign it to certain categories that are labeled for approporate retrieval at special occasions. Sometimes, if they are important enough, we say to ourselves, "I must remember that," but many times we do not go through the conscious motions, but merely carry through the process relatively automatically much as we drive a car, with many complex motor activities that have become fairly automatic and do not require conscious thought for each one to unfold in sequence.

It is through the system of labeling and coding that we gradually build up the various hierarchies of routines and subroutines that we will later use for processing new information. In the almost automatic establishment of various coding and retrieval sequences for new information lies one of the major features of the origins of imagery and fantasy. Superimposed upon this natural sequence may be particular sets toward labeling or processing that may be specific to certain types of content or may show certain generalized characteristics. For example, the specialist in a particular area of work or the connoisseur with a particular type of aesthetic interest may notice and label for retrieval certain experiences more than others. Obviously, the skilled mechanic listening to automobile engines notices little knocks or rattles that most of us cannot discriminate, and he may ticket one of these sounds for future investigation or may simply be on the alert for possible breakdown of the vehicle once having heard of it. The bird watcher may be on the alert in a woodland for colors and sounds that may suggest to him the availability of certain species in the area, whereas, for most people, all that comes out of the woods are blurs of green and vague hummings or whistles.

Cognitive Styles of Storage and Retrieval

There may be certain personality styles that lend themselves to special types of labeling processes. One possible basis for the trait of introversion may be that an individual, in general, functions as what Broadbent (1958) termed a *long processor.* For any new set of inputs this individual compares some of them with a large number of previously evaluated material before finally assigning the new material either for storage or for some kind of overt response. The *short processor,* in contrast, or the *extrovert,* may merely match new material against the most recently occurring previous material and, therefore, may process much more material, but store it much less effectively. The introvert, by having set up a complex nexus of interactive schema, will then have a greater likelihood of retrieving information and also of seeing its connections with a greater variety of information. The short processor may be strongly dependent upon the reoccurrence of a very specific external context before he is likely to retrieve earlier perceived information. There are advantages and disadvantages of both of these styles of adaptation. Yet the important thing to notice is that the set of the individual toward how to code the material probably operates fairly consistently and generates a very different pattern, not only of retrieval material for formal output, but also for rehearsal of the material in privacy.

The distinction often made clinically between the hysterical personality, who is generally viewed as more extroverted, and the obsessional personality, who is generally more introverted, can be understood from this viewpoint. The obsessional is tormented by almost too many associations and complex interactions when presented with particular questions or when thinking about a particular issue. His coding strategy is simply too complex from the start. The hysteric, on the other hand, is unlikely to recall many significant events unless placed directly in a setting conducive to the recall since he probably does not rehearse very much in the interim. This may explain why methods such as hypnosis or related regressivelike techniques seem especially effective in producing recall with hysterical patients. In effect, the context is set up similar to the one in which he originally acquired the information so he can then produce it more effectively.

Dimensions of Ongoing Imagery

The distinctions between primary and secondary process or parallel and sequential aspects of thought and imagery, as well as the distinction of McKellar (1957) made between *A* and *R* thinking, all still remain relatively gross forms of separation into categories of imagery. McKellar (1972) has attempted a more elaborate examination or categorization of imagery based on an introspective viewpoint. *Dream imagery* is what most people will generally describe as the most vivid and dramatic aspect of imagery man experiences. It must be kept in mind, however, that current evidence from the sleep laboratory suggests that most dreams are not recalled and we are left with just a fraction of the mental activity that occurs during the night in the morning. A second type of imagery McKellar described is what he calls *memory imagery*, which generally fits the category of the most common types of day-to-day imagining, recall of a variety of experiences in various sensory modalities.

McKellar's evidence, collected from hundreds of subjects, suggests that as many as 97% of the subjects report visual imagery, 93%, auditory imagery, and somewhat lower percentages report other types of imagery, but all of the main modalities are represented by at least two-thirds of his extensive sample. Most of the evidence suggests that memory imagery, except in the rare cases of eidetic imagers (Haber & Haber, 1964), is characterized by considerably less precision, fuzziness, or vagueness, and the reporting of methodologies needs to be especially carefully examined since the private criteria that individuals use may lead to great variation in what is considered relatively vivid imagery. In the case of a few individuals whom I have encountered and examined for imagery and who claim that they do not have any visual imagery, it is possible that they simply are setting too demanding a standard. They may expect that visual imagery have some of the same degree of vividness that night-dream imagery has before reporting it as imagery at all.

A third type of imagery may be viewed as *hallucinatory*. Here we again run into difficulty in separating vivid imagery from hallucination where the imagery takes on a vividness as to seem to people at the particular time it occurs to be an actual occurrence in the "real world." There is increasing evidence that a rather large number of individuals, sometimes 10% of sampled populations, reports occurrences in which imagery was so vivid that they mistook it for reality. McKellar (1972) gave examples of many well-known people who reported hallucinatorylike experiences without any indication that they were generally mentally disturbed and also pointed out a variety of physical conditions that may increase the likelihood of an anticipated event taking on the characteristics of a perception. The work of Segal (1971) on the Perky phenomenon has also pointed out the degree to which vivid imagery can be comparable to an externally generated signal. These experiments have considerable implications for the various safety hazards one faces in driving on roads or in flying under conditions that provide unsatisfactory cues or lack clear external differentiation. Under such conditions, *anticipatory* images of turns, or lights, or other signals that are useful cues may lead to gross errors of judgment and, indeed, to accidents.

McKellar gave a rather detailed account of a great variety of more specific experiences that relate at various points to imagery. These include such things as the various hypnagogic or hypnopompic images and related experiences that one finds either on falling asleep or upon awakening. Many of these experiences seem particularly closely related to the operation of the various sensory organs as they undergo functional changes in relation to oncoming sleep or awakening. Frequently these experiences have little "dynamic" significance. Nevertheless, for many people inexperienced at introspection or at attending to and noticing the variety of private experiences to which man is ordinarily prone, a disturbance may occur because of faulty labeling. The issue of attribution of various causes to such private experiences has not been studied as extensively as it ought to be. It seems likely that many kinds of private experiences such as drowsiness, awakening, or the awareness of entoptic phenomena—the lights and color displays that are a product of the phosphenes or random activity of the optic nerves that we perceive when our eyes are shut—may be frightening experiences for many individuals (Horowitz, 1970; Singer, 1966). By the same token, the effects of drugs which may modify perceptual acuity in a certain fashion or increase the intensity of particular types of imagery may also lead to labeling difficulties. Particularly distressing to many people who have used drugs, particularly LSD, has been the terrifying "flashback" effect of some of the frightening images perceived during the course of a "bad trip" (Horowitz, 1970; Matefy, 1973).

Attribution and Labeling of Private Experiences

There has been relatively little examination of the new systematic approach to attribution theory in relation to identification of imagery. Sarbin and Juhasz (1970) have taken us a step along toward a more functional orientation to understanding how imagery and role-playing orientation may be linked, yet there has been relatively little systematic work in providing an understanding of what determines how individuals will describe their imagery or related fantasy experiences, or to what causes they will attribute them. Attribution theory, as elaborated by Jones, Kanouse, Kelley, Nisbett, Valins, and Weiner (1972), places great emphasis upon the subsequent impact on behavior of the kind of causal attribution made by an individual to specific sets of social interactions or even to his own automatic responsiveness.

It would seem appropriate to extend this direction of research to our understanding of various causal attributions made to a variety of imagery experiences. There is the intriguing work generated by Piaget and now by others on ascertaining when children decide what a dream is and "where" it comes from. We need further work along this line for a variety of imagery phenomena and daydream experiences so that we can determine to what extent the labeling process itself generates subsequent behavior patterns. I mention this at this point and will return to it again in our discussion of the specific therapeutic usages of imagery because I believe that such coding is an important factor in many forms of psychotherapy and more specifically in those that involve imagery. Many clients in such treatment now learn to identify more clearly a variety of images that are associated either with fearful or positive affect and also begin to label these experiences in a form that makes them seem more subject to self-control. Indeed, the so-called "unbidden images" with which Horowitz (1970) has dealt at some length may often take on a frightening quality, much as hallucinations do, because they are inadequately identified and labeled by patients. It might be argued, from at least some evidence that has developed, that many kinds of hallucinatory experiences reported by psychotic patients are the consequences of inadequate earlier experiences with awareness of daydreams and fantasies. Under the pressure of great need or trauma, or in conditions of relative social and sensory isolation, the awareness of these fantasy or imagery patterns suddenly looms as more vivid. It is then more likely to be attributed to external causes than to the kind of ongoing natural inner process that experienced day-dreamers can identify.

An attempt at a tighter characterization of imagery in relation to various forms of thought representation has been presented by Horo-witz (1970). This table (Table III) is reproduced here because it should help the reader see some of the major distinctions made by researchers in the cognitive area for different kinds of imagery and thought process. Some clue is also provided as to the different kinds of content that characterize the ongoing stream of thought and the different rep-resentational systems involved; each representational system may also have not only somewhat different structural and functional brain sub-strata, but also different functional consequences in terms of their prac-tical usage in the behavioral repertory of the individual.

In Table III, which is derived in part from Bruner (1964), Neisser (1967), and particularly Piaget (1930), we see again the distinction between parallel and sequential processes stressed by both Neisser and Paivio. Of particular interest in terms of imagery techniques in therapy is, of course, the fact that the kinds of representation of images as-sumed to occur include signs and symbols, body image representation, and fantasies, which in Piaget's language might be viewed as anticipa-tory images, that is to say combinations of material drawn from mem-ory imagery into new structures of schema on the basis of transfor-mations of perceived events or anticipated differential outcomes. An implication of the way Table III is drawn also points to Neisser's (1972) caution that we do not view imagery by any means as a simple pictorial reproduction of a set of events. The realm of imagery, as Neisser noted, has space, volume, and a degree of complexity that is comparable in many ways to the complexity we experience in the external world.

A representation such as Table III remains limited in scope because it cannot give sufficient impression of the dynamic quality of ongoing thought. The task of such a classification, which I attempted only very crudely (Singer, 1966) in the past, has yet to be done—if it can be done at all. Certainly, however, we should eventually be able to distinguish

TABLE III

Modes of Thought Representation[a]

Mode	Sample of units	Sample of sets of units	Sample of schemata	Sample of relationships of units
Enactive	Anticipatory movements, tensions, kinesthesia	Acts Gestures Postures Facial expressions	Direction and force	This does that.
Images	Images: Tactile Gustatory Olfactory Visual Auditory	Signs Body image Fantasies Introjects	Space Volume Simultaneity Signs and signals	This is there. This is like that. This and that happen together.
Lexical	Morphemes	Grammar (phrases, sentences, paragraphs)	Linearity Sequential schemata Syllogisms	First x then y, then z. x leads to y if w but not if not w.

[a] From Horowitz, *Image Formation and Cognition*, 1970. Courtesy of Appleton-Century-Crofts, Publishing Division of Prentice-Hall, Englewood Cliffs, N.J.

between what might be called directed and undirected thought (Berlyne, 1965) or, for the kind of distinction Antrobus and I (Antrobus *et al.*, 1970) have used extensively in our various experiments on the stream of thought, *stimulus-independent thought* or *task-irrelevant mentation*.

Many investigators feel that it is useful to distinguish among fantasy, daydreaming, planning, and other characteristics of ongoing thought. My own research has not yet convinced me that such distinctions are entirely useful, particularly since I am inclined to view much of what is called daydreaming as having the same anticipatory planning implications as more consciously oriented planning behavior. We still need to know to what extent the intrusion of memory images makes a real difference in more orderly sequences of thought. Can we be sure that fantastic rearrangements of material drawn from long-term memory into scenes that are impossible of actual occurrence (for example, my fantasy of becoming a great football player or of flying to Mars, where I can become warlord) are, in essence, different from fantasies of wooing and winning an attractive girl who passes by, or planning to woo and win a girl one knows reasonably well, or simply planning one's vacation or evening meal? The data accumulated from questionnaires and interviews (Singer, 1966) does not suggest that the mere "fantastic" nature of daydreams separates normal individuals significantly from each other in this general dimension. It seems more likely that some people are simply more prone to daydreaming than others and are, therefore, more likely to engage in a great variety of mental possibilities.

In a study by Hariton and Singer (1974) of women's fantasies during sexual relations, one clear factor which emerged indicated that women generally given to daydreaming produced more fantasies during sex, irrespective of their marital satisfaction or dissatisfaction or the nature of the specific experience.

In keeping with Sarbin's (1972) view of imagining as muted role-taking, it seems more useful to regard all of the examples just cited as dependent on the stance and attribution orientation of the individual, as well as on his degree of practice with a variety of imagery and his comfort with the material he seems to be generating. As yet, we do not have the means of determining objectively whether the imagery of a fine writer is truly more vivid than that of a relatively inarticulate unskilled laborer. Certainly, we have good reason to believe that both have rather vivid private experiences in their dreams. It is hard to be certain whether the writer's communicative skills so carefully practiced enable him to describe the same experience in more detail and with the use of a greater richness of imagery or whether the writer's concentration on his imagery and its integration with various specific labeling procedures has led to an actual increase in the range and vividness of his private imagery experiences. Was Shakespeare's imagery, as documented so effectively by Spurgeon (1935), limited specifically to his verbal capacity for differentiation? As Spurgeon noted in her comparison of Shakespeare to his playwright contemporaries, he made far more use of "town" imagery, or a vividness of imagery in a variety of modalities including smell, touch, and taste, which is less "noble" than the visual or abstract imagery to which the more "lofty" Marlowe was given. It certainly seems as if Shakespeare most likely privately played out more of these kinds of experiences again and again within himself, in addition to attempting to communicate them in his poetry and in the characters of his theatrical protagonists.

The private experiences of great sensual writers such as Shakespeare, Keats, Proust, or Joyce are not available to us, obviously, and it still remains an open question as to whether their own imagery and fantasy lives were on the whole more vivid than more inarticulate souls. Mark Twain, who was one of the first writers capable of capturing the fantasy experience of children in literature, provides a humorous fantasy in his tale of the riverboat captain who goes to heaven and views a great procession of all the dignitaries of human history, as well as those from other planets. At the head of this array of Moses, Jesus, Shakespeare, and various three-headed gentlemen from Saturn, marches a young shopkeeper from Tennessee who was born with all the potential for being the greatest of God's creatures had he but the opportunity and survived. In a sense then, it is possible that our storage capacity for a great variety of images and experiences, which has been shown in recent research to be exceedingly vast (Kagan & Klein, 1973), depends in part upon its effective activation through the attitudinal set or orientation toward coding and labeling of private experience, which differ widely amongst individuals.

If nothing else, the imagery approaches in psychotherapy, whether elaborately symbolic, as in the case of the European mental imagery techniques, or more mundane, as in the behavior modification orientations, seem to be suggesting that given the proper circumstances, a much greater number of people can attend to their own imagery, generate interesting and useful sequences of such imagery, and also apparently learn to control the imagery or use it for control of their affective reactions. From the standpoint at least of our imagery capacities, there may be more of us who are "mute inglorious Miltons" than has been anticipated by psychologists, who for so many years have tended to minimize the significance of private experience.

This has been a rather lengthy review of the material increasingly available as a scientific basis for the study of imagery and fantasy processes. It has been presented chiefly because I feel that many clinicians are inclined to take imagery in their patients for granted. Many have not attempted to examine the various cognitive and affective implications of private imagery in specific detail, and many, therefore, have also missed important opportunities for a more precise understanding of the phenomena described by their patients. As I try to show in Chapter IX, much of the mystery about private experience can be cleared away when we view imagery and fantasy as natural consequences of the information-processing activity of man, keeping in mind that the affect system and cognitive system are indeed closely linked.

A good part of the research on imagery and daydreaming is still in a very early stage of development, yet we have good reason to believe that important gains have accrued. We can see that perception and imagery both are part of a general process of attempted representation of experience that involves a great deal of anticipation of new situations, as well as the filtering of much external information, coding incoming material or "reports" from long-term memory, and assigning it to retrieval programs, and also attributing various meanings or causes to experiences as they occur. These attributions themselves must be coded and labeled, and so we soon develop complex hierarchies and subroutines, which are reverberated in our stream of thought and our dreams. Novelty and complexity are almost equally available from our own long-term storage as from the outside world. The processing of material from both sources evokes affects of interest or joy, as well as fear and distress.

CHAPTER IX

A THEORETICAL FORMULATION OF THE ORIGIN AND FUNCTION OF THE STREAM OF THOUGHT

For sense sendeth over to imagination before reason have judged; and reason sendeth over to imagination before the decree can be acted; for imagination ever precedeth voluntary motion.

Francis Bacon, The Advancement of Learning

ORIGINS OF IMAGERY AND FANTASY IN CHILDHOOD

Concreteness, Abstraction, and Imagery

The human being's capacity for storing information is being increasingly recognized as a far more complex and far-reaching aspect of our behavioral repertory than had ever been suspected in the body of research generated by Ebbinghaus' original experiments. The work of Haber (1970) and Kagan (1972) and the exciting compendium of papers edited by Tulving and Donaldson (1972) point to the tremendous complexity and range of human memory processes. We have made especially good progress in the area of verbal learning and in mastering some of the rules by which words are linked to each other and stored in hierarchies of the familiarity or frequency of usage. We are just beginning theoretically to address the question of the storage of images in the various modalities. Very likely the next decade will see a great research effort in this direction.

One question that has intrigued theorists, but as yet has not been very susceptible to formal research, is whether the early thinking of the child takes place in the form of images, even without the availability of suitable verbal labels. Most researchers and students of child development are inclined to believe that this is the case, and imagery is often viewed as a basic function from this standpoint. Rohwer (1970) has questioned among the early evidence of imagery whether any is sufficient to explain adequate learning in children. He proposed that only as verbal labels and speech or other more abstract encoding processes become available, do images become effective in the learning process. Even if one does not fully accept Rohwer's position (and certainly much more research is needed in this area), the evidence provided by researchers such as Paivio (1971) and Bower (1970) make it clear that, at the very least, human memory involves two or more major systems of organization that may operate somewhat independently, but also in interaction produce the most efficient system of labeling, coding, and storage with appropriate recall or retrieval routines.

At their highest point, aesthetic or scientific, human beings manifest remarkable combinations of imagery and abstraction. Consider Shakespeare's blend of psychological and philosophical insight into the human condition with the vividness of imagery portrayed in phrases like "a tale told by an idiot, full of sound and fury, signifying nothing" or Keats' statement about truth and beauty exemplified by his vividly bringing to life the characters depicted on a Grecian urn. In science, the combination of remarkable spatial imagery with great powers of integration through mathematics that characterized the work of Einstein further attests to the power of the two systems in interaction. In thousands of humbler, but still perhaps miraculous, ways all of the learning processes and storage of daily experiences of life involve some degree of similar interaction and many of our most useful communications between people in all walks of life involve similar combinations of imagery and verbal encoding. Many of the phrases that "catch on" and eventually become what we think of as "tired cliches" were originally vivid combinations of imagery and an abstract summation of experience.

A man who comes back from work saying he had a "hellish day" may not be directly linking in his mind's eye the series of unpleasant interactions and hard physical labor he may have endured to the picture of sinners roasting on coals in banks of hellfire, tormented by pitchfork-wielding demons. A youth recounting the consequences of a series of escapades by saying "then the shit hit the fan" may not take the time to linger for a split second on the powerful synesthesia of that image. Abstractly, the phrase suffices to imply that there were serious disciplinary consequences for an infraction of rules. How much more compelling is the implication of dire consequences evoked by the image itself? As Schachtel (1959) has pointed out, we tend too often to communicate in relatively well-automated phrases without attempting fully enough to reexperience the implicit vivid experience and associated emotion that could make each moment of our lives more exciting. As I read some of the Zen philosophy, it seems essentially to be an attempt to recapture the concreteness of perceptual experience. I would question whether one need throw out the value of abstract coding systems at the same time as some Zen exponents seem to be suggesting.

Accommodation, Assimilation, and Early Imagery Development

With a view to understanding how the processes of imagery can be effective in the psychotherapeutic enterprise, let us take a closer look at how images and fantasies may get started. As I discuss this issue at much greater length elsewhere (Singer, 1973), I will try to deal with it briefly here. We can begin with Piaget's *assimilation and accommodation* as two fundamental processes by which the child organizes his experience (Piaget, 1962). The child initially is motor oriented and also perceptually attracted to moving stimuli. The child attempts in some way to use his available cognitive and motor apparatus to deal with the "booming, buzzing confusion" of the novel environment that surrounds him. His eyes follow a swinging mobile and gradually his hands, in increasingly coordinated fashion, reach for the objects within reach. These gross motor and perceptual activities reflect the child's attempt at accommodation to the novel environment and are associated initially with the innate arousal of the affects of interest and surprise (Tomkins, 1962).

The child also seeks to assimilate what it encounters into some kind of more permanent structure. At first, this assimilation is evident in simply grasping or, with improved dexterity, placing the objects into the mouth. Here, perhaps, Freud overemphasized the purely oral sensuality of this experience without seeing that orality itself might be just one phase of the general assimilative cognitive–affective process of dealing with the novel stimulation available to the child. The essentially cephalocaudal direction of development probably accounts for the greater focus on orality in the very young child, but assimilation processes must be viewed as more complex in the sense that they involve storing processes of memory, as well as the "oral incorporation" once so heavily emphasized by psychoanalysts. This somewhat reductionist position of what is essentially a far more complex encoding process is evident in Rapaport's (1960) formulation of the basic model of psychoanalytic theory along the lines of a hunger metaphor, in which the infant hallucinates the picture of the mother's breast in the delay period between arousal of the drive and its fulfillment with the arrival of the mother. I believe that a great deal more information is being organized and assimilated into the encoding system that is unrelated to specific drive satisfactions. Rather, it is related to the gradual capacity of the child to match earlier learned material with new inputs, with the resultant arousal of the affect of joy, as a high level of complex material is reduced to manageable chunks.

As the child goes through the process of accommodation and assimilation in a variety of increasingly complex environments, with increasingly diversified motor skills, he reaches into more areas and learns to differentiate more environments both physically and perceptually. The complex stored materials begin then to be organized into various subroutines and hierarchies. It is likely that at first these are organized around particular motor activities of the child or, of course, particular need-gratifying activities such as the availability of food, the reduction of pain, etc. Relatively quickly, however, the gratification of basic drives takes place efficiently and fairly quickly, and there is considerable time left over for active exploration. This exploration involves more than direct interaction with the physical environment. In periods of relative quiet or reduction of external cues, it takes the form of reverberation of memories with attempts at assimilating earlier experiences into available schema. The child's feedback of his own vocalisms, as well as his attempts to imitate the movements and sounds and visual characteristics of adults around him, all come into play at this point and are probably rehearsed and replayed in a variety of contexts. Indeed, it is quite likely that what we talk of as storage is too static a term, too dependent on the inert quality of the computer. More likely, storage in the human brain is an active process of constant play and replay of partially assimilated material, which leads to increasing novel environments that then have to be matched against other established routines.

I believe that much of the assimilation process has an intrinsic interest for the child since it involves the creation of a fairly novel environment by replay of the as yet unassimilated material. This "inner" environment is not so complex as to produce the negative affect of startle or fear. Instead, the child's control of the material leads to the more positive affect of interest characterized by a moderately increasing gradient of novel stimulation. This stage is followed (as the material does eventually get matched with established structures) by the affect of joy, and fairly soon is manifest in smiling and laughing on the part of the child.

The process I am describing, although probably a basic cognitive capacity, is not likely to be independent of social experience. The conscious efforts of the adults in the environment to engage the child by physical tickling or cuddling or by spoken phrases are important parts of the child's initial experiences, which he must then attempt to assimilate. To the extent that the child is able to accommodate to the adult by producing a smile, in turn he engenders a sequence of positive reactions that are generally pleasurable. The tragic experience of the autistic child who fails to smile back at the parent has been well documented. We still know little of the importance of the pattern of parent surrogate and child interaction in a variety of playful, positive affective ways.

The child's attempt at assimilation of the complex novel material whether from the physical environment or from social interchange is exceedingly difficult and complex since the child begins with such a limited repertory of schema. It is at this juncture that we probably see beginnings of symbolic and fantasy or make-believe processes. Sarbin's (1972) implication that imagery is muted role-taking would suggest that the attempted assimilation of adult behaviors by the young child, often with only limited vocabulary, as well as organizational schema, forms one basis for the strangeness of early childhood expressions, the very quaint cuteness of the child from the adult perspective. The efforts at imitation of adult behaviors in the child are impeded on a number of counts: there is inadequate vocal capacity, as yet insufficiently differentiated motor skill, and, in addition, only a very limited experiential base for comprehending the nature of the adult action.

The child seeking to imitate a parent who is talking on the telephone may be able to grasp some relatively simple phrases, particularly those likely to be repeated quite frequently such as "Hi, there," or, for Japanese children, "Moshi, moshi." The child may even get the intonation somewhat right after a while and manage to hold the telephone approximately in the right position, although it is unlikely to differentiate the speaking and listening ends of a telephone. It is much harder for a child to grasp the notion that the person to whom words are addressed may be miles away and not inside the telephone instrument itself.

Let us trace the child's effort to assimilate this intriguing occurrence to which children may be frequently subjected, for example, there is this shrill ringing noise and Mama puts you down to go over and pick up this black instrument and starts talking into it. The child may attempt to assimilate this experience either with the real telephone if the adult is not looking and it is within reach, or with a toy telephone that has been provided by a doting relative. It begins by imitating the motor and verbal components moderately well, but with the "cute" mishandling of the receiver and perhaps also with the repetition of key phrases without the effective sense of a full-scale conversation. Privately, the child may, in addition, add a significant component in the attempt at assimilation by picturing a person inside the telephone. This strange image may become assimilated and stored as a kind of cognitive schema that may take months or years before it is corrected.

I observed a situation in which a children's television personality, Mister Rogers, visited the Child Study Center at Yale University just as the nursery school children emerged at the end of the morning period. One of the 3 year olds ran up to him and said at once, "Mister Rogers, you're not on television, you're in real life!" After all, what basis did the child have at that point for knowing that Mister Rogers could be anything other than an image on a screen and perhaps alive inside that strange box. I suspect that some of the excitement most of us feel at seeing movie stars or television personalities in "real life" has some of the same characteristics of this child's reaction, since most of us have scarcely a better understanding of the technology that can produce movies or television images.

What I am suggesting is that a great deal of the assimilation of material from the environment that takes place for the growing person involves novel combinations that do not meet adult standards of veridicality, and, hence, may later be labeled as cute or strange or silly or bizarre, but are the only available constructs we can store at earlier ages. These stored novel combinations do get replayed by the child time and again, and, of course, gradually many of them are tested against new inputs and modified. But it is questionable whether the original materials that form the more "childlike" images or representations also associated with rather specific verbal codings are completely lost. It is likely that these continue to be actively processed by the brain in the form with which storage took place.

I am suggesting that storage in the brain is not simply a filling of material in an inert location. Here the computer analogy is unsatisfactory since the computer can shut off and continue to function once it is turned on again. I propose that brain storage involves an active process, and that the fact that much early childhood material is not recalled is more likely to be a consequence of a number of factors intrinsic to the natural developmental process. One of these is the fact that the variety of adult environments or contexts does not establish conditions likely to call up the sequence of materials associated with the early childhood assimilated images that perhaps are no longer veridical from an adult standpoint. In addition, it is quite possible that a good deal of the material has been modified by replay and new inputs so that the earliest forms of the material are associated or stored with very childlike words and phrases and are most unlikely to be touched on by the usual processes of recall. Such situations may be changed, however, by establishing adult conditions conducive to recall.

For example, as I suggested in earlier chapters, encouraging an adult to lie down on a couch in the presence of another adult partially restores the psychological situation of being a child and, therefore, increases the likelihood that one will recall images and fantasies that had been long stored as more childlike. Another possibility is that, since it is likely that the active process of storage leads to a good deal of this material occurring in dreams, the encouragement of adults to think about and recall their dreams may also lead them to become aware of childlike sequences and earlier assimilated materials. Going back either in memory or in actuality to the scenes of childhood may further unlock sequences and subroutines that have not been actively a part of consciousness for years.

Even as I have been writing this material, my attempt to reconstruct the child's experience in listening on the telephone or in watching television has led me to recall a number of early memories and faulty assimilations that were part of my own childhood experience. These included imagining that certain characters lived inside the phonograph or the radio—"Uncle Don" lived inside the box in the living room from which his voice emanated, or the humorous Gaelic accents of Sir Harry Lauder came from a quaint little man who dwelt in my aunt's mysterious Victrola. I suggest to the reader that he adopt a similar attitude for the moment and try to reestablish the mood of early childhood, choosing perhaps a particular era to see if indeed a number of comparable "faulty" assimilations and images will come back. Imagery and many of the quaint pictures that characterize childhood come almost certainly from attempts to capture strange voices and sounds in some understandable form. Perhaps this was fostered even more by the radio or phonograph for which the visual component had to be actively added by the child. It remains to be seen if we can ever discover what specific effect the omnipresence of the visual material of television has had upon child imagery development.

Origins of Symbols and Metaphors

The early faulty assimilations of children are unquestionably very idiosyncratic in the sense that no two people have identical experience, participate in identical sets of conversations with identical parents in identical environments, etc. Nevertheless, one can look to some extent for certain more universal or at least culturally widespread experiences and assimilation patterns that ultimately become the basis for the symbols and metaphors occurring in our dreams and become the basis for our religious, cultural, and aesthetic experiences. I am not proposing that archetypes in the sense of genetically established structures that take on the same symbolic meaning across cultures are inevitable. Rather, I am suggesting that there may be certain sets of experiences that all human beings have in common (obviously those related to the expression of a fairly circumscribed, but differentiated, set of affects and the satisfaction of basic drives such as hunger, thirst, sex, and pain reduction) and that, within certain environmental settings, the combination of environment and our constitutional structure interact to produce certain commonalities.

Werner and Kaplan (1963) have gone to great lengths to examine the ways in which the very nature of childhood gesture, the varieties of expressiveness of adult emotion, and certain Gestalt structures that lend themselves to our perceptual responses become incorporated with associated affects as regularities in imagery. The attempts on the part of the child to mimic complex shapes of objects by particular postures have been described by Muchow and Werner (Werner & Kaplan, 1963, p. 97), and there is a whole host of movements and imitative actions that begin to symbolize complex situations within cultures and, to some extent, across cultures. Sign language, of course, represents one obvious example, and such sign languages can be developed rather extensively as in the Hindu Indian dance routines, which are built on complex gestures that stand for sequences of behavior. It is relatively easy to learn to follow these, compared with learning the language of the people who engage in these gestures, however.

Symbolism can be seen as originating from the attempted assimilation of material in the face of limited cognitive schema or verbal encoding processes, with an attempt, therefore, at imagery representation or at imitation if the attempt is to communicate to someone else. But even this imitation is subject to the limited range of experiences or organizational Gestalt properties of the objects involved. In this sense, most cultures can generate comparable patterns of imagery for certain experiences—at least, experiences of the most widely generated type. Phallic imagery that subsequently becomes incorporated into dream symbols is one obvious example clearly related to a specific natural phenomenon that takes a certain form in all societies. The smile or the look of anger are pretty universal and can be used for symbolizing positive and negative affective conditions. The eyes shut for sleeping with the head downcast to suggest shame have also more universal characteristics and become the basis for symbols and assimilations even in early childhood.

The early experiences of childhood with tastes that are unpleasant and cannot be assimilated becomes the basis for a wide variety of verbal imagery as well as symbolic representation in many countries. In China to suffer is represented by the phrase "to eat bitterness;" a similar phrase is used as part of the Hebrew Passover seder in describing the experience of the Jews enslaved by the Egyptians in the form of eating "bitter herbs."

We need not dwell at length here on this issue since it is itself a complex area for detailed examination with the fine start made by Werner and Kaplan (1963). It is important to see that there may be certain common experiences that children share when attempting imagery representations of complex material in the absence of as yet adequate verbal encoding systems that become stored along with the attempted assimilated material. Consider the child trying to represent conditional phrases or temporal sequences for which he has yet insufficient vocabulary in imagery. Werner and Kaplan (1963) presented intriguing experimental examples of adult subjects' efforts to reproduce such phrases through imagery and ways in which certain uniformities begin to show up in the imagery. Attempts at representing in imagery the fact that one event took place before another, or the *hope* that one event might not have taken place, or one's wishes that some incident might not occur all lead to a complex and generally idiosyncratic representation. They occasionally can also take on universal characteristics.

There may be also givens in our very structure that make it necessary for the occurrence of commonality of reference. As Freud noted in relation to dreams, there can be no "negatives" in the unconscious. If we attempt to imagine ourselves not doing something in a symbolic representation, it is necessary to imagine the very thing one wishes not to do. One can then eventually develop a set of formulations about how images and particularly those especially common experiences can be organized. One way of looking at Jung's notion of archetypes is not to assume that the material is genetically coded and, therefore, inevitably occurs in dreams in the same form, but rather to view certain symbols as available early within a great variety of cultures because of their similarity to significant objects or action sequences of our experience. It seems reasonable that for most cultures in which children are reared by breast feeding somewhat curved but moderately elongated forms or parabolas can be experienced as aesthetically more pleasing.

Early Fears and Frightening Images

Thus far, I have stressed some of the more commonplace, day-to-day aspects of our environment which children try to comprehend, imitate, or assimilate into their limited cognitive repertory. Naturally one would have to view the situation in relation to different age levels and the differential cognitive capacities and environmental demands of those levels. (This is a separate question with which we will not deal in length here.) For the preschool child and even at the somewhat later phases of childhood, there are many events and experiences particularly difficult to assimilate and to match with already established structures. For the rather young child, consider the fact of lying in bed at night and seeing the shifting play of shadows on the wall. Perhaps the lights of passing automobiles cast different patterns on the wall or perhaps the flashing of neon lights creates odd shapes in a particular apartment bedroom. There are many more noises one discerns at night that take on figural properties compared with the normal background din of the daytime. These experiences are difficult to assimilate for the child and are more likely to create conditions arousing negative affects such as fear.

Much has been made in psychoanalytic literature of the child's fear of separation, rejection, or loss of the external object in the shutting of the eyes and the preparations for sleep. It would appear to me that these specific object-related fears represent only one phase of the more generally difficult assimilation process that the child faces at night. For one thing, there are, as I indicated, the external sounds and play of lights and shadows that are not readily assimilated into established schema. Because of the reduced sensory input at the onset of sleep, the child experiences a greater awareness of the processing activity of the brain and of the images and partially assimilated materials that are the prominent part of what Freud termed the *day residue,* but which I would call the *unfinished business*—the various unresolved issues or incompletely assimilated materials of the child's day-to-day life. Klinger (1970) has elaborated on the notion of the "current concerns" that are the major characteristics of adults', as well as children's, dreams and fantasies and the ongoing stream of thought. Breger *et al.* (1971) have called attention to the role of unresolved stress in generating dream and fantasy content.

In the preparation for sleep, the child, and later the adult, as our research suggests (Singer, 1966), is confronted with a vivid replay of the major unresolved issues of the day, or of the past, and of the anticipations of the following day. Most people learn simple techniques for controlling this vivid upsurge of fantasy enough so that they can fall asleep. For the child it may take a while to master this material. Even if it is not terribly threatening, it may be sufficiently complex so that, when also added to the assimilation problem of the mysterious sights and sounds of the night, the child is likely to be at a higher level of fearfulness and struggle to interpret the strange events in relation to some set of schema. Probably, the schema available to the child are those already presented by adults. These include the tales of faraway places, religious and supernatural materials that adults have already made available, the story material already provided children that is difficult to assimilate, and the consequences of teasing of children by threats of various kinds. All of these probably come together at this point and make it more likely that the child will begin to form new cognitive structures around these odd shapes and sounds. Here we have the basis for the many mythological, fairy tale, and mysterious figures that occur in our fantasies and particularly in our dreams. For the television-reared child, there is a great variety of cartoon characters, of talking animals, and of strange sights and sounds that cross the screen daily. These may be interrelated with the shadows in the night and become the basis for later "symbolic fantasies."

What I am proposing is that the mythological and symbolic combinations and complex metaphorical characteristics emerging in adult dreams or on the imagery trips that are encouraged during various forms of psychotherapy originate in the complexities of the assimilation process in early childhood. Such a process is never completely over for all of us. We still encounter new patterns of stimulation or new social situations that are not easily matched against our well-established cognitive structures. We, therefore, must puzzle these out or at least relegate them to a category of "unfinished business" so that they are more likely to emerge in our fleeting fantasies, hypnagogic reveries, and during sleep in our dreams. By adulthood we have already many complicated sets of symbols, some of them holdovers from early childhood, but many learned as part of the various allegories and metaphors that have become a part of our culture. The historical figures who represent significant aspects of our religious and historical upbringing, as well as the mythological and supernatural aspects of our particular cultural heritage, are all now available to us for linkage to new problems or unassimilable information.

The complexity of symbolism available to us today is built into our language and our communication media and so surrounds us that one need really make no assumptions of a genetic coding or archetype to explain the multilayered symbolism that emerges in mental imagery techniques and psychotherapy. With advertising men actively providing us with phallic automobiles or symbolic mistresses perched within them, proposing that behind the wheel we become as powerful as cougars, or as energetic as mustangs, what need do we have to assume a racial unconscious? Symbolism pervades our lives as part of our cultural heritage and as part of the very metaphorical characteristics that man lends to his social organization. That these should emerge in our ongoing fantasies, once we take the trouble of *carefully attending to them,* should no longer be surprising.

THE PARAMETERS
OF ADULT FANTASY AND IMAGERY

The Coding and Replay
of the Stream of Thought

One can ask, then, why the reports of symbolic imagery trips are so curious and unbelievable. Why we are surprised at the kinds of material that come up, or why do we often fail to recognize in our own dreams some of the obvious symbolism? I believe that it is very likely that this occurs because many of the events that are going on daily in the replay of our ongoing stream of thought are not actively labeled or coded by us as such. What I am suggesting is that we do not recall the degree to which we have thought about various unfinished business, or current concerns, or perhaps even tried out symbolic transformations of them during our day-to-day interior monologues because we have trained ourselves not to pay great attention to them. Hence, we do not set up formal labeling or retrieval routines that permit us to remember how much daydreaming has really gone on during a given day. As a result, many of the active internal processes that we have engaged in have not been so labeled and, therefore, come as a surprise to us when they emerge shortly before we prepare for bed or actually in the more bizarre form of our dreams.

Even in the case of nocturnal dreams, the content we recall is, generally speaking, the dream we awoke with in the morning and may not be a full representation of all the complex material that can be elicited if one is awakened periodically throughout the night at various sleep stages. The most vivid recall of dreams comes grom the Stage 1 EEG Emergent REM phase, at least for some people. These dreams do tend to have a more Freudian character than the material elicited in Stage 2, which tends to be more organized and "thoughtlike" (Foulkes, 1966; Arkin, Antrobus, Toth, & Sander, 1972). For the person who is a practiced daydreamer, that is, someone who adopts a conscious attitude of attention to the ongoing stream of thought, the accessibility of the symbolic material is probably greater. Such a person is also more likely to gain relatively quick insight into the transformations from normal English sentences that occur in the images of dreams. I believe too little attention has been paid to the individual's set toward active attention to his own inner processes and his degree of active play with this material, its replay, and assignment to it of higher priorities for recall (Singer, 1966). In a sense, as we shall see, what imagery techniques may actually provide the individual is a clearer awareness of his own processing tendencies.

It might be argued that thus far I have emphasized too much the commonplace aspects of fantasy processes, imagery, and dreaming. After all, the attraction of these processes for clinicians, as well as for the general public, has to do with the fact that they seem to be representations of major human motives. I think that a statement of this kind is obvious; part of the difficulty, however, is that it is not so easy to agree on what are major human motives. There is no doubt that much of our dreaming is built around sexual fantasies, fantasies of success or achievement, fantasies of escape from the current unpleasantnesses in our lives, and so on. McClelland (McClelland, Atkinson, Clark, & Lowell, 1953; McClelland, Davis, Kalin, & Wanner, 1972) and his collaborators have beautifully traced the many implications that grow out of the recurrent fantasies of achievement or power that are characteristic of so many of us. My concern is not to deny the importance of wishes and motives in the fantasy life of individuals, but rather to insure our recognition that the fantasy and imagery process is sufficiently general to encompass a great enough range of human motives and experiences.

I think it is more useful to view human motivation as primarily based on the affect system (Tomkins, 1962) and the principle that most people seek to maximize a positive affect of joy and interest and to minimize the negative affects of anger, distress, fear, and shame. They also are motivated as much as possible to express affects freely within the limits of personal safety and security in the society and, finally, they are motivated to control their own affective reactions. This position, therefore, does not specify some particular drives or motives as more or less basic to humanity. The main thing to consider is that the world of fantasy and imagery is at the service of a particular set of plans and hierarchical cognitive structures that given individuals have developed, and that the unfinished business, the unassimilable material of the day, and indeed of the whole life of the person are obviously related to powerful themes that have become the major processing routines for a given individual.

It is obvious that if we accumulate large samples of individual dreams or daydreams from people and categorize these systematically, we can build up a picture of their hierarchy of motives. This, however, would still be a somewhat incomplete picture of the functioning personality or even of the sources of dream and fantasy content. Many of the things that creep into dreams and daydreams are bits of unresolved or unassimilated material that are simply cognitively complex and not necessarily unresolved issues relating to major motives. Similarly, any attempt at predicting a specific behavior of individuals based on the hierarchy of motives that can be derived from an analysis of a dream log (Hall & Nordby, 1972) still will not suffice to predict what the individual may do in very specific situations that generate their own demands. My concern is to emphasize the general functions of stream of thought and the imagery process in relation to the affect system and to leave for other investigators or theoreticians the detailed exploration of the major motive systems of individuals in relation also to the situational contingency that must be taken into account if we are to predict individual behavior effectively (Singer & Singer, 1972).

Imagery and Levels of Consciousness

Let us next consider the tricky question of the relation of imagery and fantasy experiences to so-called *altered states of consciousness*. Perhaps more than ever in our history, in the United States at least, we are experiencing an interest on the part of young people in a variety of so-called states of consciousness. This new interest ranges from the kinds of self-awareness generated in the more traditional psychotherapies through religious self-sensitivity that has been a part of man's heritage for thousands of years and the even more complex emphases on special states of awareness or lack of awareness enhanced by a variety of Oriental philosophies ranging from Yoga through Zen and Sufi. We also see concern with states of body transcendence, mystical or extrasensory experiences, and the various consciousness-enhancing stages of the Arica program of Ichazo (Smith, 1973).

It would take really a separate study to examine why this new interest in the complexities of private consciousness is occurring. Probably, it represents in part a recognition by young people of a failure of the more extroverted political radicalisms of the 1960s and also an awareness that many of the radical leaders themselves were on "ego trips." In line with a greater move toward personal security and personal development in the face of social systems too complex to be radically altered, many young people are trying to "get their heads together" or to find new meanings and values. They might be responding also to the apparent failure of the more traditional religious movements. There may be important positive features to this development if we consider that man's private imagery has been a relatively neglected resource.

Whereas Freud opened up the possible understanding of conflicts through analysis, many people today recognize that analysis of one's own private products and the various transformations that occur may increase the likelihood of a variety of aesthetic and even reality-affective experiences. The question I raise, however, is whether this new interest in exploring our own consciousness has taken on excessively mystical or "gimmicky" characteristics. Consider the elaborate marketing characteristics of the DaSilva Mind Control franchise system or the commercial pretentions implied in Smith's (1973) humorous account of a stay at the Arica Institute. Despite our impressive information now on the complexities of EEG patterns and associated autonomic and motor states during sleep, we have very little clear evidence of the existence of true altered states of consciousness. What we do know is that people report different kinds of thoughts and fantasies and imagery under different kinds of experimental sets or with different degrees of reduction of external stimulation. They also bring different histories to each of these situations and, as a result, are more or less prepared for particular kinds of imagery trips. A similar finding is evident in the extensive literature on the effects of various drugs: the major share of variance consistently turns out to be the combination of previous experience of the individual, the motivational set and expectations, as well as the group atmosphere in which the drug is used (Barber, 1970).

The position I would like to propose is similar to that taken by Barber in examining the most popular of the altered states of consciousness, *hypnosis*. This dramatic state of apparent subservience, which by its very name is linked also to sleep, turns out, on extensive examination, not to be related at all to many of the measurements we make of the sleep process and, in addition, seems best explained in relation to a set of psychological variables that are perhaps more related to social experience. The extensive evidence marshaled by Barber (1970) led him to propose the following:

> three sets of consequence behaviors (*responses to test suggestions, reports of having been hypnotized, and hypnotic appearance*) are initially related to at least eight sets of antecedent variables, namely, *wording and tone of direct suggestions, task motivational instructions, definition of the situation, relaxation sleep suggestions, wording and tone of inquiry, subjects' attitudes toward the test-situation, subjects' expectations pertaining to their own performance, and experimenter role behavior* [p. 307].

It is quite possible, for example, that even the definition of a particular situation, the suggestions for relaxation or sleep, and the actual behavior of the experimenter may well be subsumed under task attitude, task expectancy, task motivation, wording and tone of direct suggestions, and wording and tone of the inquiry. This position implies that one need not posit an altered state of consciousness to understand any peculiarities of behavior in hypnotic situations, but rather this type of behavior can be viewed as a change in the role patterning of the individuals (Sarbin & Anderson, 1967).

I would add to this position the likelihood that the set of instructions and the interpersonal situation created in a presumed hypnotic trance state is one in which the individual is able to reduce drastically many of the external cues that ordinarily would be attended to and, therefore, he becomes increasingly aware of his own ongoing brain processes and imagery capacities. These in turn are selectively filtered out in the specific hypnotic situation, where that is a definition of the so-called altered state of consciousness. In the therapeutic use of imagery, however, the hypnotic aspects have not been emphasized; rather, attention to the free unrolling of imagery is the task demand. I am thus suggesting that there is something going on privately and the subject is simply not making believe entirely that he is going along with the experimenter at a purely verbal level. I believe that he is also, because of this set of instructions, increasingly aware of the private experience that he ordinarily has not labeled for retrieval—except under such special circumstances. Relaxation on a couch, acceptance of the authority of the therapist, acceptance of the mildly regressive situation, in which one plays a more childlike role, all of these are conducive to the awareness of ongoing imagery and also provide cues for retrieval of earlier memories and of the kind of more childlike assimilation activities that are ordinarily eschewed in the adult waking state. Such a view of variations in cognitive channel space seems compatible with Hilgard's (1973) recent theory of hypnosis.

Task Demands and Mental Imagery Theory

I grant that this may be a less dramatic or exciting position, but I suspect it may explain many fascinating results obtained by psychotherapy methods such as Assagioli's psychosynthesis. In such an approach, the therapist establishes an atmosphere of spiritual orientation, probably in a variety of ways, in the preparation for the experience and, by many forms of subtle suggestions, sets up the likelihood that the subject will go on a particular type of symbolic imagery trip. The establishment of a partially relaxed or regressive psychological state, the reduction of external cues, make the subject increasingly aware of private experiences. These mental events, in the case of imagery therapies, are attributed not so much to hypnosis or to some other mystical experience, but to the consequences of the particular therapeutic orientation to which the subject is exposed.

The attribution aspects of this process should not be minimized. Yet again I would argue that one must for a complete theory regard these private events as the representations of an ongoing internal souce of stimulation and not merely verbal communication patterns with the therapist. The novelty of these experiences arouses the positive affect of interest in the subject and, as connections are made or symbolic transformations deciphered so that they can match previous sets of expectations or even expectations based on suggestions of the therapist, there is the associated experience of the affect of joy. The subject obviously has a desire to continue to experience such positive affect, and is, therefore, motivated to continue this type of symbolic trip and to struggle through a phase of sometimes almost random imagery to find meanings and patterns. In effect, this very motivation with cues as to what meanings and patterns may be especially interesting to the therapist may also provide a kind of guiding format and establish a new set of subroutines by which incoming information is processed and, therefore, significantly tip the direction of any future imagery sequences toward the general theoretical model of a particular therapist.

I do not mean to suggest that therapists only get back what they put in. This would deny the patients their complex of individual differences, not only in style and capacity for awareness of fantasy processes, but also for a certain objectivity about their private experiences. It does seem very likely, however, that in the face of the great problems of orienting ourselves in a complex role, we all look for simpler formulas or methods for reducing this experience to established expectations. In this sense, the availability through the therapist of some system for translating this complexity of private experience is relieving.

It also provides the subject with a sense of control over his own private processes which he might not have felt was possible before.

SUMMARY OF THE THEORETICAL POSITION

Let me now try briefly to summarize the major theoretical points of my position on the origins and implications of imagery and fantasy processes. Imagery via specific sensory modalities is viewed as one of several major coding systems that the brain has for organizing and storing the experience. It has the special properties of being capable of parallel processing and of providing particularly vivid ongoing reenactments of previous events with the likely arousal of greater affect than the verbal encoding system. The latter has distinct advantages in terms of labeling of material and in terms of its greater abstractness and generalizability. Optimal functioning for both child and adult requires interaction between these two systems with the possibility that interactive combinations of imagery and verbal coding may have separate properties for storage and retrieval (Seamon, 1972).

Imagery and fantasy processes that are an extension of specific imagery into chained sequences develop originally out of the accommodation–assimilation cycle in which the child attempts to process information. As an additional feature of this cycle, the assimilated material, in its rehearsal, generates interest and related positive affects of joy as matchings are made with established cognitive schema. The nature of brain processing itself is not a static storage activity, but involves constant reverberation of which we become aware during moments of reduced external stimulation or, of course, at the time of sleep in the forms of dreams.

Much of the symbolism and the bizarre and mythical quality of our ongoing imagery stems from the "faulty assimilation" characteristic of childhood with a limited range of schema available. Symbolism develops through the integration of novel experiences such as a variety of inexplicable events into established schema already provided by the adult world in the form of religious and mythological or culturally generated adult surrogates and forms. Such material, although it may be increasingly less available because the situational contexts do not call for it, in later life may not be permanently lost and may be retrieved, provided external contexts are established close enough on the generalization curve to the contexts in which the material originally was stored (Tomkins, 1970).

The particular content of which we are primarily aware in the course of attending to our stream of thought or to our night dreams tends to be material stored with, in effect, a coding label that called for retrieval soon because of the unassimilability of the material into established structures. This material is, generally speaking, the unfinished business of our daily lives and, more broadly, the unfinished business of our hierarchies of motives and broader fantasy structures. The orientation of the individual toward awareness and special attention to his ongoing inner processes plays a key role in the degree to which such materials will be elaborated in consciousness and reassimilated into other cognitive structures. The particular set of an individual toward processing and reprocessing such ongoing experiences may depend heavily on social learning within the family setting or cultural orientation toward such activities. The set toward this kind of self-awareness may take a variety of forms, some of which may be worked into a creative endeavor such as writing or painting, but which also may simply function to enhance aesthetic appreciation and, to a great extent, planning ability and role-taking capacities.

Because of the combination of early humiliation often experienced in connection with make-believe and fantasy play in particular societies or subcultural groups and also because of the practical necessity of attending primarily to external environmental stimuli, including the communications of others, there is a sharp drop in attention to private processes with increasing age and, particularly, during a period of major adult responsibilities. For this reason, there is frequently a tendency not to label one's ongoing fantasy activities as such and, hence, not to have available a retrieval code for recalling that one had actually engaged in such processes earlier in the day or in the past. One of the implications of this general filtering out of such experiences is that when special external circumstances promote awareness of them, as in the case of preparation for sleep, night dreaming, or sensory-deprivation experiences (which might include natural ones such as a lengthy train ride, or artificially created ones such as those in psychological research), persons may be startled and perhaps frightened by awareness of their own ongoing processes. Indeed, they may attribute the causation of these images to external sources—as in the case of mental patients' hallucinations.

Within the specific psychotherapy setting external conditions are created that are conducive to attending to such processes; moreover, there is reinforcement from the prestigious therapist for such activity, and thus the awareness of ongoing processes has a more positive quality. First, formal training in attention and in symbolic decoding are part of the therapeutic process. In addition, the ability to produce and to report on the images is reinforced by obvious interest from the therapist, so that the individual gains not only gratification from the therapist's support, but also a more private feeling of control over these initially strange-seeming processes. This creates a considerable positive affective situation in relation to ongoing fantasy and becomes a useful part of most of the mental imagery uses for psychotherapeutic purposes.

The notion of control is an important one here since there is evidence, as Strupp (1970) has pointed out, that a major component of affective psychotherapy is the patient's experience that he has now increased his control over his own emotions and his overt behavior. In this sense, heightened awareness of one's ongoing fantasy processes also increase to some degree the extent of control over such processes so that they seem less strange and also can be called into service in connection with particular difficulty or momentary need of the individual. A particular advantage of imagery as a parallel processing transformation system is that it permits detailed scanning of rather specific events. Usually in the therapeutic situation, these events are of an interpersonal nature. The revival of a particular affect that was stored with the initial image also becomes possible. This gives the imagery transformational system special advantages in psychotherapy, which depends greatly upon *in vivo* reproductions of situations that are disturbing and threatening to the individual in his life outside the consulting room. The frequent reference to intellectualizing, as against the advantages of true feeling experiences presented by many clinicians, probably reflects the fact that the verbal encoding system by its very sequential nature is primarily effective in communication of general events or in rapid transformation or retrieval. It is less likely however, to be stored with the special emotional context with which imagery transformations are stored and, therefore, will be less obviously generalized to outside situations. In the various behavior modification approaches to psychotherapy, consequently, the power of imagery has to do with the fact that it brings the subject closer on the generalization curve to the events that are being avoided or need to be controlled systematically as part of the therapeutic aim. I attempt to elaborate on this issue in Chapter X when discussing specific therapeutic approaches.

In conclusion, the emphasis here is upon the developmental sequences and capacities at particular ages and also on the available social learning and cultural demands placed upon the individual. Imagery and fantasy must be viewed as fundamental cognitive capacities of the organism which have their special properties of storage through some form of active reprocessing that we can detect only when we inhibit to some extent our active processing of new external stimuli.

These processes carried on privately nevertheless have the same field processes as external stimuli. To the extent to which they are readily assimilable or provide differential degrees of complexity and integration into established cognitive schema, the private processes arouse positive affects such as interest and joy or negative affects such as anger, distress, and fear. Practical necessities of daily living call upon us to ignore much of the ongoing inner processing in order to function effectively in our relationships with others or to steer ourselves through the physical environment. Yet, it is likely that we can use a much greater share of the ongoing stimulus field provided by our own long-term memory system to establish positive affects and also to become aware of our major motivational tendencies, our significant unfinished businesses, and many other potentials for role rehearsal and advance planning.

CHAPTER X

THEORETICAL AND PRACTICAL IMPLICATIONS OF IMAGERY IN PSYCHOTHERAPY

Beloved Pan, and all ye other gods who haunt this place, give me beauty in the inward soul; and may the outward and inward man be at one.

Plato, Phaedrus

PSYCHOTHERAPEUTIC USAGES OF IMAGERY

Goals and Nature of Psychotherapy

Before examining the implications of imagery techniques for psychotherapy, it is necessary briefly to state the view of psychotherapy I hold. My position is closely related to that outlined in a paper by Strupp (1970). Strupp proposed that if one examines the panoply of behavior modification and psychotherapeutic techniques, one is left with the impression that the primary purpose of such treatment is essentially the development of self-control, competence, and autonomy. Examining the range of neurotic symptoms brought to the attention of the psychotherapist, he concluded that most of them can be shown to be guided by some kind of central processes, including beliefs or self-attitudes that may be implicit or frequently have evolved from symbolic transformations. Strupp takes the position that psychotherapy is essentially a technology to produce personality and behavior change, and he distinguished this position from that of some humanistic orientations, which emphasize the role of psychotherapy as a human encounter oriented toward self-development and attainment of higher potentialities. To me the latter goal suffers from a certain vagueness, arrogance, and perhaps even self-deception on the part of the therapists concerning their philosophical capacities.

I would agree with Strupp that psychotherapeutic processes involve subtle interactions between patient and therapist, and the teasing out of these interactions is often a critical feature of this relationship. Still, the ultimate function of the therapist is to make the patient's problem increasingly *specific* so that it can be addressed with some degree of precision by the means of available psychological knowledge and technique. Initially, the therapist must have the trust of the patient, and this necessitates an examination of the patient's resistances or barriers to directness, openness, and honesty, but it is hard to see how cooperation can ordinarily be obtained without some strong influence of the therapist at the outset.

The objective of psychotherapy or behavior modification is, however, to present to the patient in a reasonably systematic way methods for dealing with his own behavior that he can take with him outside the consulting room. This means that the ultimate goal of the therapeutic process is the autonomy of the patient and his development of a repertory of skills for dealing with a variety of distressing situations that may in the past have been generated by his own distorted beliefs or conditionings. Much of the evidence for the effectiveness of psychotherapy hinges on the relative specificity of outcomes produced and the nature of the problems presented (Strupp & Bergin, 1969; Meltzoff & Kornreich, 1970). This specificity of outcome does not mean that it cannot be generalized to other areas as the patient's life situation continues. Rather, with the removal of fairly specific symptoms or fully controlled behavioral tendencies, it seems likely that the patient will receive increasingly positive feedback from others in his environment and will also become aware of increased effectiveness in dealing with people and specific situations. This will inevitably lead to greater self-esteem and positive self-regard.

A critical feature in our ability to evaluate the effects of psychotherapy is our attention to the behavioral consequences of therapeutic interaction and the subsequent response of the patient. This does not mean that the private experiences of the patient are irrelevant by any means. One must recognize that private modes of self-awareness and habits of communication may change more slowly than overt behavioral responses and the overt behavior situation may lead to more rapid change in the private sector of the personality. This does not preclude the value of using techniques such as imagery in producing behavior change. It does, however, suggest that only with some reasonable evidence of overt behavioral change in areas that were clearly troublesome to the patient prior to treatment should the therapist begin to feel that satisfactory behavior modification is occurring. Too much time has been wasted in psychotherapy on elaboration of intrapsychic balances and nuances without clear attention to whether the patient was actively modifying his behavior in daily life.

To assert that psychotherapy involves a highly skilled clinical technician does not deny the humanity of the therapist–client interaction, nor does it imply that some type of mechanical reinforcement robot can soon replace the individual clinician. As Strupp (1970) noted: " . . . one cannot eliminate . . . the clinical observer and his capacity for indwelling (Polanyi, 1966), that is, to understand, in the context of an interpersonal relationship which is free from sham, deception, and facade; the patient's inner world—his fantasies, beliefs, working assumptions about himself and others [p. 401]."

Trust in the therapist, however, whether it is based on positive transference or upon a realistic appraisal of the skills of the therapist, and presumably deserved reputation are important initial components for establishing an atmosphere of individual cooperation. The therapeutic situation hinges greatly on the patient's capacity for practice either in the therapeutic session or subsequently with material elicited in therapy (Leitenberg, 1970), as it also depends strongly on the suggested outcome presented implicitly or, hopefully, explicitly by the therapist.

To say that suggestion and direct commands (Barber, 1970) have important impact on human behavior is not easily discarded as "suggestion" or "placebo effect." We still have to ask ourselves what is the psychological principle or set of operations that leads the patient to change behavior significantly on the basis of direct suggestions made. I would propose that much as in the hypnosis situation, the patient uses these suggestions to help himself focus his imagery and planning and role-taking capacities more precisely. To the extent that the therapist is himself fuzzy minded or operating under a grossly misguided theoretical position, this would imply that his direct suggestions may not help the patient and indeed might even do him harm (Bergin, 1967). Still, the major element in psychotherapy generally turns out to be the voluntary engagement of two individuals or a group with a therapist under reasonably explicit contractual circumstances. The combination of personal skill and perhaps some elements of the therapist's personality characteristics that mesh effectively with those of the patient (Witkin, Lewis, & Well, 1968) combine to enhance communication that will help the patient organize some set of procedures he can begin to practice systematically as alternatives to the poorly controlled or disordered patterns he had developed previously.

If we consider the imagery techniques in psychotherapy within this framework, we then may examine the various components present in the methods reviewed in this volume. With a few exceptions, all establish conditions in which trust of the therapist and responsiveness to his initial direction are critical. The restless and hostile patient is unlikely to lie down on the couch and to engage either in relaxation exercises or in some related form of imagery association. Locke (1971) has cleverly documented how even Wolpe engages in active establishment of rapport to insure cooperation at the outset of a behavior therapy program.

Relaxation, Meditation, and Biofeedback Conditions

Most of the imagery approaches in psychotherapy begin with some emphasis on achievement of a relaxed state. In some instances, such relaxation is closely tied with actual production of imagery or role-playing, as in the case of autogenic training (Schultz & Luthe, 1959) or hypnosis (Barber & Hahn, 1964). The most commonly used method that depends predominantly on kinesthetic feedback is, of course, the Jacobsen (1938) *progressive relaxation technique.* On theoretical grounds, the relaxation exercises seem crucial only in relation to Wolpe's theory of *reciprocal inhibition* or *counterconditioning.* In the *desensitization method,* presumably the degree of relaxation should provide an inhibiting element for the anxiety aroused by the phobic images. The evidence that the Jacobsen method actually does produce what might be termed a relaxed state of any degree of consistency is rather dubious, however. Jacobsen's original studies are not methodologically satisfactory because of statistical limitations in analysis, the differential interpersonal contact between experimenter and client for the relaxation and control group, and other specific considerations (Mathews, 1971).

In general, the data on relaxation methods summarized by Mathews (1971) yield rather mixed results with regard to the consistency and degree of relaxation possible in the clinical situation. The evidence suggested by the results of Wolpe and Flood (1970) and Van Egeren,

Feather, and Hein (1971) and others seems, on the whole, to be contrary to the original notion of the counterconditioning effect of the relaxation. If anything, the data suggests, as Mathews (1971) concluded, that "relaxation may augment both vividness and the autonomic effects of imagery, while at the same time maximizing the response decrement with repeated presentations [p. 88]." In other words, there is some slight support for the fact that there are autonomic changes associated with various relaxation exercises and varieties of autogenic training (Geissman & Noel, 1961), but the task demands of the situation and the relationship to the therapist seem equally crucial. There is also the likelihood that concentration and the reduction of external stimulation that characterize the relaxation instructions produce a situation conducive to the occurrence or awareness of imagery and ongoing daydreaming (Antrobus, 1968; Antrobus et al., 1966).

There are indications that, to some extent, subjects who are new to the hypnotic situation (Barber, 1970) or subjects producing vivid imagery manifest some increase in autonomic responsiveness, a finding that again would be contrary to the presumed relaxation effect (Chapman & Feather, 1971; Van Egeren et al., 1971). Perhaps the most extensive study in this area was carried out by Grossberg and Wilson (1968) with indications that the correlation between heart rate and vividness of imagery was $r = .60$. The general results of this study led to the conclusions that phobic imagery can indeed arouse predictable autonomic reactions, but these autonomic responses decline with *repetition primarily* and not necessarily only in conjunction with the relaxed state. The work of May and Johnson (1973) on heart-rate increases associated with arousing words also indicated that subjects reported more vivid imagery for words like "mutilate" or "massacre."

The demand characteristics of the situation and the attribution process (since there are indications that habituation of autonomic responses such as GSR may actually precede the reduction of anxiety (Leitenberg, Agras, & Barlow, 1969) raise serious questions about the specific theory of desensitization in relation to relaxation. At the same time, it seems reasonable to suppose that a major consequence of the relaxation instructions is to establish conditions that enhance attention to one's own ongoing imagery processes. Relaxation should also reduce hyperalertness to external stimulation that would blur the vividness of imagery and overload the visual system, which must handle both imagery derived from long-term memory and incoming stimulation. Wilkins (1971) is inclined to conclude that an attribution model based on the subject's self-perception and relabeling of his experience may be more critical in producing reduction of phobic reactions than the inhibition of anxiety by relaxation. The relaxation exercises seem to be part of a gradual introduction of the patient to circumstances that allow him to experience his imagery vividly. In the case of phobic imagery, the patient has already developed massive avoidance tendencies so as to restrict contact either with the actual phobic object or situation and also to avoid even imaginary contemplation of the thing or situation. The relaxation experience permits the patient to engage in the imagery under controlled conditions and to become aware that he can indeed confront this situation.

As Bandler, Madaras, and Bem (1968) demonstrated in a study of the experienced intensity of shock when directly endured or escaped, an experience that one "lives through" may be evaluated as less painful than one that has been avoided. In this sense, the subject under the relaxation conditions has now reduced external stimulation to some degree and can become aware of his own imagery more fully and project the image of the phobic object. Having realized that he can do so undoubtedly plays a role in reducing the attribution of high intensity of fear to the image and increases the likelihood that he will engage in that imagery again. This is a necessary step toward the goal of directly confronting the frightening situation.

Viewed in this context, then, relaxation exercises would appear to be valuable primarily as inducements to the production of imagery and to helping the patient develop a sense of capacity for control over imagery. In addition, the relaxation procedures themselves involve a distraction from the press of external stimulation of the repetitive awareness of particularly frightening internal messages rather than images. They substitute an alternative ritual for the obsessional ritual the patient has been carrying on in the form of thoughts such as, "I must not go near so and so, I better make sure that such an event does not occur which might make it necessary for me to go near this place, etc." Relaxation comes close, in this way, to many of the goals of various meditation exercises. If we ignore for the moment the complex superstructure of religious belief and mysticism associated with various approaches to meditation, we can see how systematic attention to one's own breathing, repetition of certain phrases, and the exercises in various forms of meditation may lead to systematic reduction of the external stimuli that have to be processed and also to the reduction of repetitive internal formulas associated with fear and avoidance responses. Fischer (1971) attempted an elaborate description of the relation of meditative states to the general range of consciousness under what he calls "hyperaroused" and "hypoaroused" states, and he also related these experiences to the sensitivity level of inner experiences and to brain rhythms.

Although Fischer's (1971) more precise correlation of brain waves and psychophysiological measurements with these states is far from being demonstrated, the continuity of various meditative states and relaxation is suggested. Less clear is the degree to which he puts hallucination at the far end of the continuum, along with creativity and sensitivity, whereas it is entirely possible that many aspects of the awareness of one's own private experiences and fantasies occur during conditions of low autonomic responsiveness (Antrobus et al., 1970). Indeed, it is also true that Zen and Yoga meditative states generally seem to be attempts to avoid rumination or fantasy. Yet systematic inquiry and control studies have not really been carried out to test this reduction of consciousness and private experience during these states. Maupin (1965) found evidence that subjects with considerable fantasy capacity and awareness of their own ongoing imagery were most likely to be good candidates for Zen meditation. Furthermore, Linden (1971) found that school children trained in meditation became more field independent.

It seems to me that a more probable value of the relaxation, in addition to its establishment of conditions conducive to imagery and control of thought processes, is that it may also play a role in enhancing alertness to one's ongoing feedback processes from autonomic and muscular systems. As suggested earlier, it is likely that some day Schultz will be recognized as a forerunner of the biofeedback movement. This emphasis on the self-control of autonomic responses and capacity to control brain rhythms such as the *alpha,* has some apparent relationship to relaxation and, in certain subjects, occurrence of imagery as well (Antrobus et al., 1964). But the fact remains that we are very far from consistent data on self-control of psychophysiological responses. The research program of Green, Green, and Walter (1970), despite considerable technological advance, still remains a program with only a few individual case studies to support the long-range potential of the method.

Nevertheless, it behooves psychotherapists to be attentive to the fact that they can help patients through relaxation exercises or related methods to become aware and capable of discriminating their various affective states (Izard, 1972) and the nature of their ongoing imagery processes. In my own view, it appears unnecessary to include the many elaborate, rather mystical notions drawn from oriental philosophy or based on pseudoscientific elaborations in order to justify this relatively simple kind of exercise in self-awareness. It is one thing to appreciate some of the philosophical implications of various ideologies or quasi-religious orientations and to appreciate aesthetically their great contribution to art and culture. It is quite a different matter to overload the already confused client with this kind of superstructure when the process of self-awareness and behavioral control are grasped relatively easily in relation to reasonably well-defined operations of the imagery and daydreaming capacities with which we are all endowed.

Training Imaginative Capacities

The implication of the position toward which I have been guiding the reader is that various imagery techniques in psychotherapy represent examples of training the patient for more effective use of his own imaginative capacities. The reviews of Mathews (1971), Wilkins (1971), and Morganstern (1973), as well as the various attribution studies and the role-oriented approaches of Sarbin (1972) and Barber (1970), all emphasize the fact that cognitive factors, expectancies of change, and discrimination of various settings and situations in which behavior is to be shown contribute to behavior modification as a consequence of imagery approaches. If it is true that we have available as a basic resource the ongoing processing of our brain, which is actively dealing with a variety of stored materials by a continuous transformation, then the attitudinal set we take toward our own imagery may be a critical factor in ultimate control of this process. One of the major biofeedback methods available to us is a heightened sensitivity to our ongoing fantasy processes. By covert rehearsal, discrimination of different images, and use of positive images as a distraction and a shift away from recurring frightening scenes, there is the likelihood that we can increasingly master our social and physical world through a more effective resort to our storehouse of experience. Freud called thought "experimental action"; indeed, this is the position that seems most useful to adopt. We can, as we become aware of our imagery, try out many different possibilities and roles with relative inpunity. A recent study by Rychlak (1973) indicates that more emotionally stable adolescents produce more positively-toned future fantasies.

In fact, for many patients the first step—realizing that thoughts do not necessarily lead to action—may be a significant therapeutic step. One patient of mine became aware of a series of thoughts that she might harm her children. It was possible to show her that such thoughts came when there were situations with her husband or family that had made her extremely angry. The thoughts essentially reflected her anger, rather than any necessary likelihood of overt action against the children. Once realizing this, she was on the one hand greatly relieved and, on the other, relatively quick to ignore such thoughts if they occurred. The patient also learned to use the thoughts as signals that there was something troubling in her interpersonal situation that ought to be addressed. The more frightening notion that she was psychotic and that thoughts were as dangerous as actions (a belief that could be traced back to early childhood experiences in her family setting) was dispelled relatively quickly. This case is a simple example of the combination of an attribution therapy with the increase of cognitive schema available to the patient so that she can now assimilate these thoughts more effectively and is less likely to experience distress or negative affect when they occur.

An important first step, then, in psychotherapeutic application of imagery techniques involves the establishment of conditions in which the patient can identify his ongoing stream of thought, perceive it as ego-syntonic, that is, a natural part of his own development, and learn that he can begin to use, to some extent, the material presented for some type of self-understanding or self-control. This awareness was probably one of the major factors in the attraction to psychoanalysis on the part of so many young intellectuals. The therapist's reinforcement of the recall of dreams and fantasies and the possibility that these could be analyzed was extremely exciting. Indeed, the almost narcissistic gratification associated with extensive examination of one's daily dreams and fantasies may have led to the prolongation of analyses when only limited external improvement was occurring. Patients could come back day after day for years and enjoy the attention to their own ongoing thought processes or the analysis of the elements of their dreams and not have to face up to the urgent responsibilities of change in their daily interactions.

As I suggested earlier, the controlled awareness of one's ongoing stream of thought provides an interesting alternative stimulus field, which, since it provides only moderately complex material, arouses the affect of interest and, as it is examined and reformulated, leads to a reduction of this arousal and the occurrence of the affect of joy (Tomkins, 1962). McGhee (1971), in his review of the development of humor, also seems to present evidence and increasingly consistent theoretical indications for a position similar to the one I am proposing concerning the combination of the affects of interest and joy in dealing with novel materials of moderate complexity. By its very nature as an amazingly diverse processing system, our brain is capable of providing us with a set of outputs that create variety and novelty to an amazing degree. Our attention to these processes, provided we have been prepared for their strangeness and seemingly metaphoric and symbolic qualities, can be an important addition to our behavior repertory.

I am far from suggesting that withdrawal from social interaction into endless private rumination will be indefinitely satisfying. As a matter of fact, it is likely that a condition of hopeless withdrawal from society may lead ultimately to a reduction in the tendency to fantasize and daydream (Singer, 1966). At the same time, there are ample indications that persons who have already developed gifts for introspection or for elaborate development of fantasy and imaginative or philosophical thought have been able to tolerate long periods of social isolation reasonably well. A number of significant philosophical works has been composed in prison. One thinks, for example, of Bertrand Russell's productivity during his imprisonment during World War I and Cervantes' composition of *Don Quixote*. A distinguished architect and planner, Herman Field, told me about his prolonged imprisonment as a presumed American agent by the Czechoslovak government in the 1950s under conditions of severe social and sensory deprivation. He managed to pass the time and resist his captors' efforts to extract a false confession by mentally composing a novel based on his experiences and also by elaborate imagination of the captors' thoughts and expectations so that he could gradually win certain rights including access to pen and paper. Experimental studies also indicate that time seems to pass more rapidly under conditions in which one is carrying out fantasy activities that have a positive affective tone (Wheeler, 1969).

The Cognitive–Affective Basis for Mental Imagery Therapies

Thus far I have been describing the more general gains made through the use of imagery in psychotherapy. These generally positive consequences are valuable in introducing the patient to therapy, encouraging him to continue, and providing him with an important new asset that will increase his experience of self-control and autonomy. I, however, have not yet dealt with the manner in which the imagery can help in the relief of specific symptoms or in the reduction of undesirable behavioral tendencies. Here, of course, the situation becomes more complicated since there is such a variety of symptoms and behavioral situations that lead people to see psychotherapists. (The interested reader may review the presentations in earlier chapters of the various approaches to psychotherapy and behavior modification and pursue in more detail the literature cited on these techniques.) I propose that a cognitive–affective model based more on reasonably

well-defined operations and the language system close to the information-processing tasks of the individual is most useful in examining
what goes on in the attempt to treat particular symptoms or behavior
patterns.

The patient brings to a given therapist a set of expectations of
process and outcome that may be partly a function of long-standing
transference distortions growing out of the family experience of the
patient, but may also have some degree of reality. After all, the information already available about the particular orientation of the therapist or soon made available by the therapist may play a part in the
role enactment of the patient as patient. We may expect, for example,
that a patient consulting a Jungian or a mental imagery practitioner
anticipates to some extent what is expected of him and also conceivably
has some idea that what ails him has been partly shunted aside as part
of a gross avoidance mechanism.

If he is provided the atmosphere for relaxing, attending to his imagery, given a certain amount of perhaps unwitting reinforcement for
certain types of imagery productions, and encouraged by his "guide" to
confront frightening images more directly (as in desensitization or
implosive techniques), the patient may feel his own private experiences
become, in general, less threatening or frightening. Indeed, he begins
to be aware, even though he may be talking in symbolic terminology, of
the interpersonal relationships mirrored by his imagery travels. The
encouragement of the patient to reexperience his daily trip and write
down and then discuss the material at the beginning of the next session
(Frétigny & Virel, 1968) also establishes an atmosphere for a reflective
appraisal of this material and the translation of it into interpersonal
terms. Despite the assertions of various mental imagery practitioners
that the trip is all that is necessary, my own reading of the case material
of some of the patient–therapist interactions suggests that there is more
of a cognitive reorientation taking place with some understanding of
how this symbolic material can be translated into one's own daily
experiences.

Many of the symbolic trips that take place in mental imagery
therapies seem to involve gradual approaches to feared situations
which were systematically avoided in imagery, as well as in reality, in
the past. The symbolic mode seems to make it somewhat easier for the
patient to approach the situation. In the session itself or afterward, in
retrospect, the subject recognizes the actual situation that was represented symbolically in climbing a mountain or entering a cave. He realizes that he endured the situation with little pain or with the addition of
some magical gimmick from the guide; he now can mentally rehearse

the reenactment of the same behavior, thus opening the way for more overt practice of the new behavioral approach. The considerable power of covert rehearsal has recently been supported in some very careful experiments by McFall and Twentyman (1973) in studying so complex a behavior as assertiveness. It is likely that many of the important benefits accruing from a variety of mental imagery techniques, as well as behavior modification methods, relate to the fact that conditions have been established whereby the patient not only can identify more clearly a specific area of difficulty and can entertain it mentally, but then is provided with a certain amount of "coaching" (McFall & Twentyman, 1973) in the form of suggested alternative behaviors, which can be used in both covert and overt rehearsal to modify behavior.

I am suggesting that a closer scrutiny of the rambling, somewhat romantic, or seemingly mystical character of many mental imagery techniques may indicate that their effectiveness depends on the following:

1. The patient can discriminate more clearly his own ongoing fantasy processes.
2. He can get some clues from the therapist as to alternative ways of approaching these situations.
3. He can become aware within this area of imagery situations that he has avoided.
4. He is encouraged in a variety of fashions to engage in covert rehearsal of alternatives.
5. He ultimately is less afraid to make overt approaches to these situations.

Associated with all of these activities, I would suggest, is an increase in the generally positive affective state. The novelty of the fantasy activity, the sense of mastery of difficulty situations, the joy of recognition when symbolic material can be translated into recognizable current interpersonal dilemmas—all of these lead to increased positive affect and a sense of self-control.

If we consider Leuner's (1969) approach to the mental imagery method, we see that his particularly systematic procedure provides even more structure to help the patient delineate the various conflict areas in his life. Presented with such a structure, the patient who arrives at the therapist somewhat confused and disorganized about the difficulties he has been having suddenly sees more organized ways of approaching the material. He can now engage in the symbolic transformations of imagery with some sense that these relate to major areas of his life. The use of the relaxation method, reclining on a couch, and the encouragement of a mildly hypnagogic state comparable to that experienced at the onset of sleep permit the patient to establish a context more likely to be conducive to recall of structures stored at earlier ages in the partially unassimilated form more characteristic of early childhood. This may account for the greater degree of mythological or fairy tale references that occur in many of the European mental imagery cases. It is interesting that in the behavior modification approaches making extensive use of imagery, for example, Cautela's, where the emphasis is on the patient's providing imagery related to his immediate life situation, relatively little mythology imagery is reported. It would be interesting to ascertain whether the relatively direct approach of the behavior modification group in imagery is effective generally or whether some patients might, because of their fears of direct imaging of the distressing material, prefer the rather more roundabout symbolic journey of the European imagery methods.

One may speculate at some length about how to translate the European methods into more operational–information-processing or cognitive–affective terminology. What seems more important for the future is that we consider the possibilities of formal investigation to determine whether the more parsimonious and direct approaches of the kind that Cautela, Bandura, McFall and Twentyman advocate are sufficient to deal with the vast array of problems people bring to the psychotherapist. If this is indeed the case, then one need not resort to the more complex and theoretically dubious approach of the European mental imagery method.

My own experience is somewhat mixed in this regard. On the whole, I have found more direct use of imagery, when tied in with a sensitivity to the broader life pattern of the patient and to transference possibilities, to be most effective. On the other hand, there have been a few instances when I found that patients' resistance to direct examination of their current experience or their inability to articulate some of their immediate interpersonal difficulties precluded so direct an approach. In these cases, I have employed variants of the mental imagery techniques, particularly Leuner's approach. The effect has been rather dramatic in the sense that a great deal of interesting narrative emerged from patients who had seemed hitherto relatively inarticulate. In addition, the vividness of the imagery, the variations in the imagined settings, and, at least in one case, the depth of aesthetic sensitivity demonstrated by the patient were revelations both to the therapist and to the patient. In this last instance, the patient had presented himself as a querulous, narrow, and embittered person, yet the range of imagery, the love of nature, and facility in communicating the imagery material suddenly elucidated important areas of competence for the patient. This new personality dimension was then explored more actively in a direct fashion with the patient, who was able to use this skill in a working situation that helped build up his confidence somewhat more and overcome some of his phobic tendencies.

I would propose, on the basis of my experience in a number of cases, that the use of indirect methods through dreams, sometimes projective techniques, or the kind of imagery association technique I just cited may have a valuable impact on the therapist, which will also feed back into the therapeutic relationship. Many times when patients do seem to be incapable of addressing directly personal problems or are seemingly unimaginative in face-to-face communication, unable to describe incidents, or given to talking in cliches or generalities, the therapist may be easily discouraged and in subtle ways communicate such discouragement to the patient. The experience of boredom on the part of the therapist is difficult to overcome and certainly leads to a generally negative affective tone in the sessions. A shift to the symbolic or imagery mode generally makes the material presented more interesting by its variety and moderate unpredictability. The therapist's affective situation becomes more positive, and he can begin to communicate some of his enthusiasm to the patient, as well. This again seems to be a major asset of the use of symbolic imagery techniques in pyschotherapy. The therapist's interest may not only be buoyed up, but also he may begin to see patterns of relationship expressed in this transformed medium which were less clear previously in the cliche language of the patient; he also may begin to see, as I have suggested, significant new dimensions and creative possibilities that the patient has suppressed in himself. My position is that so much is going on in the complex information processes and man has such a vast storage capacity that almost any broadening of attention to such private processes is bound to foster not only increased self-awareness of the patient but the emergence of new skills, intentions, and behavioral potentiality.

IMAGERY IN MORE EXTENDED
DYNAMIC PSYCHOTHERAPY:
SOME CASE REPORTS

Positive-Emotive Imagery
for Desensitization

In continuing our examination of a cognitive–affective approach to imagery and therapy, it may be useful to exemplify various behavior modification uses of positive emotive imagery with case material. In referring to the specific uses I have made of these methods, it is important to stress that my orientation has been essentially a neo-Freudian psychoanalytic one over many years and my general approach has been one of understanding the patient's life situation within the context of his broader history and social milieu. At the same time, I have become increasingly aware that examination of a person's life, even with the tools of dream analysis and transference analysis, often did not address itself satisfactorily to the relief of specific dilemmas, phobias, and poorly controlled impulses, which seriously troubled the patient and limited his chances for significant change in his life situation.

My feeling is that it is not simply a matter of personal preference or taste for the therapist to alter his method and therapeutic style in response to the needs of specific patients. On the contrary, I feel that it is his ethical responsibility to pay serious attention to the available scientific literature in his field and to modify his methods when it is evident that new approaches that are reasonably well validated become available. For some reason, clinicians trained in systematic psychoanalytic positions or oriented toward the humanistic approach have focused extensively on "understanding" the patient, but have not taken seriously enough, I believe, the necessity for helping the patient deal with the day-to-day difficulties of his life situation. These difficulties often were created, not by primarily external necessities, but by the individual's own fears or phobias, distortions in cognitive orientation, deficiencies in social experience, and so on. My decision to use some behavior modification methods involving imagery and, to a lesser extent, some of the European imagery methods has not been arrived at lightly. I have introduced their usage very cautiously into my practice.

The first instance I should like to describe involves the use of positive-emotive imagery with a phobic patient. I had seen this patient, a married woman in her early thirties, for a number of years in a more traditional psychoanalysis; during this time, she made quite satisfactory progress both in terms of self-understanding and in important improvements in her life situation. Some years after treatment stopped, she returned to therapy with the specific complaint of a series of handicapping phobias. These had only been hinted at in the earlier period of therapy and, at no time in the past, had been expressed in behavioral difficulties. They now had become full blown—to the point of nearly crippling of her effectiveness in the running of her household.

Because of the intensive background of analytic work, it was possible to identify quickly the origins of the phobic responses in relation to significant relations between the patient and her family and husband. At the same time, it also seemed clear that very little new material was emerging in the discussions with the patient, and the paralyzing phobias persisted. A course of desensitization was then proposed to the patient. She was at first startled. Nevertheless, she was prepared to undergo this method. Generally speaking, the Wolpe desensitization approach was applied with the variation that I introduced at that time on the basis of a cognitive–affective approach [not having as yet been familiar with the Lazarus' (1971) *positive-emotive imagery*]. The patient was encouraged to develop, along with the hierarchy of phobic situations, a series of situations associated with strong positive affect. In the case of this young woman, she had many associations to a lake resort that she loved and to certain scenes from peaceful European settings that once they came to mind, she found particularly compelling and enjoyable to contemplate for periods of time. An important part of the treatment was the delineation of the hierarchy of fears into relatively fine points. These were then systematically juxtaposed against the positive imagery. Another important feature for treatment was the patient's ability to enter what appeared to be a relatively deep state of relaxation, almost hypnotic in appearance. This undoubtedly reflected some of the positive transference the patient had developed to the therapist. Her capacity to focus upon imagery was quite intense. During various imagery trials there were occasional loud noises or sounds outside the office: on one occasion, an explosion occurred in the street. It startled me, yet produced no overt response at all in the patient!

One of my obvious concerns in using this technique was the degree to which the patient might be experiencing a master–slave or Svengali–Trilby relationship, which could create problems of dependency and limited independence later on. This problem had been dealt with to some extent in earlier phases of the treatment, but I was concerned lest it recur in this more dramatic psychotherapeutic approach. Such concerns were relatively quickly dispelled by the fact that at various times in the course of presentation of imagery to the patient, she was able to interrupt, while seemingly completely concentrating on her imagery, to say, "You're going too fast! Cut it out and let me do this myself!"

The systematic desensitization with positive imagery proved to be effective quite rapidly with the young woman in relieving a variety of symptoms. As a matter of fact, the effect was so dramatic as to lead her to be somewhat suspicious. Her husband, who was an English professor with a strong intellectual background in Jungian psychoanalysis, was particularly distressed at the introduction of this method of treatment and at first felt that the therapist had gone mad. He was converted relatively soon when he realized that his wife was now not only rid of the phobic material, but in consequence, feeling more free, in greater control of her emotions, and more open with him and with various friends and neighbors. The value of the use of positive imagery was also demonstrated very dramatically at an early point in the desensitization when the patient developed a considerable feeling of pressure and, for a few days, was quite despairing. The use of positive imagery during a session led quickly to a remarkable change in her mood. Again, a demonstration that she could, through her own imagery capacities, control much of her affect was extremely encouraging.

The value of this combination of relaxation and positive imagery methods in my experience was that it could be easily learned by a fairly intelligent and sensitive person and it could then become an asset to be used by private practice of these methods to avert any recurrences of anxiety on many future occasions. This proved to be the case, for this young woman relatively soon began practicing extensively at home and was able to dispel significant moments of anxiety or depression with the method. The therapeutic interviews continued for some time after the desensitization was pretty well discontinued and focused upon significant aspects of the patient's life situation. In effect, with the termination of this phobic episode in her life, the patient was now ready to explore a variety of new experiences. This in turn led to concern about some of the major philosophical and existential problems in her life, as well as to a heightened awareness of certain limitations in the nature of her relationship to her husband. These could then be explored more fruitfully in direct communication. There was ultimately a successful termination of treatment and no recurrence of the phobic symptoms has been reported by her during several contacts over a period of years subsequent to termination.

I presented this interesting individual story in the briefest of terms here without some of the dynamically intriguing aspects involving the origins of the phobias, their relations to early childhood experiences, and all kinds of other material that emerged, but did not in my opinion lead to the decrease in the phobic symptoms. I believed that the factor of regular practice in the session and outside, willingness to contemplate in detail the frightening scenes, and at the same time to learn to shift attention from them to a positive image associated with strong positive affect led the patient to experience greater control over her imagery capacities. By making the various frightening situations fully discriminable and conscious, the technique led her gradually to practice them openly and to find that she could indeed endure these situations. Each success brought with it more positive self-regard and a sense of autonomy. In this respect, I feel that denunciation of behavior modification approaches as mechanical or dehumanizing are utterly unwarranted. If anything, it was my impression that the patient and others with whom I have worked using similar methods have been greatly encouraged by the fact that these techniques are not in any way mysterious once tried and they are tools that one can use effectively without dependence upon the therapist.

Aversive Imagery for Behavior Control

The next case I should like to present also grew out of a more intense analytic experience, in this case with a young man, a minister in his twenties who was also a gifted mathematician. Again, the reader must take my word for the fact that this treatment was a more extended, dynamically oriented one with a considerable review of the overall life pattern of the patient in relation to specific problems he presented and with considerable examination of dream material, transferential data, and scrutiny of his interpersonal perspectives and reactions. A very troubling symptom that the patient had presented at the outset, and had not changed over several years in treatment, was a persisting inclination to voyeurism. It was possible to trace the origin of the symptom, with considerable affect expressed, to early childhood memories and a frequent exposure to his mother's nakedness. She was an entertainer who was largely unavailable to the child as a companion or full-fledged mother figure. In general, the patient showed all of the symptoms of a classical Oedipus complex, and account of which need not detain us further at this point. The voyeurism, which had persisted for 15 years or more, was chiefly manifested in an interest in pornographic movies (then unavailable in public places) and, what was especially disconcerting to the patient, the great need to peek into windows and often to use high-powered field glasses to scan windows of suburban homes or the windows in the apartment complex in the suburb where he dwelt in search of partially undressed women. The patient would then masturbate while watching the woman through his field glasses. The symptom itself had never led to any grossly illegal act and was relatively circumscribed within the patient's life situation. He had some normal sexual outlets and with therapeutic help moved even more effectively into such activities, eventually marrying. The persistence of the voyeurism had, however, a humiliating effect upon him and he felt hesitant to move toward effective social relationships or to contemplate marriage while he was aware of this very strong tendency on his part.

An examination of the pattern of the voyeurism brought out several important points that led to a decision to attempt a behavior modification approach. One was the fact that the symptom persisted despite considerable gain in insight about his life style and actual improvement in many areas. It was, as indicated, relatively circumscribed and autonomous in structure, and specifically related to the fact that much of his work as a mathematician was carried out in a solitary office or in his apartment. There would be periods of intense concentration followed by restlessness, a not unusual experience for writers, scholars, or scientists who work under conditions which require extended solitary mental activity. Even though he had been relatively recently engaging in satisfactory sexual relations with women whom he cared about, the tendency to fill the unoccupied time by the long-established habit emerged, and the young man found himself compulsively going through the sequence of voyeuristic acts. An additional feature of this experience was that because of his shame about the voyeurism going back to early childhood, he had a strong tendency to avert his eyes to avoid looking lustfully at young women whom he passed on the street. In fact, when he was seriously involved with a young woman, he felt that any attention to other girls on his part amounted to infidelity, about which he felt guilty.

The treatment approach then proposed first involved a detailed analysis of the sequence of acts engaged in prior to, and in the course of, the voyeuristic compulsion. The patient was relaxed in order to help introduce vivid imagery; then he was encouraged to develop a series of noxious images that would evoke very strong negative affect. In his case, the images took the form of men with various loathsome skin diseases, some of which he had seen in a hospital where he had worked and also on a tour of the Far East. The patient then was encouraged to imagine sequentially each step of the process by which he would be working on a problem, become restless, arise, attempt to resist, then go to the window with his glasses and scan the neighboring homes. At each point of the sequence he was encouraged to imagine himself as vividly as possible in the situation and immediately juxtapose against this scene the noxious image. Again, there was considerable cooperation from the patient, who practiced at home with the method, as well as in the session.

Within a relatively few weeks, the daily instances of voyeurism had dropped sharply and within a few months they had disappeared. There were a few brief recurrences over a period of several months, generally under circumstances explainable in relation to particular moments of upset that had occurred in the personal relationships of the patient with various women. Gradually the episodes disappeared and have not recurred by report from the patient in about 4 years.

Considering the fact that this was a nearly daily habit over a period of 15 years, the result is indeed encouraging.

A second phase of the treatment of this problem made use of an attribution approach. To some extent, the patient was encouraged to recognize that looking at young women to lust after them, that is, allowing his eyes to stray over the attractive shape of a young woman passing on the street, was a fairly common and natural response for a young man, and that women themselves, by the very nature of their dress, encouraged this. Again, it was a question of helping him see that this kind of fantasy activity about passing women need not be translated into action and did not involve any significant faithlessness to his intended wife—provided it was done casually and not in a compulsive fashion. The patient felt considerably liberated by this possibility and actually was able then to shift his pattern so that he was less likely to become tense and avert his gaze in such situations. At the same time, he did not develop any tendencies toward infidelity when he was actively dating someone. He subsequently married and has done well in the marriage. Some of his interests in pornography were put to the test when the Supreme Court decision on obscenity made it possible for a great variety of prurient films to be shown in metropolitan theatres. What happened then was that the young man was able to invite his wife to join him at one or two of these films—only to find that they no longer had the appeal and demanding character they once had. His interest in them quickly diminished.

Theoretically, one can perceive that in a certain sense the compulsive act of voyeurism, or viewing pornography in this case, had some of the same characteristics as a phobic situation. The very humiliating tone and negative character of the act gave it a special meaning for him that he had to separate from any other aspects of natural daily living. As a result, he could not actively try out alternatives or discuss the situation and examine it in relation to more natural kinds of looking behaviors. The imagery exploration of this situation at first created for him a sense again of being able to control the act through the extremely noxious images with which he could link it and which literally made him nauseated. This increased control then led him to try alternative behaviors and also to feel some degree of autonomy in the situation. Once he had experienced a sense of control over the behavior, its triviality became more and more apparent to him and in many ways laughable. This was also true for the viewing of the pornographic movies, which seemed rather less exciting.

The question arises as to whether the noxious imagery had a special kind of conditioning effect, as Cautela might argue. That is hard to prove. For conditioning, one ought to have a very precise timing. This kind of timing did not seem all that precise in the clinical situation. I am rather inclined to believe that the availability of the noxious imagery provided him with an additional cognitive tool for quickly identifying each step of the sequence, which in the past that had unrolled itself automatically. He could now interpose a contrary tendency on his own part. The noxious imagery was simply a particularly strong means of directing his attention to the unpleasantness of the task that he was engaging in at the moment. I see the function, therefore, of the noxious imagery, at least in this case, as having more of a signaling function rather than one of establishing a new conditioned response. It is, of course, possible that one could interpret this result by means of the kind of conditioned inhibitor described by Rescorla (1969; Rescorla & Solomon, 1967; Rescorla & Wagner, 1972). Again, this seems to me unlikely. Since conditioning ordinarily depends strongly upon precise timing, and individual practice, and activity in the therapy office, it is difficult to say that control over the juxtaposition of the images was ever that good.

Let me cite another case that made a similar use of aversive imagery, but added a form of positive reinforcement. The case involved extended dynamic treatment of a young man who had a rather dramatic form of Oedipus complex. The patient was an only child, born shortly after the sudden death of his father. For a reason never learned by him, the patient's mother brought him up without mentioning his father. There were no pictures in the home and no references to the father until the patient was well into school age. Then, he began to learn about his father's existence from relatives and from the inquiries of teachers and friends. His mother clearly had chosen him to replace the father and to develop in him a set of responses and guilt patterns that were remarkably effective in inducing him to remain at home, living with her through his adult years. The particular problem for which he sought treatment had to do with great concern about homosexuality and a strong desire to control his compulsive tendency to meet young men in a specific hangout for homosexuals or in the pornographic movie houses that had sprung up in the New York metropolitan area.

I will not discuss the elaborate ramifications of this complex treatment process, but only wish to point out that the approach was one of first ascertaining the degree to which there was a true commitment to giving up the homosexual pattern in favor of a heterosexual life style and then working from that point. Initially, treatment focused on the patient's guilt and his severe problems with his mother. Treatment followed a reasonably normal course in which the patient gradually was able to free himself from the closeness to the mother, move to his own apartment in a suburban area, and develop a somewhat independent social life. Despite important gains in a number of areas, the compulsive homosexual pattern persisted. This pattern involved "cruising," primarily in theaters, quite frequently during a given week. It became clear that the patient's life style was not a homosexual one in the sense of his commitment or involvement in any way with homosexual society. He was, as far as could be ascertained, committed to a heterosexual life. The patient was a young professional man, quite successful in his work and well respected. He worked in a setting where there were many young women who found him attractive and frequently made overtures to him. There was also evidence that he had at one time been able to have a successful heterosexual relationship and had been very hurt by the rejection, which had been based on social and religious grounds.

It seemed clear then that the homosexual pattern, while it did date back to early exposure at about age 10 or 11, was still relatively circumscribed and might be susceptible to a more direct assault. Again, a noxious imagery technique, much as that described in the previous case, was employed. Although this particular patient was somewhat less imaginative in the sense of being able to produce a great variety of images, it was found that the use of some of the kinds of descriptive materials (such as Cautela developed) were effective in producing very vivid and distressing affects in connection with the scene. The patient was encouraged to practice these sequences at home in connection with a variety of temptation scenes built on his actual day-to-day experiences.

Because the patient had been inhibited and backward with women for some time as a consequence of his earlier frustrating experience, an effort was also made to help him develop positive imagery in association with scenes connected with women. He was able to imagine particular girls from his work setting and associate them with sexual encounters. At various points in the treatment, the positive association with women was introduced at a point where the patient had shifted away from homosexual scenes by the use of the noxious imagery. The shift away from the noxious imagery then took place toward the imagery of the attractive girl and to the positive scenes and positive affective reaction. This was practiced patiently over a period of a month or two, several times a week, in my office and at the patient's home. Soon there followed a very dramatic drop in instances of overt homosexual acts. A chart of these over a period of 6 months would have been dramatic in showing the decline from a very high and persisting plateau of interest and overt encounter to a near-zero frequency with occasional relapses generally traceable to disruptive incidents with the patient's mother.

In the meantime, the patient began to explore heterosexual encounters and dating more actively. Eventually, he met and married a young woman, who fortunately was relatively uninhibited sexually and at the same time a very warm and loving person. There were important therapeutic encounters not specifically involving imagery that stemmed from the patient's need to prove to himself that he could be as honest as possible with his wife about his past. He faced these with remarkable courage and integrity.

In this case an important element in the patient's willingness to undergo treatment and an important feature of his acceptance of heterosexuality was undoubtedly the father transference he had with the therapist. His lack of a significant male image had been a serious handicap, and he attempted to make this up by various kinds of symbolic modeling with the therapist. Nevertheless, this did not produce an excessive dependence on the therapist and the patient was ready to terminate therapy once he had established his independence of his mother, had married, and made important improvements in his work situation.

Personality Dynamics, Transference, and Imagery Training

The case just described leads into an area I should like to elaborate on briefly because it points to some of the issues that, in the past, have divided behavior modification therapists from the more psychoanalytically or humanistically oriented therapists. The patient just described was clearly relying upon the therapist as a kind of big brother or father, who could serve to some extent as a male role model. This orientation encouraged him to try harder in his own self-analysis, as well as to attempt to use some of the imagery methods. It was clear that his need was for a supportive father rather than for a lover. The therapist's role, however, was not one of friendship or direct advice.

The stance that I maintained was strictly a professional one, although I made it clear that I was concerned about this young man and that I respected him in the dilemmas he faced. In fact, my own experience made it clear that the decision as to what sexual direction he wanted to take was basically his. It was important that he have every opportunity to explore all of his thoughts and feelings on the subject fully to make sure that he was not deceiving himself in his belief that he wanted very much to lead a heterosexual life and be able to marry and have a family. An important part of the mutual respect in the relationship had to do with my own recognition that he was competent in certain areas of decoration and household activities more traditionally assigned in this society to the feminine role. I believe I was able to convey to him my feeling that these interests did not preclude his assuming a male role in a heterosexual relationship and becoming a father in a family.

One of the ways in which the therapeutic situation involved his shift toward heterosexuality was based on the therapist's ease in discussing sexual situations with him and in helping him to use the imagery about contact with attractive women in the overall imagery sequences employed. An important part of the treatment also involved helping the patient separate the young women whom he met socially from the image of his mother and various other elderly females with whom he had grown up. He grew to realize that many young women could be loving, attentive, and tender, and yet at the same time free of much of the prudishness, feigned incompetence, and gossiping qualities he experienced so commonly in these family figures.

It is important to view the use of imagery against the background of the fact that there was attention paid to the therapist–patient relationship in its more subtle forms and also to the various hidden agendas that the patient had brought into the therapeutic situation. The patient not only made effective use of the imagery techniques in the formal sense of having aversive scenes juxtaposed against moments of temptation toward his compulsive behavior. He also occasionally used the image of the therapist as a kind of imaginary companion with whom he discussed certain problems or whose image appeared to him when he was at a choice point. Even the aversive imagery gradually changed its form from some of the noxious scenes developed in the session itself into a picture of large black letters saying "Stop!," which would come to him at the moment he was aware of an inclination to take off in the afternoon and head for one of the pick-up places he had frequented in the past. What seemed important to this young man amid other gains was that he now had his own imaginative capacities working for him as an asset in the determination to modify his own behavioral style.

Concern that such a person could become excessively dependent upon the therapist did not prove justified. The patient's new-found capacities for imagery and fantasy seemed to provide him with an alternative to the direct availability of the therapist. In addition, he was able to find resources of masculinity within himself that were strongly reinforced in the relationship with the young woman he eventually married. She was by no means a shrinking violet. Indeed, she was an effective and forceful young woman with a career in her own right, but at the same time with considerable respect for this young man's strengths and also with a strong attraction to him physically. Where his homosexual relationships had all been "one-night stands" with a host of faceless men whose names he never even learned, his relationship with this woman was a complex and differentiated one that gave him the sense of being a much more genuine person.

It should be clear that in this case, along with the use of a somewhat ritualized form of behavior modification, the approach was set in a much broader context of overall personality change. The personality change, it must be stressed, was manifested not merely in a different pattern of verbalizations by the patient about himself or relationships, but also in the trying of new behavioral patterns and the opportunity to obtain different kinds of reinforcement from those he had received in the past. In effect, a way was established for the patient to enter a new sequence of relationships that could feed back new experiences to him and that would lead to further broadening of his personality potentialities. In this sense, one can also see that symptom removal or a direct attack on particular problems can have a broadening effect on the total personality.

THE ROLE OF THE THERAPIST
IN IMAGERY METHODS OF PSYCHOTHERAPY

The position I am taking is that the psychotherapist is first of all a technically skilled expert who offers his services to clients on the basis of his practice of a scientific discipline. Research suggests that empathic capacities, sensitivity to nuances of interpersonal behavior, and freedom from severe personal problems are all important components of the personality of the therapist that play a positive role in his effectiveness in practice. Nevertheless, I believe it is urgent for the mental health professions to recognize that they are not simply in the business of providing loving kindness. Although some of the value of psychotherapy is indeed reflected in Schofield's phrase, "the purchase of friendship," it would be a shame if this was all that therapists could offer. Hopefully, the therapist should be able to establish circumstances that make his services no longer necessary so that the patient is in a position to find his own friends and engage in an extended personal life without further recourse to the therapist or, at worst, with occasional brief contacts over the years.

If one reads the case reports of European practitioners, there seems little question that their stance is one of a professional relationship in which they do offer their particular technology whether it is more analytically oriented or a mental imagery approach. It is likely that even in the mental imagery methods, the therapist's role is more than just that of a kind of neutral guide, and he may be the subject of some additional transference reactions. The effectiveness of the treatment, however, at least as reported in the case studies accumulated by Leuner or Fretigny and Virel, make it clear that patients do not become excessively dependent in the course of imagery trips.

In some ways the psychotherapist can be viewed as a teacher, as well as a technician. This does not mean that he gives formal lectures, for even good teachers know that they are not always the best method of influencing their pupils. Still, the therapist's role is to help the patient not only find out about himself, but also try out new ways of relating to others and new ways of looking at a variety of life situations. The therapist, like the teacher, has a background of formal knowledge beyond the patient's, as well as his personal experiences. These he has to communicate to the patient in a fashion that can be as useful as possible. Examples of this approach include the kinds of shifts in attribution that the therapist can help the patient make. Even in the behavior modification cases described variously by Wolpe and Lazarus, among others, one sees again and again examples of the therapist actively conveying new information to the patient or guiding the patient to a realization that he has a false or distorted set of expectations about certain kinds of relationships or about sexual behavior.

Ellis' *rational-emotive therapy* (Ellis, 1973) is one of the most explicit expressions of this position. The therapist, without ignoring the importance of affective involvement on the part of the patient, is concerned with helping the patient examine the range of assumptions he makes about social or sexual behavior and consider alternative possibilities. Here again, the therapist's experience with the effectiveness of imagery is employed to provide technical means for the patient to enhance certain affects. Ellis has recognized earlier than many clinicians how imagery is often used adaptively to produce certain states of sexual arousal or to shift attention away from distracting or distressing behavior. Research supports the general notion that sexual fantasies of women during intercourse can be used for adaptive purposes (Hariton & Singer, 1974). The knowledgeable therapist cannot only help the patient reexamine his situation, but can also provide some techniques that will further develop skills of the patient in self-analysis, interpersonal communication, and in dealing with fears or aversions.

In the case described earlier, I referred to the therapist as a role model in specific instances for the patient. This is a particularly dangerous game to play if engaged in to a large degree without attention to the distorting aspects of transference so extensively documented by psychoanalytic clinicians. It seems to me to have been especially mishandled by a number of "guru"-type humanist therapists, and more specifically by someone like Frederick Perls in his Esalen days. One is often faced with the dilemma that therapists generally have achieved their status through considerable self-discipline in earlier years, attention to their studies, and, in general, by meeting the formal demands of society. They may feel they have become too inhibited and now yearn for greater freedom in their later years. Patients, however, generally come for therapy, as Strupp has pointed out so effectively, because they seek to control their emotionality, which has run rampant and led them into embarrassing or painful situations, or because they are too dependent or socially limited in a variety of ways. The patients generally admire the self-discipline and control and effectiveness of the analyst, and it is this which they seek to emulate for themselves. For therapists to encourage a loosening of controls and great freedom and flexibility in social interchange may often be useful for a very small group of overintellectualized, inhibited patients, but the larger group of patients probably are more in need of development of skills for self-restraint or more discriminating kinds of flexibility.

It would seem more appropriate that modeling behavior on the part of the therapist be limited primarily to the demonstration of the kinds of skills that do not prejudge the many differences between the patient's and therapist's lives. In this sense, the therapist's demonstration that imagery skills are available and can be used, and even therapist's ability to interpret dreams or occasionally to show some self-awareness or willingness to examine his own imagery, may be a useful example that the patient can take away with him.

The therapist may also be a useful imaginary companion for the patient in the sense that I have described. For example, in the instance of one patient who was phobic about traveling and concerned about a long driving trip in a foreign country, I encouraged her to help pass the time by imagining that she was narrating the details of the trip to me or to some other person in her life. There was some practice during the session in this technique in imaginary form, and then the patient subsequently found that she was able to use this approach on a few instances when she became aware of mounting anxiety during the course of the actual automobile trip. The modeling usage of the therapist should be limited to providing the patient with new potential skills or with an awareness of alternative ways of reacting to certain situations. It seems arrogant for a therapist to assume that one's personal way of life is automatically generalizable to a large number of individuals from very different backgrounds who go back after the therapy session to very diverse family and work situations.

I have left for last the role of the therapist as psychoanalyst. I believe even here that most psychoanalysis involves some combination of the guide, teacher, and model roles. The analytic stance, perhaps more than any other, however, is one that imposes an ascetic demand for sober self-examination at each point in the course of the therapeutic encounter. The analyst is concerned that the patient explore dreams, fantasies, fleeting passing thoughts, as well as review, in detail, significant interpersonal exchanges. The approach of Socrates implies that the unexamined life is not worth living and involves essentially interminable self-examination. This orientation and ideal is at once the strength and limitation of analysis. It has some of the elements of a lifetime activity and of a kind of philosophical quest since, after all, it is never entirely possible to ascertain when an analysis of this kind has terminated. Nevertheless, the therapeutic stance that involves serious attention to the examination of the patient's transference distortions, the nuances of the relationship, the elaborate nature of ongoing fantasies and dreams may be something that can also be transferred to the patient. Care must be taken lest this tendency be used in an obsessive and ruminative fashion as sometimes happens to make analytic patients such utter social bores. An important outcome of the analytic style is the patient's awareness that his own private products, his thoughts, daydreams, and night dreams are important and significant features of his life situation and worthy of sustained attention and study.

A REVIEW OF THE SPECIFIC USES
OF IMAGERY IN PSYCHOTHERAPY

The patient who comes for psychotherapy or relief of symptomatic difficulties brings with him generally the same basic capacity for imagery as all human beings. What is noteworthy, however, is that often enough the awareness of ongoing imagery or the sustained attention to such imagery characterizing certain individuals (Singer & Antrobus, 1972) shows wide individual differences in the general population. Most of us, as I mentioned earlier, have learned to ignore much of the ongoing processing of our brain in order to steer ourselves through the external environment. One of the first steps, then, in the use of imagery in therapy is that the therapist, by calling attention to the importance of private processes, dreams, fantasies and by noting the possibility that imagery can be used as a resource in the treatment, opens up a dimension that has been glimpsed only briefly by many patients in the past. The therapeutic process in effect calls attention to the ongoing interior monologue which most people ignore except for their thrill of recognition when they see it in the writings of a fine novelist. The same situation holds for the increased awareness of dreams and the gradual accumulation by the patient of his own dream log and awareness that the dreams are to some extent aspects of his own personality and reasonably interpretable.

A second important feature of the use of imagery is the fact that the patient now becomes aware that many of his thoughts about people, some of his fantasies or expectations, and indeed some of his judgments actually represent poorly assimilated childhood information about human relationships or sexual functions that are no longer appropriate for his current life situation. Thus, he begins to pay increasing attention to his own expectations about people or specific situations and to ascertain the degree to which they may be reflections of fantasy situations. In this sense, therapeutic work makes increasingly explicit the kind of theorizing that Miller *et al.* (1960) have proposed for the normal pattern of day-to-day behavior, the important function of anticipatory planning and cognitive structures in the ways in which the individual moves through the world. If the therapist is appropriately conscious of what he is doing in encouraging this type of examination, he can help the patient develop a very significant asset for his further autonomous development—a heightened capacity for examining his wishes and plans in relation to a variety of alternative possibilities and options in his life situation. Once again, the patient thus is in a position to experience a control over his own thought processes.

Another important function of imagery has to do with the patient's recognition that he has indeed stored a great many more experiences than he ordinarily notices. The establishment of various contexts for the revival of earlier memories makes it clear to a patient that his past, indeed many of his earlier experiences, are more accessible to him than he believed. Such heightened awareness and the use of this material reflect a significant gain in ego functioning. The recall of earlier events also is often associated with a vivid revival of emotion. Again, the patient becomes aware that cognition and emotion are closely intertwined and that he is not as much a creature of cliche as he might have expected. He finds that he can in effect savor his emotions; thereby he experiences greater control over them, as well as a greater capacity to express them—both important human motivations, as Tomkins (1962) has pointed out.

Specifically related to the issue of emotion is the important discovery a patient can make that his capacity for producing positive affect through specific imagery or for shifting away from a negative affective pattern by this means is an extremely valuable asset. At the simplest level we have, of course, the *Power of Positive Thinking* or some form of a Coué ritual. I believe this experience goes far deeper, however. The patient does not simply rely on ritualized phrases or cliches. He has generated powerful and important personal experiences that he can now manipulate to elaborate on his own ongoing mood or can use to distract himself from a seemingly serious negative affect that may lead him to impulsive action or create overt difficulties for him in his significant relationships. It is nonsense to believe that the awareness of the fact that imagery can produce affective change will help a patient overcome the natural grief at the loss of a loved one or at a natural catastrophe. To paraphrase Freud, the goal of psychotherapy is to deal with the excessive burden of childhood neuroses or other distorted difficulties in order to allow us strength to face the real horrors that surround us in our human condition. The advantage of the imagery is this: under conditions in which unexpected negative affects occur, or under which one cannot change a mood and is being led deeper into a morass, the use of the positive imagery method may be particularly effective. Izard (1971) has elaborated even further on the various uses of affect discrimination in the therapeutic process. Here, again, imagery may play a useful role in providing one with situations that are likely to evoke differential affective reactions.

Still another function of imagery in the therapeutic process involves its immediacy and parallel processing aspects. The patient who finds himself going on in a rather stereotyped fashion about the fact that there is nothing to say or nothing of interest to report and the days have been pretty much the same, etc. may find that quietly sitting back and allowing pictures to come to his mind will lead to a fruitful new direction of exploration. The sequential characteristics of language can be usefully circumvented by reliance on imagery, which not only provides a detailed picture of the situation, and is likely to establish a context for the revival of relevant emotion, but also, often enough, will also provide some clue as to the bases for resistance which the patient may be experiencing toward moving in certain directions. Resistance, as many therapists are aware, is often manifested by elaborate verbalization, but without any reliance on imagery-related words. The resort to imagery may catch the patient by surprise and outwit his defenses, as Reyher (1963) has so strongly argued.

Of course, excessive imagery can also serve defensive or resistive purposes. Individuals who are shy or hesitant to engage in direct interaction may find themselves resorting extensively to their ongoing fantasy lives as a comfort, on the one hand, and as a means of avoiding contact or communication with others. In Chekhov's *The Cherry Orchard,* the sadly ineffective aristocratic brother of the heroine is much given to playing mental games of billiards and in the midst of ordinary conversation, he suddenly makes comments such as "six ball to the left pocket." Obviously, he is indulging in an elaborate imagery reproduction of his favorite game, rather than attending carefully to the conversation of persons around him. The same dilemma can occur in psychotherapy when patients frequently bring in such elaborate dreams that hour after hour is taken up in narration without any possibility of real understanding or self-awareness. These situations are, however, not that common and probably could be dealt with fairly effectively by some of the thought-stopping techniques. We do, however, need more research on the use of related thought-stopping methods for the control of severe obsessional ruminations which in the past have been recalcitrant to therapeutic intervention.

CREATIVITY AND THE ENHANCEMENT OF AESTHETIC APPRECIATION

It is not necessary at this point to review other uses of imagery that have been dealt with at length in this volume—the specific behavior modification techniques or the mental imagery trips. I should like to close this chapter with some mention of an important dimension not sufficiently attended to in the imagery sphere that can be a valuable outgrowth of psychotherapeutic activity. I refer to the likelihood that the increased awareness of imagery and willingness to use it on the part of the patient as a consequence of its effective use in the treatment may also open up a new aesthetic dimension for many persons who have, in the past, ignored the variety and colorful quality of private experiences. This can include enhanced creativity. By creativity I do not necessarily mean the capacity to produce a great work of art or science. There are many kinds of creative ways of relating in normal human interaction, which can be heightened by sensitivity to fantasy and the transformations of dreams or daydreams. Just the ability to use imagery in expressing oneself or the possibility of mentally trying out a variety of odd alternatives prior to some social situation may lead to a unique or interesting approach by the patient in that new situation. Here we deal with the kind of creativity also fostered by someone like Gordon (1961) in his development of *synectics*—an approach particularly oriented toward scientists and engineers to help them develop original orientations to problem solutions.

Self-disclosure in imagery form can also be a meaningful way of communicating with another person and suggesting deeper feeling. Remember the song, "I'll tell you my dream, you tell me yours." In addition to increasing ability to use divergent thinking (Guilford, 1967), the awareness of imagery and greater control in the use of one's own daydreams and fantasies make it possible for a subtler appreciation of many aspects of art and culture.

Much of the significant literature in Western civilization has been produced by rather introspective individuals who, in poetry, fiction, or philosophical essays, have paid considerable attention to their own ongoing streams of thought. The person whose sensitivity to imagery has been deepened will more quickly experience the shock of recognition and the associated affect of joy in reading material from many of the great classic writers, as well as the sensitive new novelists or poets. Much of the world's art represents either in fairly direct or abstract form some attempt to capture private experience and present it in a form that is reasonably recognizable to members of a particular culture. Greater sensitivity to one's own imagery will increase awareness of what the painter or sculptor may have been striving to communicate as drawn from *his* own experience.

A similar possibility exists for the appreciation of humor. McGhee (1971) has noted that we still know too little about the role of fantasy in humor, but he has emphasized the arousal and then recognition pattern that seems to be characteristic of the humor sequence. It is my own guess that the ability to "take an attitude toward the possible," as Kurt Goldstein (1940) used to put it, makes for the creation and appreciation of humor. Much humor is, of course, closely related to obvious tabu subjects such as sex or excretory functions. A considerable amount of the greatest humor, however, has a somewhat different orientation and is built more upon an arousal of an expectation and then a shift from it — sometimes even with a hint of sadness. Remember the Charles Addams cartoon of the lone unicorn gazing wistfully after the departing Noah's Ark. Wild shifts of focus, such as those appearing in some of the Chaplin or Woody Allen movies, represent similar examples of a play with divergent processes leading to a situation that is humorous by its very dramatic shift from a conventional expectation. For the person not much given to playing with his own thoughts and fantasies, some of this kind of humor will not seem at all funny. It will, if anything, seem so complex and unassimilable as to arouse some fear or startle reaction without any opportunity to match this up against one's own previous established schema for outlandish thoughts. The more active fantasizer given to playing with a variety of possibilities in his own thought will be more prepared for the wild shift of focus of a great comedian and, while startled momentarily by the shift, can then make a connection and reduce the aroused condition so that the experience of joy or laughter follows.

In Chaplin's "Modern Times," the little tramp sees a red flag fall off a passing construction truck. He picks it up and runs after the truck, waving. Suddenly a Communist parade comes around the corner just behind him and, needless to say, he becomes embroiled in a melee with the awaiting police. In Woody Allen's "Bananas," the hero under pursuit from police inadvertently picks up a cross-shaped tire tool and joins a religious procession that is passing, thus managing to avoid detection. The scene is funny in its own right, but even funnier if one can make the additional match to the Chaplin scene before it which Allen clearly had in mind.

An important asset, then, that can come from therapeutic experience or from the many kinds of imagery training now being explored in the human potential movement or in research on child training (Singer, 1973) is a general enrichment of one's behavioral repertory. It should be clear that we are on the threshold of important new areas of study and practical application of the great storage and imagery capacities of our brain. The various psychotherapeutic uses of imagery may suffer from vagueness and imprecision of definition. Nevertheless, their significant achievements in ameliorating symptomatic distress and in broadening personal horizons for patients cannot be ignored. The time at last seems ripe for scientists and clinicians to work more closely to explore a human capacity whose potential we have only begun to tap for psychotherapy, education, and creative living.

REFERENCES

Ahsen, A. *Basic concepts in eidetic psychotherapy.* New York: Eidetic Publ., 1968.

Alexander, E. D. From play therapy to encounter marathon. *Psychotherapy,* 1969, **6,** 188–193.

Allen, D. T. The crib scene: A psychodramatic exercise. *Psychotherapy,* 1969, **6,** 206–208.

Anant, D. D. A note on the treatment of alcoholics by a verbal aversion technique. *Canadian Psychologist,* 1967, **1,** 19–22.

Antrobus, J. S. Information theory and stimulus-independent thought. *British Journal of Psychology,* 1968, **59,** 423–430.

Antrobus, J. S., Antrobus, Judith S., & Singer, J. L. Eye movements accompanying daydreaming, visual imagery, and thought suppression. *Journal of Abnormal and Social Psychology, 1964,* **69,** 244–252.

Antrobus, J. S., Coleman, R., & Singer, J. L. Signal-detection performance by subjects differing in predisposition to daydreaming. *Journal of Consulting Psychology,* 1967, **31,** 487–491.

Antrobus, J. S., & Singer, J. L. Visual signal detection of a function of sequential variability of simultaneous speech. *Journal of Experimental Psychology,* 1964, **68,** 603–610.

Antrobus, J. S., Singer, J. L., Goldstein, S., & Fortgang, M. Mindwandering and cognitive structure. *Transactions of the New York Academy of Sciences,* 1970, **32,** 242–252.

Antrobus, J. S., Singer, J. L., & Greenberg, S. Studies in the stream of consciousness. *Perceptual and Motor Skills,* 1966, **23,** 399–417.

Arieti, S. *The intrapsychic self.* New York: Basic Books, 1967.

Arkin, A. M., Antrobus, J. S., Toth, M., & Sander, K. The effects of REM deprivation on sleep mentation—progress report no. 2. In M. H. Chase, W. C. Stern, & P. L. Walter (Eds.), *Sleep research.* Vol. 1. Los Angeles: Brain Research Institute, 1972.

Ascher, L. M., & Cautela, J. Covert negative reinforcement: An experimental test. *Journal of Behavior Therapy and Experimental Psychology,* 1972, **3,** 1–5.

Aserinsky, E., & Kleitman, N. Regularly occurring periods of eye motility, and concomitant phenomena during sleep. *Science,* 1953, **118,** 273–274.

Ashem, B., & Donner, L. Covert sensitization with alcoholics. A controlled replication. *Behavior Research and Therapy,* 1968, **6,** 7–12.

Assagioli, R. *Dynamic psychology and psychosynthesis.* New York: Psychosynthesis Research Foundation, 1959.

Assagioli, R. *Psychosynthesis: A manual of principles and techniques.* New York: Hobbs, Dorman, 1965.

Assagioli, R. Symbols of transpersonal experiences. *Journal of Transpersonal Psychology* 1969, **1**, 30–37.

Ayer, W. Implosive therapy: A review. *Psychotherapy*, 1972, **9**, 242–250.

Bach, G. *Intensive group psychotherapy.* New York: Ronald, 1954.

Bachélard, G. *On poetic imagination and reverie.* New York: Bobbs-Merrill, 1971.

Bachélard, G. *The psychoanalysis of fire.* Boston: Beacon, 1964.

Bachélard, G. *The poetics of reverie.* Boston: Beacon, 1969.

Bakan, P. Hypnotizability, laterality of eye movements and function of brain asymmetry. *Perceptual and Motor Skills*, 1969, **28**, 927–932.

Bakan, P. The eyes have it. *Psychology Today*, 1971, **4**, 64–68.

Baker, B. L. Symptom treatment and symptom substitution in enuresis. *Journal of Abnormal Psychology*, 1969, **74**, 42–49.

Bandler, R. J., Madaras, G. R., & Bern, D. J. Self-observation as a source of pain. *Journal of Personality and Social Psychology*, 1968, **9**, 205–209.

Bandura, A. *Principles of behavior modification.* New York: Holt, Rinehart & Winston, 1969.

Bandura, A. *Psychological modeling.* New York: Atherton, 1971.

Bandura, A., & Barab, P. Processes governing disinhibitory effects through symbolic modeling. *Journal of Abnormal Psychology*, 1973, **82**, 1–9.

Bandura, A. Blanchard, E. B., & Ritter, B. Relative efficacy of desensitization and modeling approaches for inducing behavioral, affective, and attitudinal changes. *Journal of Personality and Social Psychology*, 1969, **13**, 173–199.

Bandura, A., Grusec, J. E., & Menlove, F. L. Observational learning as a function of symbolization and incentive set. *Child Development*, 1966, **37**, 499–506.

Bandura, A., & Jeffrey, R. The role of symbolic coding, cognitive organization and rehearsal processes in observational learning. *Journal of Personality and Social Psychology*, 1973, **26**, 122–130.

Bandura, A., & Menlove, F. Factors determining vicarious extinction of avoidance behavior through symbolic modeling. *Journal of Personality and Social Psychology*, 1968, **8**, 99–108.

Barber, T. X. *LSD, marihuana, yoga and hypnosis.* Chicago: Aldine, 1970.

Barber, T. X., & Hahn, K. W., Jr. Experimental studies in "hypnotic" behavior: Physiological and subjective effects of imagined pain. *Journal of Nervous and Mental Disease*, 1964, **139**, 416–425.

Barlow, D. H., Leitenberg, H., & Agras, W. S. Experimental control of sexual deviation through manipulation of the noxious scene in covert sensitization. *Journal of Abnormal Psychology*, 1969, **74**, 596–600.

Barolin, G. Spontane Altersregression in Symboldrama und ihre klinische Bedeutung. *Zeitschrift für Psychotherapie und Medizinsche Psychologie*, 1961, **3**, 11.

Beck, M. Rehabilitation eines chronischen Trinkers mit des Methode des katathymen Bilderlebens. *Praxis Psychotherapie*, 1968, **13**, 3, 97–103.

Berdach, E., & Bakan, P. Body position and free recall of early memories. *Psychotherapy*, 1967, **4**, 101–102.

Berecz, J. M. The modification of smoking behavior through self-administered punishment of imagined behavior: A new approach to aversion therapy. *Journal of Consulting and Clinical Psychology*, 1972, **38**, 244–250.

Bergin, A. E. Further comments on psychotherapy research and therapeutic practice. *International Journal of Psychiatry*, 1967, **3**, 317–323.

Bergin, A. E. A technique for improving desensitization via warmth, empathy, and emotional re-experiencing of hierarchy events. In R. Rubin & C. M. Franks (Eds.) *Advances in behavior therapy.* New York: Academic Press, 1969.

Berlyne, D. E. *Structure and direction in thinking.* New York: Wiley, 1965.

Berne, E. *Games people play.* New York: Grove, 1964.

Bertini, M., Lewis, H., & Witkin, H. Some preliminary observations with an experimental procedure for the study of hypnogogic and similar phenomena. *Archivio di psicologia, neurologia, e psichiatria,* 1964, **25,** 495–535.

Binet, A. *L'étude experimentale de l'intelligence.* Paris: Alfred Costes, 1922.

Bion, W. R. Experience in groups: I. *Human Relations,* 1948, **1,** 314–320.

Bonime, W. *The clinical use of dreams.* New York: Basic Books, 1962.

Borkavec, T. D. Effects of expectancy on the outcome of systematic desensitization and implosive treatments for analogue anxiety. *Behavior Therapy,* 1972, **3,** 29–40.

Boulogouris, J., & Marks, I. M. Implosion (flooding): A new treatment for phobias. *British Medical Journal,* 1969, **2,** 309–319.

Boulogouris, J., Marks, I. M., & Marset, P. Superiority of flooding (implosion) to desensitization for reducing pathological fear. *Behavior Research and Therapy,* 1971, **9,** 7–16.

Bower, G. H. Imagery as a relational organizer in associative learning. *Journal of Verbal Learning and Verbal Behavior,* 1970, **9,** 529–533.   (a)

Bower, G. H. Mental imagery and associative learning. In L. Gregg (Ed.) *Cognition in learning and memory.* New York: Wiley, 1973.

Breger, L., Hunter, I., & Lane, R. W. *The effect of stress dreams.* New York: International Universities Press, 1971.

Breger, L., & McGaugh, J. L. Critique and reformulation of "learning-theory" approaches to psychotherapy and neurosis. *Psychological Bulletin,* 1965, **63,** 338–358.

Broadbent, D. E. *Perception and communication.* New York: Pergamon, 1958.

Bruner, J. S. The course of cognitive growth. *American Psychologist,* 1964, **19,** 1–15.

Caligor, L., & May, R. *Dreams and symbols.* New York: Basic Books, 1968.

Carlin, M. T. The effects of modeled behavior during imposed delay on the observer's subsequent willingness to delay rewards. *Dissertation Abstracts,* 1966, **26,** 6834–6835.

Cautela, J. R. Treatment of compulsive behavior by covert sensitization. *Psychological Record,* 1966, **16,** 33–41.

Cautela, J. R. Covert sensitization. *Psychological Reports,* 1967, **20,** 459–468.

Cautela, J. R. Behavior therapy and self-control: Techniques and implications. In C. M. Franks (Ed.) *The assessment and status of the behavior therapies and associated developments.* New York: McGraw-Hill, 1969.

Cautela, J. R. Covert reinforcement. *Behavior Therapy,* 1970, **1,** 33–50.

Cautela, J. R. Covert extinction. *Behavior Therapy,* 1971, **2,** 192–200.

Cautela, J. R. Reinforcement survey schedule: Evaluation and current applications. *Psychological Reports,* 1972, **30,** 683–690.

Cautela, J. R. Covert conditioning. Unpublished manuscript, 1974.

Cautela, J. R., & Kastenbaum, R. A reinforcement survey schedule for use in therapy, training, and research. *Psychological Reports,* 1967, **20,** 1115–1130.

Cautela, J. R., Steppen, J., & Wish, P. An experimental test of covert reinforcement. *Journal of Consulting and Clinical Psychology,* 1974 (in press).

Cautela, J. R., Walsh, K., & Wish, P. The use of covert reinforcement in the modification of attitudes toward the mentally retarded. *The Journal of Psychology,* 1971, **77,** 257–260.

Cautela, J. R., & Wisocki, P. A. Covert sensitization for the treatment of sexual deviations. *Psychological Record,* 1971, **21,** 37–48.

Chapman, C., & Feather, R. Sensitivity to phobic imagery: A sensory decision theory analysis. *Behavior Research and Therapy,* 1971, **9,** 161–168.

Chase, M., Stern, C. S., & Walter, P. L. *Sleep research,* Vol. 1. Los Angeles: Brain Research Institute, 1972.

Chateau, J. *L'enfant et le jeu.* Paris: Scarabee, 1967.

Chittenden, G. E. An experimental study in measuring and modifying assertive behavior in young children. *Monographs of the Society for Research in Child Development*, 1942 (**1**, Serial No. 31).

Clark, P. The phantasy method of analysing narcissistic neuroses. *Psychoanalytic Review*, 1925, **13**, 225–232.

Crampton, M. The visual "Who am I?" method: An approach to experience of the self. *Psychosynthesis Research Foundation*, 1968, **23**, 19–40.

Darwin, P. L., & McBrearty, J. F. The subject speaks up in desensitization. In R. Rubin & C. M. Franks (Ed.), *Advances in behavior therapy*, 1968. New York: Academic Press, 1969.

Daudet, L. *Le rêve éveillé*. Paris: Bernard Grasset, 1926.

Davison, G. C. Elimination of a sadistic fantasy by a client-controlled counter-conditioning technique: A case study. *Journal of Abnormal Psychology*, 1968, **73**, 84–90.

Davison, G. C., & Wilson, G. T. Critique of "Desensitization: Social and cognitive factors underlying the effectiveness of Wolpe's procedure." *Psychological Bulletin*, 1972, **78**, 28–31.

Day, M. E. An eye-movement indicator of type and level of anxiety: Some clinical observations. *Journal of Clinical Psychology*, 1967, **23**, 428–441.

Desoille, R. *Exploration de l'affectivité subconsciente par la méthode du rêve éveillé*. Paris: D'Autry, 1938.

Desoille, R. *Le rêve éveillé en psychothérapie (essaie sur la fonction de régulation de l'inconscient collectif)*. Paris: P.O.F., 1945.

Desoille, R. *Theorie et pratique du rêve éveillé dirigé*. Geneva: Mont-Blanc, 1961.

Desoille, R. Groupe d'études du rêve éveillé dirigé en psychothérapie. Séance du 26 mai 1966. *Bulletin de la Société de recherches psychothérapiques de langue française*, 1966, **IV**, 52–59.

Donnars, J. Troubles de la sphère ano–genito–urinaire révelés par l'imagerie mentale. *Proceedings of 3rd International Congress of Le Société Internationale des Techniques d'Imagerie Mentale, Cortina, Italy, 1970*.

Drucker, E. Studies on the role of temporal uncertainty in the deployment of attention. Unpublished doctoral dissertation. The City University of New York, 1969.

Dunn, S., Bliss, J., & Siipola, E. Effects of impulsivity, introversion and individual values upon association under free conditions. *Journal of Personality*, 1958, **26**, 61–76.

Dweck, C. The role of expectations and attributions in the alleviation of learned helplessness in a problem-solving situation. *Dissertation Abstracts International*, 1972, **33**, 2317, 2318.

Ekman, P., Friesen, W. V., & Ellsworth, P. *Emotions in the human face: Guidelines for research and a review of findings*. New York: Pergamon, 1971.

Ellis, A. The no cop-out theory. *Psychology Today*, 1973, **7**, 56–60.

Fazio, A. F. Treatment components in implosive therapy. *Journal of Abnormal Psychology*, 1970, **76**, 211–219.

Feingold, L. An automated technique for aversive conditioning in sexual deviations. In R. Rubin & C. M. Franks (Eds.), *Advances in behavior therapy*. New York: Academic Press, 1969.

Feldman, M. P. Aversion therapy for sexual deviations: A critical review. *Psychological Bulletin*, 1966, **65**, 65–79.

Feldman, M. P., & MacCulloch, M. J. The application of anticipatory avoidance learning to the treatment of homosexuality. I: Theory, technique and preliminary results. *Behavior Research and Therapy*, 1965, **2**, 165–183.

Feldstein, S. REM sleep deprivation and waking thought. Unpublished doctoral dissertation, City University of New York, 1972.

Fenichel, O. *The psychoanalytic theory of neurosis.* New York: Norton, 1945.

Filler, M. S., & Giambra, L. M. Daydreaming as a function of cueing and task difficulty. *Perceptual and Motor Skills,* 1974, in press.

Fischer, R. A cartography of ecstatic and meditative states, *Science,* 1971, **174,** 897–904.

Foulkes, D. *The psychology of sleep.* New York: Scribners, 1966.

Frétigny, R., & Virel, A. Imagerie mentale et odeurs. Proceedings of the 2nd Conference of the International Society of Mental Imagery Techniques, Paris, 1967.

Frétigny, R., & Virel, A. *L'imagerie mentale.* Geneva: Mont-Blanc, 1968.

Freud, S. Studies on hysteria. (Breuer, J., and Freud, S.) In J. Strachey (Ed.), *The standard edition.* Vol. 2. London: Hogarth, 1955.

Freud, S. The interpretation of dreams. In J. Strachey (Ed.), *The standard edition.* Vols. 4, 5. London: Hogarth, 1962.

Freud, S. Freud's psychoanalytic procedure. In J. Strachey (Ed.), *The standard edition.* Vol. 7. London: Hogarth, 1962. Pp. 249–254.

Freud, S. Project for a scientific psychology. In J. Strachey (Ed.), *The standard edition.* Vol. 1. London: Hogarth, 1966. Pp. 283–344.

Freyberg, J. T. Increasing the imaginative play of urban disadvantaged kindergarten children through systematic training. In J. L. Singer, *The child's world of make-believe.* New York: Academic Press, 1973.

Fromm, E. *The forgotten language.* New York: Rinehart, 1951.

Fusella, V. Blocking of an external signal through self-projected imagery: The role of inner-acceptant personality style and categories of imagery. Unpublished doctoral dissertation, City University of New York, 1972.

Geissman, P., & Noel, C. EEG study with frequency analysis and polygraphy of autogenic training. *Proceedings of the 3rd World Congress of Psychiatry,* 1961, **3,** 468–472.

Gendlin, E. T. Focusing. *Psychotherapy,* 1969, **6,** 4–15.

Gerard, R. Psychosynthesis: A psychotherapy for the whole man. *Psychosynthesis Research Foundation.* Issue no. 14, 1964.

Gerst, M. S. Symbolic coding process in observational learning. *Journal of Personality and Social Psychology,* 1971, **19,** 9–17.

Gold, S., & Neufeld, I. L. A learning approach to the treatment of homosexuality. *Behavior Research and Therapy,* 1965, **2,** 201–204.

Goldfried, M. Systematic desensitization as training in self-control. *Journal of Consulting and Clinical Psychology,* 1971, **37,** 228–234.

Goldstein, K. *Human nature in the light of psychopathology.* Cambridge, Massachusetts: Harvard University Press, 1940.

Gordon, W. J. J. *Synectics: The development of creative capacity.* New York: Harper and Brothers, 1961.

Gottlieb, S. Modeling effects upon fantasy. In J. L. Singer, *The child's world of make-believe.* New York: Academic Press, 1973.

Green, E. E., Green, A. M., & Walters, E. D. Voluntary control of internal states: Psychological and Physiological. *Journal of Transpersonal Psychology,* 1970, **2,** 1–26.

Green, M., Ullman, M., & Tauber, E. Dreaming and modern dream theory. In J. Marmor (Ed.), *Modern psychoanalysis.* New York: Basic Books, 1968.

Greene, R. J. & Reyher, J. Pain tolerance in hypnotic analgesic and imagination states. *Journal of Abnormal Psychology,* 1972, **79,** 29–38.

Grey, A. Oedipus in Hindu dreams, Gandhi's life and Erikson's concepts. *Contemporary Psychoanalysis,* 1973, **9,** 327–355.

Grossberg, J. M., & Wilson, H. Physiological changes accompanying the visualization of fearful and neutral situations. *Journal of Personality and Social Psychology,* 1968, **10,** 124–133.

Guilford, J. P. *The nature of human intelligence.* New York: McGraw-Hill, 1967.

Haber, R. N. How can we remember what we see? *Scientific American,* 1970, **222,** 104–112.

Haber, R. N., & Haber, R. B. Eidetic imagery, I. Frequency. *Perceptual and Motor Skills,* 1964, **19,** 131–138.

Hall, C. S., & Lind, R. E. *Dreams, life and literature: A study of Franz Kafka.* Chapel Hill, North Carolina: Univ. of North Carolina Press, 1970.

Hall, E. S., & Nordby, V. J. *The individual and his dreams.* New York: Signet, 1972.

Hammer, M. The directed daydream technique. *Psychotherapy,* 1967, **4,** 173–181.

Happich, C. Das Bildewusstein als ansatzstelle psychischer Behandlung. *Zentreblatt Psychotherapie,* 1932, **5.**

Hariton, B., & Singer, J. L. Women's fantasies during marital intercourse. *Journal of Consulting and Clinical Psychology.* 1974. (In press.).

Hartmann, H. *Ego psychology and the problem of adaptation.* New York: International Universities Press, 1958.

Hebb, D. O. The American revolution. *American Psychologist,* 1960, **15,** 735–745.

Hebb, D. O. Concerning imagery. *Psychological Review,* 1968, **75,** 466–477.

Hilgard, E. R. *Hypnotic susceptibility.* New York: Harcourt, 1965.

Hilgard, E. R. A neodissociation interpretation of pain reduction in hypnosis. *Psychological Review,* 1973, **80,** 396–411.

Hodgson, R. J., & Rachman, S. An experimental investigation of the implosion technique. *Behavior Research and Therapy, 1970,* **8,** 21–28.

Hogan, R. A., & Kirchner, J. H. A preliminary report of the extinction of learned fears via short term implosive therapy. *Journal of Abnormal Psychology,* 1967, **72,** 106–111.

Hogan, R. A., & Kirchner, J. H. Implosive, eclectic, verbal and bibliotherapy in the treatment of fears of snakes. *Behavior Research and Therapy,* 1968, **6,** 167–171.

Holt, R. Imagery: The return of the ostracized. *American Psychologist,* 1964, **19,** 254–264.

Holt, R. Beyond vitalism and mechanism. In J. H. Massenman (Ed.), *Science and psychoanalysis,* Vol. XI. New York: Grune & Stratton, 1967.

Holt, R. On the nature and generality of mental imagery. In P. Sheehan (Ed.), *The function and nature of imagery.* New York: Academic Press, 1972.

Horowitz, M. J. *Image formation and cognition.* New York: Appleton, 1970.

Howlett, S., & Nawas, M. M. Exposure to aversive imagery and suggestion in systematic desensitization. In R. Rubin, H. Fensterheim, A. A. Lazarus, & C. M. Franks (Eds.), *Advances in behavior therapy.* New York: Academic Press, 1971.

Hume, D. *An Inquiry concerning human understanding.* Chicago: Open Court, 1912.

Izard, C. E. *The face of emotion.* New York: Appleton, 1971.

Izard, C. E. *Patterns of emotions.* New York: Academic Press, 1972.

Jackson, J. H. *Selected writings,* 2 vols. New York: Basic Books, 1958.

Jacobs, A., & Sachs, L. B. *The psychology of private events.* New York: Academic Press, 1971.

Jacobsen, E. *Progressive relaxation.* Chicago: Univ. of Chicago Press, 1938.

Jaensch, E. R. *Eidetic imagery and typological methods of investigation.* New York: Harcourt, 1930.

James, W. *Principles of psychology.* New York: Holt, 1890.

Janda, L. H., & Rimm, D. C. Covert sensitization in the treatment of obesity. *Journal of Abnormal Psychology.* 1972, **80,** 37–42.

Johnsgard, K. W. Symbol confrontation in a recurrent nightmare. *Psychotherapy,* 1969, **6,** 177–187.

Johnson, L. C. Are stages of sleep related to waking behavior? *American Scientist,* 1973, **61,** 326–338.

Jones, E. E., Kanouse, D. E., Kelly, H. H., Nisbett, R., Valins, S. & Weiner, B. *Attribution.* Morristown, New Jersey: General Learning Press, 1972.

Jones, M. C. The elimination of childrens' fears. *Journal of Experimental Psychology*, 1924, **7**, 382–390.

Jung, C. G. *Contributions to analytical psychology.* London: Kegan, Paul, Trench, Trubner, 1928.

Jung, C. G. *Man and his symbols.* New York: Dell, 1968.

Kagan, J. Reflection-impulsivity: The generality and dynamics of conceptual tempo. *Journal of Abnormal Psychology*, 1966, **71**, 17–24.

Kagan, J., & Klein, R. Cross-cultural perspectives in early development. *American Psychologist*, 1973, **28**, 947–961.

Kamil, L. J. Psychodynamic changes through systematic desensitization. *Journal of Abnormal Psychology*, 1970, **76**, 199–205.

Kantor, J. R. *Problems of physiological psychology.* Bloomington, Indiana: Principia Press, 1947.

Kanzer, M. Image formation during free association. *The Psychoanalytic Quarterly*, 1958, **27**, 465–484.

Kaplan, E. K. Gaston Bachelard's philosophy of imagination: An introduction. *Philosophy and Phenomenological Research*, 1972, **33**, 1–24.

Keen, S. A conversation about ego destruction with Oscar Ichazo. *Psychology Today*, 1973, **7**, 64–96.

Kelly, G. A. *The psychology of personal constructs*, Vol. II. *Clinical diagnosis and psychotherapy.* New York: Norton, 1955.

Kinsbourne, M. The control of attention by interaction between the cerebral hemispheres. Paper presented at the Fourth International Symposium on Attention and Performance, Boulder, Colorado, 1971.

Kirchner, J. H., & Hogan, R. A. The therapist variable in the implosion of phobias. *Psychotherapy*, 1966, **3**, 102–104.

Klein, G. Peremptory ideation: Structure and force in motivated ideas. In R. R. Holt (Ed.), *Motives and thought.* New York: International Universities Press, 1967.

Kleitman, N. *Sleep and wakefulness.* Chicago: University of Chicago Press, 1963.

Klinger, E. *Structure and function of fantasy.* New York: Wiley, 1970.

Kocel, K., Galin, D., Ornstein, R., & Merrin, E. L. Lateral eye movement and cognitive mode. *Psychonomic Science*, 1972, **27**, 223–228.

Koch, W. Psychotherapeutische Kurzbehandlung Somnambuler Flucht-Zustände mit dem Symboldrama nach Leuner. *Praxis der Psychotherapie*, 1962, **7**, 5, 214–217.

Koch, W. Experience catathyme des symboles. *Informations de la Société Internationale des Techniques d'imagerie Mentale* (Proceedings of the 1st annual Congress). Paris: SITIM, 1968.

Kolvin, I. Aversive imagery treatment in adolescents. *Behavior Research and Therapy*, 1967, **5**, 506–515.

Kornadt, H. J. Der Zusammenhang zwischen allegemeinen Anspruchniveau und bestimmten Merkmalen bildhafter Verstellungen. *Referat vom Internationalen Kongress für Psychologie*, Bonn, 1960.

Kosbab, F. P. Symbolism, self-experience and the deductic use of affective imagery in psychiatric training. *Zeitschrift für Psychotherapie und Medizinische Psychologie*, 1972, **22**, 210–224.

Krapfl, J. E. Differential ordering of stimulus presentation and semi-automated versus live treatment in the systematic desensitization of snake phobia. Unpublished doctoral dissertation, University of Missouri, 1967.

Kretschmer, E. Gestufte Aktivhypnose zweigleisige standard Methode. *Handbuch der Neurosenlehre und Psychotherapie*, 1959, **IV**, 130–141.

Krippke, D., & Sonnenschein, R. A 90 minute daydream cycle. *Proceedings of the Association for the Psychophysiological Study of Sleep*, San Diego, California, 1973.

Kroth, J. A. The analytic couch and response to free association. *Psychotherapy: Theory, Research and Practice,* 1970, **7,** 206–208.

Kubie, L. The use of induced hypnotic reveries in the recovery of repressed amnesic data. *Bulletin of the Menninger Clinic,* 1943, **7,** 172–183.

Kubie, L. The use of induced hypnotic reverie in the recovery of anamnesic data. *Bulletin of the Menninger Clinic,* 1972, **7,** 172–183.

Lashley, D. S. *Brain mechanisms and intelligence.* Chicago: Univ. of Chicago Press, 1929.

Lazarus, A. A. Group therapy of phobic disorders by systematic desensitization. *Journal of Abnormal and Social Psychology,* 1961, **63,** 505–510.

Lazarus, A. A. *Behavior therapy and beyond.* New York: McGraw-Hill, 1971.

Lazarus, A. A., & Abramovitz, A. The use of "emotive imagery" in the treatment of children's phobias. *Journal of Mental Science,* 1962, **108,** 191–195.

Leask, J., Haber, R. N., & Haber, R. B. Eidetic imagery in children, II. Longitudinal and experimental results. Unpublished manuscript, University of Rochester, 1968.

Lefkowitz, M. M., Blake, R. R., & Mouton, J. S. Status factors in pedestrian violation of traffic signals. *Journal of Abnormal and Social Psychology,* 1955, **51,** 175–183.

Leitenberg, H. Practice as a psychotherapeutic variable: An experimental analysis within single cases. *Journal of Psychiatric Research,* 1970, **7,** 215–225.

Leitenberg, H., Agras, W. S., Barlow, D. H., & Oliveau, D. C. Contribution of selective positive reinforcement and therapeutic instructions to systematic desensitization therapy. *Journal of Abnormal Psychology,* 1969, **74,** 113–118.

Leuner, H. Kontrolle der Symbolinterpretation im experimentellen Verfahren. *Zeitschrift für Psychotherapie und Medizinische Psychologie,* 1954.

Leuner, H. Symbolkonfrontation, ein nicht-interpretierendes Vorgehen in der Psychotherapie. *Schweiz Archiv Neurologie und Psychiatrie,* 1955.

Leuner, H. Das Landschaftsbild als Metaphor dynamischer Strukturen. In *Festschrift zum 70. Geburtstag von E. Speer.* Munchen: Lehmanns Verlag, 1959.

Leuner, H. Guided affective imagery (GAI): A method of intensive psychotherapy. *American Journal of Psychotherapy,* 1969, **23,** 4–22.

Levis, D. J., & Carrera, R. Effects of ten hours of implosive therapy in the treatment of out-patients: A preliminary report. *Journal of Abnormal Psychology,* 1967, **72,** 504–508.

Lewis, H. R., & Streitfeld, S. *Growth games.* New York: Harcourt, 1971.

Linden, W. Meditation, cognitive style and reading in elementary school children. Unpublished doctoral dissertation, New York University, 1971.

Locke, E. Is "behavior therapy" behavioristic? (An analysis of Wolpe's psychotherapeutic methods). *Psychological Bulletin,* 1971, **76,** 318–327.

Luchins, A. S., & Luchins, E. J. Learning a complex ritualized social role. *Psychological Record,* 1966, **16,** 177–187.

McClelland, D. C., Atkinson, J. W., Clark, R. A. & Lowell, E. L. *The achievement motive.* New York: Appleton, 1953.

McClelland, D. C., Davis, W., Kalin, R., & Wanner, E. *The drinking man: Alcohol and human motivation.* New York: Free Press, 1972.

McFall, R. M., & Twentyman, C. T. Four experiments on the relative contributions of rehearsal, modeling, and coaching to assertion training. *Journal of Abnormal Psychology,* 1973, **81,** 199–218.

McGhee, P. Development of the humor response: A review of the literature. *Psychological Bulletin,* 1971, **76,** 328–348.

McGuigan, F. J. *Thinking: Studies of covert language processes.* New York: Appleton, 1966.

McKellar, P. *Imagination and thinking.* New York: Basic Books, 1957.

McKellar, P. Imagery from the standpoint of introspection. In P. Sheehan (Ed.), *The function and nature of imagery.* New York: Academic Press, 1972.

Malleson, N. Panic and phobia: A possible method of treatment. *Lancet,* 1959, **1,** 225–227.

Marks, D. Individual differences in the vividness of visual imagery and their effect on function. In P. Sheehan (Ed.), *The function and nature of imagery*. New York: Academic Press, 1972.

Marks, I. M. *Fears and phobias*. New York: Academic Press, 1969.

Marshall, H., & Hahn, S. C. Experimental modification of dramatic play. *Journal of Personality and Social Psychology*, 1967, **5**, 119–122.

Masters, R., & Houston, J. *Mind games*. New York: Viking Press, 1972.

Matefy, R. E. Behavior therapy to extinguish spontaneous recurrences of LSD effects: A case study. *Journal of Nervous and Mental Disease*, 1973, **156**, 226–231.

Mathews, A. Psychophysiological approaches to the investigation of desensitization and related procedures. *Psychological Bulletin*, 1971, **76**, 73–91.

Maupin E. W. Individual differences in response to a Zen meditation exercise. *Journal of Consulting Psychology*, 1965, **29**, 139–145.

May, J. & Johnson, H. Physiological activity to internally elicited arousal and inhibitory thoughts. *Journal of Abnormal Psychology*, 1973, **82**, 239–245.

Meichenbaum, D. The effects of instructions and reinforcement on thinking and language behaviors of schizophrenics. *Behavior Research and Therapy*, 1969, **7**, 101–114.

Meichenbaum, D. Examination of model characteristics in reducing avoidance behavior. *Journal of Personality and Social Psychology*, 1971, **17**, 298–307. (a)

Meichenbaum, D. Cognitive factors in behavior modification: Modifying what people say to themselves. Paper presented at the 5th annual meeting of the Association for the Advancement of Behavior Therapy, Washington, D.C., 1971. (b)

Meichenbaum, D. Clinical implications of modifying what clients say to themselves. Research Report No. 42, University of Waterloo, Waterloo, Ontario, 1972.

Meichenbaum, D. & Goodman, J. Reflection-impulsivity and verbal control of motor behavior. *Child Development*, 1969, **40**, 785–797.

Meichenbaum, D. & Goodman, J. Training impulsive children to talk to themselves. *Journal of Abnormal Psychology*, 1971, **77**, 115–126.

Meltzoff, J., & Kornreich, M. *Research in psychotherapy*. New York: Atherton, 1970.

Meskin, B., & Singer, J. L. Daydreaming, reflective thought and laterality of eye-movements. *Journal of Personality and Social Psychology*, 1974. (In press.)

Miller, G., Galanter, E., & Pribram, K. *Plans and the structure of behavior*. New York: Holt, 1960.

Moreno, J. L. Reflections on my method of group psychotherapy and psychodrama. In H. Greenwald (Ed.), *Active psychotherapy*. New York: Atherton, 1967.

Morgan, R., & Bakan, P. Sensory deprivation hallucinations and other sleep behavior as a function of position, method of report, and anxiety. *Perceptual and Motor Skills*, 1965, **20**, 19–25.

Morgenstern, L. Implosive therapy and flooding procedures: A critical review. *Psychological Bulletin*, 1973, **79**, 318–334.

Mumford, L. *The myth of the machine*. London: Secker & Warburg, 1967.

Neisser, U. *Cognitive psychology*. New York: Appleton, 1967.

Neisser, U. Changing conceptions of imagery. In P. Sheehan (Ed.), *The function and nature of imagery*. New York: Academic Press, 1972.

Nerenz, K. Die musikalische Beeinflussung des experimentellen katathymen Bilderlebens und ihre psychotherapeutische Wirkung. Dissertazionen Göttingen, 1965.

Nerenz, K. Das musikalische Symboldrama als hilfsmethode in der Psychotherapie. *Zeitschrift für Psychotherapie und Medizinische Psychologie*, 1969.

O'Connor, R. D. Modification of social withdrawal through symbolic modeling. *Journal of Applied Behavior Analysis*, 1969, **2**, 15–22.

Orne, M. T. The nature of hypnosis: Artifact and essence. *Journal of Abnormal and Social Psychology*, 1959, **58**, 277–299.

Oswald, I. *Sleeping and waking.* New York: Elsevier, 1962.

Paivio, A. *Imagery and verbal processes.* New York: Holt, Rinehart & Winston, 1971.

Paul, G. L. *Insight vs. desensitization in psychotherapy.* Stanford, California: Stanford Univ. Press, 1966.

Paul, G. L. Insight vs. desensitization in psychotherapy two years after termination. *Journal of Consulting Psychology,* 1967, **31,** 333–348.

Paul, G. L. Two-year follow-up of systematic desensitization in therapy groups. *Journal of Abnormal Psychology,* 1968, **73,** 119–130.

Perky, C. W. An experimental study of imagination. *American Journal of Psychology,* 1910, **21,** 422–452.

Perls, F. *Gestalt therapy verbatim.* New York: Bantam, 1970.

Perls, F. *In and out of the garbage pail.* New York: Bantam, 1972.

Perls, F., Goodman, P., & Hefferline, R. *Gestalt therapy.* New York: Dell, 1951.

Piaget, J. *The child's conception of physical causality.* New York: Harcourt, 1930.

Piaget, J. *Language and thought of the child.* New York: Harcourt, 1932.

Piaget, J. *Play, dreams, and imitation in childhood.* New York: Norton, 1962.

Pflaum, G. Erste Ergebnisse des musikalischen Katathymee Bilderlebens in seiner Anwendung als gruppen Therapie. Medizinische Dissertationen Göttingen, 1968.

Polanyi, M. *The tacit dimension.* New York: Doubleday, 1966.

Premack, D. Toward empirical behavior laws: I. Positive reinforcement. *Psychological Review,* 1959, **66,** 219–233.

Rachman, S. Aversion therapy: Chemical or electrical? *Behavior Research and Therapy,* 1965, **2,** 289–300.

Rachman, S. *Phobias: Their nature and control.* Springfield, Illinois: Charles C Thomas, 1968.

Rachman, S. The treatment of anxiety and phobic reactions by systematic desensitization psychotherapy. *Journal of Abnormal and Social Psychology,* 1959, **58,** 259–263.

Rachman, S. & Teasdale, J. *Aversion therapy and behavior disorders: An Analysis.* Coral Gables, Florida: University of Miami Press, 1969.

Rapaport, D. *Organization and pathology of thought.* New York: Columbia University Press, 1951.

Rapaport, D. The psychoanalytical theory of motivation. In *Nebraska Symposium on Motivation.* Lincoln, Nebraska: University of Nebraska Press, 1960.

Reese, H. W. Imagery and contextual meaning. *Psychological Bulletin,* 1970, **73,** 404–414. (a)

Reese, H. W. Imagery in children's paired associate learning. *Journal of Experimental Psychology,* 1970, **9,** 174–178. (b)

Reese, H. W. Implications of mnemonic research for cognitive theory. Paper read at Southeastern Conference on Research in Child Development. Athens, Georgia, 1970 (mimeographed). (c)

Reich, W. *Character analysis.* (2nd ed.) New York: Orgone Institute Press, 1945.

Reppucci, N. D., & Baker, B. Self-desensitization: Implications for treatment and teaching. In R. Rubin & C. M. Franks (Eds.), *Advances in behavior therapy, 1968.* New York: Academic Press, 1969.

Rescorla, R. A. Pavlovian conditioned inhibition. *Psychological Bulletin,* 1969, **72,** 77–94.

Rescorla, R. A., & Solomon, R. L. Two-process learning theory: Relationships between Pavlovian conditioning and instrumental learning. *Psychological Review,* 1967, **74,** 151–182.

Rescorla, R. A., & Wagner, A. R. A theory of Pavlovian conditioning: Variations in the effectiveness of reinforcement and nonreinforcement. In A. Black & W. F. Prokasy (Eds.), *Classical conditioning II.* New York: Appleton, 1972.

Reyher, J. Free imagery: An uncovering procedure. *Journal of Clinical Psychology*, 1963, **19**, 454–459.

Reyher, J., & Morishige, H. EEG and rapid eye movements during free imagery and dream recall. *Journal of Abnormal Psychology*, 1969, **74**, 576–582.

Reyher, J., & Smeltzer, W. The uncovering properties of visual imagery and verbal association: A comparative study. *Journal of Abnormal Psychology*, 1968, **73**, 218–222.

Richardson, A. *Mental imagery*. New York: Springer, 1969.

Rigo, L. L. La psicoterapia con il rêve éveillé dirigé. *Archivio di Psicologia, Neurologia e Psychiatria*, 1962, **25**, 45.

Rigo, L. L. Histoire de notre image (d'André Virel). Une guistificazione genetico-historica dei fondamenti tecnici della psicoterapia con il rêve évieillé de Desoille. *Mierva Medico-psicologica, Torino (Italy)*, 1966, **7**.

Rigo, L. L. L'imagerie di gruppo negli adulti. Proceedings of the 3rd International Congress of the Société International des Techniques d'Imagerie Mentale. Cortina, Italy, 1970.

Rigo-Uberto, S. Un caso di sintomatologia neurolica grave fobico-ossessiva in un S. preadolescente trattato con un tecnica psicoterapica includente anche l'imagerie mentale. Paper read at the 3rd International Congress of the Société International des Techniques d'Imagerie Mentale. Cortina, Italy, 1970.

Robertiello, R. Encouraging the patient to live out sexual fantasies. *Psychotherapy: Theory, Research and Practice*, 1969, **6**, 183–187.

Rohwer, W. D., Jr. Images and pictures in children's learning. *Psychological Bulletin*, 1970.

Rotter, J. Social learning and clinical psychology. Englewood Cliffs, New Jersey: Prentice-Hall, 1954.

Rubinstein, B. Explanation and more descriptions: a meta-scientific examination of certain aspects of the psychoanalytical theory of motivation. In R. Holt (Ed.), *Motives and thought: Psychoanalytic essays in honor of David Rapaport. Psychological Issues*, 1967, **5** (no. 2-3, monograph 18/19).

Rychlak, J. Time orientation in the positive and negative free phantasies of mildly abnormal versus normal highschool males. *Journal of Consulting and Clinical Psychology*, 1973, **41**, 175–180.

Salter, A. *Conditioned reflex therapy*. New York: Farrar, Strauss, 1949.

Sanderson, R., Campbell, D., & Laverty S. An investigation of a new aversive conditioning technique for alcoholism. In C. M. Franks (Ed.), *Conditioning techniques in clinical practice and research*. New York: Springer, 1964. Pp. 165–177.

Sarbin, T. R. Imagining as muted role-taking: A historical–linguistic analysis. In P. Sheehan (Ed.), *The function and nature of imagery*. New York: Academic Press, 1972.

Sarbin, J. R., & Anderson, M. L. Role-theoretical analysis of hypnotic behavior. In J. E. Gordon (Ed.), *Handbook of clinical and experimental hypnosis*. New York: Macmillan, 1967.

Sarbin, T. R., & Juhasz, J. B. Toward a theory of imagination. *Journal of Personality*, 1970, **38**, 52–76.

Schachtel, E. *Metamorphosis*. New York: Basic Books, 1959.

Schaub, A. On the intensity of images. *American Journal of Psychology*, 1911, **22**, 346–368.

Scheidler, T. Use of fantasy as a therapeutic agent in latency age groups. *Psychotherapy*, 1972, **9**, 299–303.

Schilder, P. *Medical psychology*. New York: International Universities Press, 1953.

Schlosberg, H. Three dimensions of emotion. *Psychological Review*, 1954, **61**, 81–88.

Schultz, J. H. *Le Training autogène*. Paris: Paris University Press, 1967.

Schultz, J. H., & Luthe, W. *Autogenic training: A physiologic approach in psychotherapy*. New York: Grune & Stratton, 1959.

Schutz, W. C. *Joy: Expanding human awareness.* New York: Grove Press, 1967.

Schwartz, A. N., & Hawkins, H. L. Patient models and affect statements in group therapy. *Proceedings of the 73rd Annual Convention of the American Psychological Association,* 1965, 265–266.

Schwartz, G. E. Cardiac responses to self-induced thoughts. *Psychophysiology* 1971, **8,** 462–467.

Seamon, J. Imagery codes and human information retrieval. *Journal of Experimental Psychology,* 1972, **96,** 468–470.

Seamon, J. Coding and retrieval processes and the hemispheres of the brain. In S. J. Dimond & J. G. Beaumont (Eds.), *Hemisphere function in the human brain.* London: Paul Elek, 1973.

Segal, E. M., & Lachman, R. Complex behavior or higher mental process: Is there a paradigm shift? *American Psychologist,* 1972, **27,** 46–55.

Segal, S. J. (Ed.), *Imagery: Current cognitive approaches.* New York: Academic Press, 1971.

Segal, S. J., & Glickman, M. Relaxation and the Perky effect: The influence of body position and judgments of imagery. *American Journal of Psychology,* 1967, **60,** 257–262.

Sheehan, P. Functional similarity of imagery and perceiving: individual differences in vividness of imagery. *Perceptual and Motor Skills,* 1966, **23,** 1011–1033.

Sheehan, P. *The function and nature of imagery.* New York: Academic Press, 1972.

Sheffield, F. D. Theoretical considerations in the learning of complex sequential tasks from demonstration and practice. In A. A. Lumsdaine (Ed.), *Student response in programmed instruction.* Washington, D. C.: National Academy of Sciences – National Research Council, 1961, 117–131.

Shorr, J. E. The existential question and the imaginary situation as therapy. *Existential Psychiatry,* 1967, **6,** 443–462.

Shorr, J. E. *Psycho-imagination therapy.* New York: Intercontinental Medical Book Corporation, 1972.

Silberer, H. On symbol formation. In D. Rapaport (Ed.), *Organization and pathology of thought.* New York: Columbia Univ. Press, 1951.

Simpson, H. M., & Paivio, A. Changes in pupil size during an imagery task without motor involvement. *Psychonomic Science,* 1966, **5,** 405–406.

Singer, D. L. Aggression arousal, hostile humor, catharsis. *Journal of Personality and Social Psychology Monograph Supplement,* 1968, **8,** 1–4.

Singer, E. *Key concepts in psychotherapy.* New York: Random House, 1965.

Singer, J. L. *Daydreaming.* New York: Random House, 1966.

Singer, J. L. Drives, affects and daydreams. In J. S. Antrobus (Ed.), *Cognition and affect.* Boston: Little, Brown, 1970.

Singer, J. L. The influence of violence portrayed in television or movies upon overt aggressive behavior. In J. L. Singer (Ed.), *The control of aggression and violence.* New York: Academic Press, 1971. (a)

Singer, J. L. Imagery and daydream techniques employed in psychotherapy: Some practical and theoretical implications. In Charles Spielberger (Ed.), *Current topics in clinical and community psychology,* Vol. 3. New York: Academic Press, 1971. (b)

Singer, J. L. *The child's world of make-believe: Experimental studies of imaginative play.* New York: Academic Press, 1973.

Singer, J. L., & Antrobus, J. S. A factor-analytic study of daydream and conceptually-related cognitive and personality variables. *Perceptual and Motor Skills, Monograph Supplement,* **3-VI7,** 1963.

Singer, J. L., & Antrobus, J. S. Eye movements during fantasies, *A.M.A. Archives of General Psychiatry,* 1965, **12,** 71–76.

Singer, J. L., & Antrobus, J. S. Daydreaming, imaginal processes, and personality: A normative study. In P. Sheehan (Ed.), *The function and nature of imagery.* New York: Academic Press, 1972.

Singer, J. L., Antrobus, J. S., & Auster, N. Stimulus-independent thought content and tolerance for silence. In preparation.

Singer, J. L., Greenberg, S., & Antrobus, J. S. Looking with the mind's eye: Experimental studies of ocular motility during daydreaming and mental arithmetic. *Transactions of the New York Academy of Sciences,* 1971, **33,** 694–709.

Singer, J. L., & Singer, D. Personality. *Annual Review of Psychology,* 1972, **23,** 375–412.

Skinner, B. F. *Science and human behavior.* New York: MacMillan, 1953.

Smilansky, S. *The effects of sociodramatic play on disadvantaged preschool children.* New York: Wiley, 1968.

Smith, Adam (Jerry Goodman). Alumni notes—Altered States U. *Psychology Today,* 1973, **7,** 75–79.

Spurgeon, C. *Shakespeare's imagery and what it tells us.* Cambridge: Cambridge Univ. Press, 1935.

Stampfl, T. G., & Levis, D. J. Essentials of implosive therapy: A learning theory-based psychodynamic behavioral therapy. *Journal of Abnormal Psychology,* 1967, **72,** 496–503.

Starker, S. Daydreaming styles and nocturnal dreaming. *Journal of Abnormal Psychology,* 1974, **83,** 52–55.

Sternberg, S. Memory scanning: Mental processes revealed by reaction-time experiments. *American Scientist,* 1969, **57,** 421–457.

Strupp, H. H. Specific vs. non-specific factors in psychology and the problem of control. *Archives of General Psychiatry,* 1970, **23,** 393–401.

Strupp, H. H., & Bergin, A. E. Some empirical and conceptual bases for coordinated research in psychotherapy: A critical review of issues, trends, and evidence. *International Journal of Psychiatry,* 1969, **7,** 18–90.

Sullivan, H. S. *Clinical studies in psychiatry.* New York: Norton, 1956.

Tauber, E. S., & Green, M. G. *Prelogical experience.* New York: Basic Books, 1959.

Tolman, E. *Purposive behavior in animals and men.* New York: Appleton, 1932.

Tomkins, S. *Affect, imagery, and consciousness,* Vol. I, Vol. II. New York: Springer, 1962–1963.

Tomkins, S. A theory of memory. In J. S. Antrobus (Ed.), *Cognition and affect.* Boston: Little, Brown, 1970.

Tomkins, S., & Messick, S. (Eds.) *Computer simulation of personality.* New York: Wiley, 1963.

Truax, C. B., & Carkhuff, R. R. *Toward effective counseling and psychotherapy.* Chicago: Aldine, 1967.

Tulving, E., & Donaldson, W. (Eds.) *Organization of memory.* New York: Academic Press, 1972.

Vaihinger, H. *Philosophy of "as if."* New York: Harcourt, 1925.

Van Egeren, L. F. Psychophysiology of systematic desensitization: Individual differences and the habituation model. *Journal of Behavior Therapy and Experimental Psychiatry,* 1970, **1,** 249–255.

Van Egeren, L. F., Feather, B. W., & Hein, P. L. Desensitization of phobias: Some psychophysiology propositions. *Psychophysiology,* 1971, **8,** 213–228.

Van Hekken, S. M. J. The influence of verbalization on observational learning in a group of mediating and a group of non-mediating children. *Human Development,* 1969, **12,** 204–213.

Wagner, M. K., & Bragg, R. A. Comparing behavior modification methods for habit decrement-smoking. V.A. Hospital, Salisbury, North Carolina, 1969 (mimeographed).

Watson, J. B. *Behaviorism.* Chicago: University of Chicago Press, 1930.

Watson, J. P., & Marks, I. M. Relevant and irrelevant fear in flooding – a crossover study of phobic patients. *Behavior Therapy,* 1971, **2,** 275–293.

Weiner, H. Real and imagined cost effects upon human fixed-interval responding. *Psychological Reports,* 1965, **17,** 659–662.

Weitzman, B. Behavior therapy and psychotherapy. *Psychological Review,* 1967, **74,** 300–317.

Werner, H., & Kaplan, B. *Symbolic realization.* New York: Wiley, 1963.

Wheeler, J. Fantasy, affect and the perception of time. Unpublished doctoral dissertation, City University of New York, 1969.

White, R. W. Motivation reconsidered: The concept of competence. *Psychological Review,* 1959, **66,** 297–333.

White, R. W. Competence and psychosexual stages of development. In M. R. Jones (Ed.), *Nebraska symposium on motivation.* Lincoln, Nebraska: University of Nebraska Press, 1960.

White, R. W. *Ego and reality in psychoanalytic theory. Psychological Issues,* 1964, **3,** monograph II.

Wilkins, W. Desensitization: Getting it together with Davison & Wilson. *Psychological Bulletin,* 1972, **78,** 32–36.

Wilkins, W. Desensitization: Social and cognitive factors underlying the effectiveness of Wolpe's procedure. *Psychological Bulletin,* 1971, **76,** 311–317.

Wilkins, W., & Domitor, P. J. The role of instructed attention shifts in systematic desensiization. Paper presented at the 81st meeting of the American Psychological Association, Honolulu, 1973.

Witkin, H. A., Lewis, H. B., & Weil, E. Affective reactions and patient-therapist interactions among more differentiated and less differentiated patients early in therapy. *Journal of Nervous and Mental Diseases,* 1968, **146,** 193–207.

Wolpe, J. Reciprocal inhibition as the main basis of psychotherapeutic effects. *Archives of Neurology and Psychiatry,* 1954, **72,** 205–226.

Wolpe, J. *Psychotherapy by reciprocal inhibition.* Stanford, California: Stanford Univ. Press, 1958.

Wolpe, J. The systematic desensitization treatment of neuroses. *Journal of Nervous and Mental Disease,* 1961, **132,** 189–203.

Wolpe, J. *The practice of behavior therapy.* New York: Pergamon, 1969.

Wolpe, J., & Flood, J. The effect of relaxation on the galvanic skin response to repeated phobic stimuli in ascending order. *Journal of Behavior Therapy and Experimental Psychiatry,* 1970, **1,** 195–200.

Wolpe, J., & Lazarus, A. A. *Behavior therapy techniques.* New York: Pergamon, 1966.

Wolpin, M. Guided imagining to reduce avoidance behavior. Psychotherapy, 1969, **6,** 122–124.

Wolpin, M., & Raines, J. Visual imagery, expected roles, and extinction as possible factors in reducing fear and avoidance behavior. *Behavior Research and Therapy,* 1966, **4,** 25–37.

Wolstein, B. *Transference.* New York: Grune & Stratton, 1954.

Zachary, R. Massed aversive imagery ("implosion") in the treatment of maladaptive fear responses: A cognitive-affective model. In preparation, 1974.

SUBJECT INDEX